Manasara Series No. V

Architecture of Manasara

Illustrations of Architectural and Sculptural Objects

With a Synopsis

Prasanna Kumar Acharya

LOW PRICE PUBLICATIONS
Delhi-110052

First Published 1934
Reprinted in **LPP** 1995, 1998, 2006, 2013

ISBN 10: 81-7536-349-5
ISBN 13: 978-81-7536-349-6

Published by
Low Price Publications
A-6, Nimri Commercial Centre,
Ashok Vihar Phase-IV, Delhi-110052
Phone: +91-11-27302453 Fax: +91-11-47061936
e-mail: info@Lppindia.com
website: www.Lppindia.com

Printed at:
IIP Printers
D-17, Raja Garden, New Delhi

PRINTED IN INDIA

"What the learned world demand of us in India is to be quite certain of our data, to place the monumental record before them exactly as it now exists, and to interpret it faithfully and literally."

ILLUSTRATIONS
OF
ARCHITECTURAL AND SCULPTURAL OBJECTS

CHAPTER VI
GNOMONS AND PEGS

Plate no.	Figure	Description
I	Gnomons	Varying in accordance with the variation of light shadow in different months.
II	Fig. 1	General method of finding cardinal points (for orientation of buildings).
	Fig. 2	Alternative method of finding cardinal points
	Fig. 3	Method of fixing foundation pegs.

CHAPTER VII
SITE PLANS OF THIRTY-TWO VARIETIES

Plate no.	Figure	Description
III	First variety	Sakala plan of 1 plot.
	Second variety	Pechaka plan of 4 plots.
	Third variety	Pīṭha plan of 9 plots.
IV	Fourth variety	Mahāpīṭha plan of 16 plots.
	Fig. 1A	Same, arranged differently.
V	Fifth variety	Upapīṭha plan of 25 plots.
VI	Sixth variety	Ugrapīṭha plan of 36 plots.
VII	Seventh variety	Sthaṇḍila plan of 49 plots
VIII	Eighth variety	Chaṇḍita plan of 64 plots, square.
IX	Eighth variety	Same, circular.
X	Ninth variety	Parama-śāyika plan of 81 plots, square
XI	Ninth variety	Same, circular.
XII	Ninth variety	Same, triangular.
XIII	Tenth variety	Āsana plan of 100 plots, square.
XIV	Tenth variety	Same, circular.

Plate no.	Figure	Description
		Not illustrated
	Eleventh variety	Sthānīya plan of 121 plots
	Twelfth variety	Deśya plan of 144 plots.
	Thirteenth variety	Ubhaya-chaṇḍita plan of 169 plots.
	Fourteenth variety	Bhadra plan of 196 plots.
	Fifteenth variety	Mahāsana plan of 225 plots.
	Sixteenth variety	Padma-garbha plan of 256 plots.
	Seventeenth variety	Triyuta plan of 289 plots.
	Eighteenth variety	Karṇāshṭaka plan of 324 plots.
	Nineteenth variety	Gaṇita plan of 369 plots.
	Twentieth variety	Sūrya-viśālaka plan of 400 plots.
	Twenty-first variety	Susaṁhita plan of 441 plots.
	Twenty-second variety	Supratikānta plan of 484 plots.
	Twenty-third variety	Viśālaka plan of 529 plots.
	Twenty-fourth variety	Vipra-garbha plan of 576 plots.
	Twenty-fifth variety	Viveśa plan of 625 plots.
	Twenty-sixth variety	Vipula-bhoga plan of 676 plots.
	Twenty-seventh variety	Viprakānta plan of 729 plots.
	Twenty-eighth variety	Viśālāksha plan of 784 plots.
	Twenty-ninth variety	Vipra-bhakti plan of 841 plots.
	Thirtieth variety	Viśveśa-sāra plan of 900 plots.
	Thirty-first variety	Īśvarakānta plan of 961 plots.
	Thirty-second variety	Chandrakānta plan of 1024 plots.

CHAPTER IX

VILLAGE SCHEMES OF EIGHT TYPES

Plate no.	Figure	Description	
XV	First type	Lay-out plan	of Daṇḍaka village.
XVI	Second type	Ditto	of Sarvatobhadra village
XVII	Third type	Ditto	of Nandyāvarta village.
XVIII	Fourth type	Ditto	of Padmaka village.
XIX	Fifth type	Ditto	of Svastika village.
XX	Sixth type	Ditto	of Prastara village.
XXI	Seventh type	Ditto	of Kārmuka village.
XXII	Eighth type	Ditto	of Chaturmukha village.

CHAPTER X

TOWN-PLANS OF EIGHT TYPES AND FORTS AND FORTRESSES OF FIFTEEN TYPES

Plate no.	Figure	Description
XXIII	First type	Lay-out plan of Rājadhānīya city.
XXIV	Fifth type	Left side figure—General outline of Kharvaṭa town.
	Sixth type	Right side top figure—General outline of Kheṭa town.
	Seventh type	Right-side bottom figure—General outline of Kubjaka town.
		Not illustrated
	Second type	Nagara—City without King's palace.
	Third type	Pura – Ordinary residential town.
	Fourth type	Nagarī—City of certain type.
	Eighth type	Pattana—Commercial port on sea-side.
XXV	Eleventh type	Left-side top figure—Jala-durga (water-fort).
	Fourth type	Left-side bottom figure, Droṇaka—A fortress or fortified commercial town.
	First type	Right-side top figure, Śibira—Encampment.
		Right-side bottom figure—Details of Fort-gates.
		Not illustrated
	Second type	Vāhinī-mukha.
	Third type	Sthānīya.
	Fifth type	Saṁviddha.
	Sixth type	Kolaka.
	Seventh type	Nigama.
	Eighth type	Skandhāvāra.
	Ninth type	Giri-durga—Mountain fort.
	First variety	Fort on the top of a mountain.
	Second variety	Fort in the valley of a mountain.
	Third variety	Fort on the mountain-slope.
	Tenth type	Vana-durga—Forest fort.
	Twelfth type	Paṅka-durga—Marsh (or clay) fort.
	Thirteenth type	Ratha-durga—Chariot fort.
	Fourteenth type	Deva-durga—Divine fort.
	Fifteenth type	Miśra-durga—Mixed fort.

CHAPTER XII

FOUNDATIONS AND BRICKS

Plate no.	Figure	Description
XXVI	Foundation	Left-side middle figure—Suggested section of foundation.
	Bricks	Right-side top figure—Intermediate size bricks.
	Ditto	Right-side middle figure—Small size bricks.
	Ditto	Ditto Large size bricks.

CHAPTER XIII

PEDESTALS OF COLUMNS OF THREE CLASSES COMPRISING TWELVE TYPES AND PROFILES OF MOULDINGS OF SOME FIFTY VARIETIES

Plate no.	Figure	Description
		MOULDINGS
XXVII	Fig. 1	Vājana.
		Prativājana.
		Ratna-paṭṭa.
		Nimna.
		Splay.
		Vajra-paṭṭa.
		Subsidiary mouldings based on Vājana types
		Classic fillets
	Fig. 2	Padma, cyma recta and cyma reversa.
	Fig. 3	Karṇa or cavetto.
	Fig. 4	Kumuda or torus.
	Fig. 5	Antarita or scotia.
	Fig. 6	Gopāna or ovolo.
	Fig. 7	Prati and Pratimukha.
	Fig. 8	Kapota or bird's beak.
	Fig. 9	Kumbha and Dhārā-kumbha.

Not illustrated separately but employed

First type	Abja, Ambuja, or Saroruha—cyma.
Second type	Antara, Antarāla or Antarika—fillet.
Third type	Aṅghri—a pillar-like moulding.
Fourth type	Aṁśu—a moulding between cyma and corona
Fifth type	Argala—a bolt-like moulding.
Sixth type	Ādhāra—a flat moulding used as a support.

Plate no.	Figure	Description
	Seventh type	Āliṅga—a fillet with greater projection.
	Eighth type	Āsana—a seat-like moulding.
	Ninth type	Bhadra—a portico-like moulding.
	Tenth type	Bodhikā—a corbel-like moulding.
	Eleventh type	Dala—a petal-like moulding.
	Twelfth type	Gala, Grīva, Kaṇṭha or Kandhara—dado.
	Thirteenth type	Ghaṭa—a pot-like moulding.
	Fourteenth type	Gopānaka—ovolo or corona.
	Fifteenth type	Hāra—a bead-like moulding.
	Sixteenth type	Janman—a plinth-like moulding.
	Seventeenth type	Kampa or Kampana—fillet.
	Eighteenth type	Kumuda—torus or astragal.
	Nineteenth type	Kendra—a point-like moulding.
	Twentieth type	Kshepaṇa—a projecting fillet.
	Twenty-first type	Mushṭi-bandha - a fist-like moulding.
	Twenty-second type	Mūla—a root-like moulding.
	Twenty-third type	Mṛiṇāla or Mṛiṇālikā—a stalk-like moulding.
	Twenty-fourth type	Nāṭaka—a theatre-like moulding.
	Twenty-fifth type	Nāsi, Nāsī or Nāsikā—a vestibule-like moulding.
	Twenty-sixth type	Paṭṭa or Paṭṭikā—fillet.
	Twenty-seventh type	Pratika—a crescent moulding.
	Twenty-eighth type	Prati-vaktra—a face-like moulding.
	Twenty-ninth type	Prati-vājana—a concave moulding like the cavetto.
	Thirtieth type	Prati-bandha—a band-like moulding.
	Thirty-first type	Pratima—an image-like moulding of the base
	Thirty-second type	Pāduka—a foot-like moulding.
	Thirty-third type	Prastara—corona.
	Thirty-fourth type	Phalakā—abacus.
	Thirty-fifth type	Ratna-kampa—a jewel-fillet.
	Thirty-sixth type	Ratna-vapra—a jewel-cavetto.
	Thirty-seventh type	Tāṭikā—tenia.
	Thirty-eighth type	Tuṅga—a vault-like moulding.
	Thirty-ninth type	Uttara—a corona or upper fillet.
	Fortieth type	Upāna—a rectangular plinth-like moulding.
	Forty-first type	Vapra or vapraka—cavetto.
	Forty-second type	Valabha or valabhī—a thatch-like moulding

Plate no.	Figure	Description	
		Compound mouldings	
	Forty-third type	Kampa-karṇa—a fillet-ear.	
	Forty-fourth type	Karna-padma—an ear-cyma.	
	Forty-fifth type	Khudra-kampa—a small fillet.	
	Forty-sixth type	Kshudra-padma or Kshudrāmbuja—a small cyma.	
	Forty-seventh type	Mahāmbuja—a large cyma.	
	Forty-eighth type	Padma-kampa—a cyma-fillet.	
	Forty-ninth type	Ratna-kampa—a jewel-fillet.	
	Fiftieth type	Ratna-paṭṭa—a jewel-fillet.	
	Fifty-first type	Vajra-paṭṭa—a club-fillet.	
		PEDESTALS	
XXVIII	First type	Vedibhadra class of Pedestals,	of 24 parts.
	Second type	Ditto	of 12 parts.
	Third type	Ditto	of 18 parts.
	Fourth type	Ditto	of 12 parts.
XIX	First type	Pratibhadra class of Pedestals,	of 26 parts.
	Second type	Ditto	of 32 parts.
	Third type	Ditto	of 33 parts.
	Fourth type	Ditto	of 36 parts.
XXX	First type	Mañchabhadra class of Pedestals,	of 30 parts.
	Second type	Ditto	of 31 parts.
	Third type	Ditto	of 33 parts.
	Fourth type	Ditto	of 34 parts.

CHAPTER XIV
BASES OF COLUMNS OF EIGHTEEN CLASSES COMPRISING SIXTY-FOUR TYPES

Plate no.	Figure	Description	
XXXI	First type	Pāda-bandha class,	of 24 parts.
	Second type	Ditto	of 29 parts.
	Third type	Ditto	of 27 parts.
	Fourth type	Ditto	of 28 parts.
XXXII	First type	Uraga-bandha class,	of 18 parts.
	Second type	Ditto	of 20 parts.
	Third type	Ditto	of 22 parts.
	Fourth type	Ditto	of 24 parts.

Plate no.	Figure	Description	
XXXIII	First type	Pratikrama class,	of 21 parts.
	Second type	Ditto	of 22 parts.
	Third type	Ditto	of 23 parts.
	Fourth type	Ditto	of 24 parts.
XXXIV	First type	Kumuda-bandha class,	of 27 parts.
	Second type	Ditto	of 27 parts.
	Third type	Ditto	of 29 parts.
	Fourth type	Ditto	of 29 parts.
XXXV	Fifth class	Vapra-bandha base,	of 31 parts.
	First type	Puspa-pushkala class,	of 32 parts.
	Second type	Ditto	of 32 parts.
	Third type	Ditto	of 32 parts.
	Fourth type	Ditto	of 32 parts.
XXXVI	Seventh class	Vapra-bandha base,	of 19 parts.
	First type	Śrībhoga class,	of 25 parts.
	Second type	Ditto	of 27 parts.
XXXVII	First type	Śrībandha class,	of 28 parts.
	Second type	Ditto	of 28 parts.
	Third type	Ditto	of 28 parts.
	Fourth type	Ditto	of 26 parts.
XXXVIII	First type	Mañcha-bandha class,	of 26 parts.
	Second type	Ditto	of 26 parts.
	Third type	Ditto	of 26 parts.
	Fourth type	Ditto	of 26 parts.
XXXIX	First type	Śreṇi-bandha class,	of 18 parts.
	Second type	Ditto	of 22 parts.
	Third type	Ditto	of 23 parts.
	Fourth type	Ditto	of 24 parts.
XL	First type	Padma-bandha class,	of 20 parts.
	Second type	Ditto	of 22 parts.
	Third type	Ditto	of 22 parts.
	Fourth type	Ditto	of 19 parts.
XLI	First type	Kumbha-bandha class,	of 22 parts.
	Second type	Ditto	of 21 parts.
	Third type	Ditto	of 24 parts.
	Fourth type	Ditto	of 24 parts.
	Fifth type	Ditto	of 25 parts.

Plate no.	Figure	Description	
XLII	Fourteenth class	Ratna-bandha base,	of 26 parts.
	Fifteenth class	Paṭṭa-bandha base,	of 20 parts.
	Sixteenth class	Śrīkānta base,	of 38 parts.
	Seventeenth class	Kampa-bandha base,	of 36 parts.
XLIII	First type	Kukshi-bandha class,	of 18 parts.
	Second type	Ditto	of 19 parts.
	Third type	Ditto	of 27 parts.
	Fourth type	Ditto	of 26 parts.
	Fifth type	Ditto	of 24 parts.

CHAPTER XV

COLUMNS OF FIVE ORDERS OF SEVERAL GROUPS

Plate no.	Figure	Description
XLIV	First group	Chitra-kaṇṭha class, similar to Roman Doric in proportion; Whole order of 6 parts comprising: Pedestal 1 part. Base 1 part. Shaft 2 parts. Capital 1 part. Entablature 1 part. Diameter $\frac{1}{8}$th height or $\frac{1}{2}$ part.
	First and third orders	Brahma-kānta of square plan and Rudrakānta of circular or sixteen-sided plan.
	Second order	Vishnu-kānta of octagonal plan.
	Fifth order	Skanda-kānta of hexagonal plan.
	Fourth order	Śiva-kānta of pentagonal plan.
XLV	Second group	Padma-kānta class, similar to Ionic order in proportion;
	Third group	Chitra-skambha class, similar to Corinthian order in proportion; Whole order of 6 parts comprising: Pedestal 1 part. Base 1 part. Shaft 2 parts. Capital 1 part Entablature 1 part Diameter of Padma-kānta $\frac{1}{9}$th height. Diameter of Chitra-skambha $\frac{1}{10}$th height.

Plate no.	Figure	Description
XLV	First and third orders	Brahma-kānta of square plan and Rudrakānta of circular or sixteen-sided plan.
	Second order	Vishṇu-kānta of octagonal plan.
	Fifth order	Skanda-kānta of hexagonal plan.
	Fourth order	Śiva-kānta of pentagonal plan.
	Fifth order	Chitra-skambha of square, circular, sixteen-sided, octagonal, hexagonal, or pentagonal plan.
XLVI	Fourth group	Pālikā-stambha class. Whole order of 6 parts comprising : Pedestal 1 part. Base 1 part. Shaft 2 parts. Capital 1 part. Entablature 1 part. Diameter $\frac{1}{11}$th height.
	First and third orders	Brahma-kānta of square plan and Rudra-kānta of circular or sixteen-sided plan.
	Second order	Vishṇu-kānta of octagonal plan.
	Fifth order	Skanda-kānta of hexagonal plan.
	Fourth order	Śiva-kānta of pentagonal plan.
XLVII	Fifth group	Kumbha-stambha class;
	Sixth group	Koshtha-stambha class, similar to Grecian Anta ; Whole order of 6 parts comprising : Pedestal 1 part. Base 1 part. Shaft 2 parts. Capital 1 part. Entablature 1 part. Diameter of both $\frac{1}{12}$th height.
	First and third orders	Brahma-kānta of square plan and Rudra-kānta of circular or sixteen-sided plan.
	Second order	Vishṇu-kānta of octagonal plan.
	Fifth order	Skanda kānta of hexagonal plan.
	Fourth order	Śiva-kānta of pentagonal plan.
	Fig. 5	Koshṭha-stambha pilaster.

Plate no.	Figure	Description
XLVIII	Seventh group	Five other orders from Agamas without pedestal and entablature;
		Whole order of 4 parts comprising:
		Base 1 part.
		Shaft 2 parts.
		Capital 1 part.
		Diameter ¼th height.
	First and fourth orders	Śrikara of circular plan and Priya-darśana of square plan.
	Third order	Saumukhya of octagonal plan.
	Second order	Chandra-kānta of sixteen-sided plan.
	Fifth order	Śubhaṁkari of square, octagonal or mixed plan.
XLIX	Eighth group	Five other orders from Purānas and Brihat-saṁhitā;
		Whole order of 10¾ parts comprising:
		Pedestal 1 part.
		Base 1 part.
		Shaft 6 parts.
		Capital 1 part.
		Entablature 1¾ parts.
	First and fifth orders	Ruchaka of square plan and Vritta of circular plan.
	Second order	Vajra of octagonal plan, similar to Tuskan order in proportion.
	Third order	Dvi-vajra of sixteen sided plan.
	Fourth order	Pralinaka of thirty-two-sided plan.

CHAPTER XVI

ENTABLATURES OF EIGHT TYPES AND ROOFS OF FIVE TYPES

Plate no.	Figure	Description
L		ENTABLATURES
	First type	of 27 parts.
	Second type	of 34½ parts.
	Third type	of 36½ parts.
	Fourth type	of 30½ parts.
	Fifth type	of 30½ parts.
	Sixth type	of 29 parts.
	Eighth type	of 34 parts.

Plate no	Figure	Description
		Not illustrated
	Seventh type	of 26 parts.
		Roofs
	First type	Flat roof of quadrangular and other shapes.
	Second type	Pent roof of various shapes.
	Third type	Spherical roof of various shapes.
	Fourth type	Oval roof of various shapes.
	Fifth type	Round roof of various shapes.

CHAPTER XVII
JOINERY OF EIGHTEEN TYPES

Plate no.	Figure	Description
L1	First type	Joint between horizontal and vertical pieces on the middle of the latter.
	Second type	Nandyāvarta order.
	Third type	Sarvatobhadra order.
	Fourth type	Svastika order.
	Fifth type	Malla-bandha (A) or Nalyed joint.
	Sixth type	Malla-bandha (B) or Scarfed joint.
	Seventh type	Mahāvṛitta joint of Mesha-yuddha type.
	Eighth type	Mesha-yuddha or Mortise and Tenon joint.
	Ninth type	Śūkara-ghrāṇa joint.
	Tenth type	Joints in frieze.
		Not illustrated
	Eleventh type	Malla-bandha joint between two pieces of wood looking like two wrestlers wrestling against each other.
	Twelfth type	Brahma-rāja joint between three and four pieces of wood having four heads like the four-headed deity Brahmā.
	Thirteenth type	Veṇu-parva joint between five pieces of bamboos.
	Fourteenth type	Pūga-parva joint between six pieces of wood like areca or betel-nut joints.

Plate no.	Figure	Description
	Fifteenth type	Deva-sandhi joint between seven pieces of wood.
	Sixteenth type	Ṛishi-sandhi joint between eight pieces of wood.
	Seventeenth type	Ishu-parva joint between nine pieces of wood looking arrow-shaped.
	Eighteenth type	Daṇḍika joint between ten or more pieces of wood.

CHAPTER XVIII

GENERAL FEATURES OF EDIFICES

Not illustrated but employed

Plate no.	Figures	Description
	Porches	Several varieties.
	Domes	Several varieties.
	Dome-nails	Several varieties.
	Three main styles	Nāgara, Vesara, Drāvida : depending on the shape of upper portions.
	Three groups	Śuddha, Miśra, Saṁkīrṇa : depending on materials.
	Four classes	Jāti, Chhanda, Vikalpa, Ābhāsa. : depending on units of measurement.
	Three postures	Sthānaka, Asāna, Śayana : depending on postures of images in case of temples.
	Three standards	Saṁchita, Asaṁchita, Apasaṁchita : depending on height, breadth, or length as the regulator of the whole structure.
	Three sexes	Puṁliṅga or masculine, Strīliṅga or feminine, Napuṁsaka or neuter : depending on equiangular or rectangular shape, but in case of temples on the sexes of the deities in addition to shapes.
	Five shapes	Square, octagonal, oval, round, circular.
	Three sizes	Large, intermediate, small,

CHAPTER XIX

SINGLE STOREY BUILDINGS OF EIGHT TYPES

Plate no.	Figure	Description
LII	First type	Vaijayantika, of small proportion, used both as temples and dwelling-houses with slight alteration. Elevation towards the breadth.
LIII	First type	Typical plan.
LIV	Second type	Bhoga, of small proportion, used both as temples and dwelling-houses with slight alteration. Elevation towards the breadth
LV	Third type	Śrīviśāla, of intermediate proportion, used both as temples and dwelling houses with slight alteration. Elevation towards the breadth.
LVI	Eighth type	Keśara, of large proportion, used both as temples and dwelling-houses with slight alteration. Elevation towards the breadth.
LVII	Eighth type	Cross-section.
		Not illustrated
	Fourth type	Svasti-bandha, used both as temples and dwelling-houses.
	Fifth type	Śrīkara, used both as temples and dwelling-houses.
	Sixth type	Hasti-prishṭha, used both as temples and dwelling-houses.
	Seventh type	Skanda-tāra, used both as temples and dwelling houses.

CHAPTER XX

TWO-STOREYED BUILDINGS OF EIGHT TYPES

Plate no.	Figure	Description
LVIII	First type	Srīkara, of small size, used both as temples and dwelling-houses with slight alteration. Elevation towards the breadth.
LIX	First type	Of intermediate size, elevation towards the breadth.

Plate no.	Figure	Description
LX	First type	Typical plan based on intermediate size.
LXI	First type	Large size, elevation towards the breadth.
LXII	First type	Cross-section based on large size.
		Not illustrated
	Second type	Vijaya, used both as temples and dwelling-houses.
	Third type	Siddha, used both as temples and dwelling-houses.
	Fourth type	Paushṭika, used both as temples and dwelling-houses.
	Fifth type	Kānti, used both as temples and dwelling-houses.
	Sixth type	Prabhūta, used both as temples and dwelling-houses.
	Seventh type	Svastika, used both as temples and dwelling-houses.
	Eighth type	Pushkala, used both as temples and dwelling-houses.

CHAPTER XXI

THREE-STOREYED BUILDINGS OF EIGHT TYPES

Plate no.	Figure	Description
LXIII	Third type	Sukhālaya, of small size, used both as temples and dwelling-houses. Elevation towards the breadth.
LXIV	Eighth type	Kailāśa, of intermediate size, used both as temples and dwelling-houses. Elevation towards the breadth.
LXV	Second type	Āsana, of large size, used both as temples and dwelling-houses. Elevation towards the breadth.
LXVI	Second type	Cross-section based on large size.
LXVII	Second type	Typical plan (ground floor) based on large size.

Plate no.	Figure	Description
		Not illustrated
	First type	Śrīkara, used both as temples and dwelling-houses.
	Fourth type	Kesara, used both as temples and dwelling-houses.
	Fifth type	Kamalāṅga, used both as temples and dwelling-houses.
	Sixth type	Brahmakānta, used both as temples and dwelling-houses.
	Seventh type	Merukānta, used both as temples and dwelling-houses.

CHAPTER XXII
FOUR-STOREYED BUILDINGS OF EIGHT TYPES

Plate no.	Figure	Description
LXVIII	First type	Vishṇu-kānta, of small size, used both as temples and dwelling-houses with slight alteration. Elevation towards the breadth.
LXIX	Fourth type	Rudra-kānta, of intermediate size, used both as temples and dwelling-houses with slight alteration. Elevation towards the breadth.
LXX	Fourth type	Cross-section, based on intermediate size.
LXXI	Fourth type	Typical plan (ground floor), based on intermediate size.
LXXII	Second type	Chaturmukha, of large size, used both as temples and dwelling-houses with slight alteration. Elevation towards the breadth.
		Not illustrated
	Third type	Sadāśiva, used both as temples and dwelling-houses.
	Fifth type	Īśvara-kānta, used both as temples and dwelling-houses
	Sixth type	Mañcha-kānta, used both as temples and dwelling-houses.
	Seventh type	Vedi-kānta, used both as temples and dwelling-houses.
	Eighth type	Indra-kānta, used both as temples and dwelling-houses

CHAPTER XXIII

FIVE-STOREYED BUILDINGS OF NINE TYPES

Plate no.	Figure	Description
LXXIII	First type	Airāvata, used both as temples and dwelling-houses with slight alteration. Elevation towards the breadth.
LXXIV	First type	Cross-section.
LXXV	First type	Typical plan (ground floor).
		Not illustrated
	Second type	Bhūta-kānta, used both as temples and dwelling-houses.
	Third type	Viśva-kānta, used both as temples and dwelling-houses.
	Fourth type	Mūrti-kānta, used both as temples and dwelling-houses.
	Fifth type	Gṛiha-kānta, used both as temples and dwelling-houses.
	Sixth type	Mahā-kānta, used both as temples and dwelling-houses.
	Seventh type	Kalyāṇa, used both as temples and dwelling-houses.
	Eighth type	Yajña-kānta, used both as temples and dwelling-houses.
	Ninth type	Brahma-kānta, used both as temples and dwelling-houses.

CHAPTER XXIV

SIX-STOREYED BUILDINGS OF THIRTEEN TYPES

Plate no.	Figure	Description
LXXVI	First type	Padma-kānta, used both as temples and dwelling-houses with slight alteration. Elevation towards the breadth.
LXXVII	First type	Cross-section.
LXXVIII	First type	Typical plan (ground floor).

Plate no.	Figure	Description
		Not illustrated
	Second type	Kāntāra, used both as temples and dwelling-houses.
	Third type	Sundara, used both as temples and dwelling-houses.
	Fourth type	Upakānta, used both as temples and dwelling-houses.
	Fifth type	Kamalāksha, used both as temples and dwelling-houses.
	Sixth type	Ratna kānta, used both as temples and dwelling-houses.
	Seventh type	Vipulāṅka, used both as temples and dwelling-houses.
	Eighth type	Jyotishkānta, used both as temples and dwelling-houses.
	Ninth type	Saroruha, used both as temples and dwelling-houses.
	Tenth type	Vipulākṛitika, used both as temples and dwelling-houses.
	Eleventh type	Svasti-kānta, used both as temples and dwelling-houses.
	Twelfth type	Nandyāvarta, used both as temples and dwelling-houses.
	Thirteenth type	Ikshu-kānta, used both as temples and dwelling-houses.

CHAPTER XXV

SEVEN-STOREYED BUILDINGS OF EIGHT TYPES

Plate no.	Figure	Description
LXXIX	First type	Puṇḍarīka, used both as temples and dwelling-houses with slight alteration.
LXXX	First type	Cross-section.
LXXXI	First type	Typical plan (ground floor).

Plate no.	Figure	Description
		Not illustrated
	Second type	Śrīkānta, used both as temples and dwelling-houses.
	Third type	Śrībhoga, used both as temples and dwelling-houses.
	Fourth type	Dhāraṇa, used both as temples and dwelling-houses.
	Fifth type	Pañjara, used both as temples and dwelling-houses.
	Sixth type	Āśramāgāra, used both as temples and dwelling-houses.
	Seventh type	Harmya-kānta, used both as temples and dwelling-houses.
	Eighth type	Hima-kānta, used both as temples and dwelling-houses.

CHAPTER XXVI

EIGHT-STOREYED BUILDINGS OF EIGHT TYPES

Plate no.	Figure	Description
LXXXII	First type	Bhū-kānta, used both as temples and dwelling-houses with slight alteration. Elevation towards the breadth.
LXXXIII	First type	Cross-section.
LXXXIV	First type	Plans in general :
	Fig. 1	With 17 parts } Small size of Bhū-kānta.
	Fig. 2	With 18 parts } Small size of Bhū-kānta.
	Fig. 3	With 21 parts, of the intermediate size of Svarga-kānta.
	Fig. 4	With 22 parts, of the large size of Mahā-kānta.
		Not fully illustrated
	Second type	Bhūpa-kānta, used both as temples and dwelling-houses.
	Third type	Svarga-kānta, used both as temples and dwelling-houses.

Plate no	Figure	Description
	Fourth type	Mahā-kānta, used both as temples and dwelling-houses.
	Fifth type	Jana-kānta, used both as temples and dwelling-houses.
	Sixth type	Tapas-kānta, used both as temples and dwelling-houses.
	Seventh type	Satya-kānta, used both as temples and dwelling-houses.
	Eighth type	Deva-kānta, used both as temples and dwelling-houses.

CHAPTER XXVII

NINE-STOREYED BUILDINGS OF SEVEN TYPES

Plate no.	Figure	Description
LXXXV	First type	Saura-kānta, used both as temples and dwelling-houses. Elevation towards the breadth.
LXXXVI	First type	Cross-section.
LXXXVII	First type	Plans in general :
	Fig. 1	With 20 parts, of small size of Saura-kānta.
	Fig. 2	With 27 parts, of large size of Viśva-kānta.
	Fig. 3	With 24 parts, of intermediate size of Vivṛita.
		Not fully illustrated
	Second type	Raurava, used both as temples and dwelling-houses.
	Third type	Chaṇḍita, used both as temples and dwelling-houses.
	Fourth type	Bhūshaṇa, used both as temples and dwelling-houses.
	Fifth type	Vivṛita, used both as temples and dwelling-houses.
	Sixth type	Suprati-kānta, used both as temples and dwelling-houses.
	Seventh type	Viśva-kānta, used both as temples and dwelling-houses.

CHAPTER XXVIII

TEN-STOREYED BUILDINGS OF SIX TYPES

Plate no.	Figure	Description
LXXXVIII	First type	Bhū-kānta, used both as temples and dwelling-houses with slight alteration. Elevation towards the breadth.
LXXXIX	First type	Cross-section.
XC	First type	Plans in general.
		Not illustrated
	Second type	Chandra-kānta, used both as temples and dwelling-houses.
	Third type	Bhavana-kānta, used both as temples and dwelling-houses.
	Fourth type	Antariksha-kānta, used both as temples and dwelling-houses.
	Fifth type	Megha-kānta, used both as temples and dwelling-houses.
	Sixth type	Abja-kānta, used both as temples and dwelling-houses.

CHAPTER XXIX

ELEVEN-STOREYED BUILDINGS OF SIX TYPES

Plate no.	Figure	Description
XCI	First type	Śambhu-kānta, used both as temples and dwelling-houses with slight alteration.
XCII	First type	Cross-section.
XCIII	Fig. 1	Small size plan, of 19 parts of Śambhu-kānta.
XXIII	Fig. 2	Intermediate size plan, of 21 parts, of Vajra-kānta.
XXIII	Fig. 3	Large size plan, of 30 parts, of Chakra-kānta.
		Not fully illustrated
	Second type	Īśa-kānta, used both as temples and dwelling-houses.
	Third type	Chakra-kānta, used both as temples and dwelling-houses.

Plate no.	Figure	Description
	Fourth type	Yama kānta, used both as temples and dwelling-houses.
	Fifth type	Vajra-kānta, used both as temples and dwelling-houses.
	Sixth type	Akra-kānta, used both as temples and dwelling-houses.

CHAPTER XXX

TWELVE-STOREYED BUILDINGS OF TEN TYPES AND STEPS AND STAIRCASES OF VARIOUS KINDS

Plate no	Figure	Description
XCIV	First type	Pañchāla, used both as temples and dwelling-houses with slight alteration. Elevation towards the breadth.
XCV	First type	Cross-section.
XCVI	First type	Plans in general :
	Fig. 1	Small size, of 28 parts, of Pañchāla and Drāviḍa.
XCVI	Fig. 2	Intermediate size, of 31 parts, of Virāṭa-kānta.
XCVII	Fig. 1	Intermediate size, of 33 parts, of Madhya-kānta.
	Fig. 2	Intermediate size, of 34 parts, of Kerala-kānta.
XCVIII	Fig. 1	Intermediate size, of 33 parts, of Kāliṅga-kānta.
	Fig 2	Intermediate size, of 34 parts, of Vaṁśaka-kānta.
		Not fully illustrated
	Second type	Drāviḍa, used both as temples and dwelling-houses.
	Third type	Madhya-kānta, used both as temples and dwelling-houses.
	Fourth type	Kāliṅga-kānta, used both as temples and dwelling-houses.
	Fifth type	Virāṭa-kānta, used both as temples and dwelling-houses.

Plate no.	Figure	Description
	Sixth type	Kerala-kānta, used both as temples and dwelling-houses.
	Seventh type	Vaṁśaka-kānta, used both as temples and dwelling-houses.
	Eighth type	Māgadha-kānta, used both as temples and dwelling-houses.
	Ninth type	Janaka-kānta, used both as temples and dwelling-houses.
	Tenth type	Sphūrjaka (? Gurjaraka), used both as temples and dwelling-houses.
		STEPS AND STAIRCASES
XCIX	Figs. 1 and 2	Plans showing various positions of steps and staircases (fixed).
	Fig. 3	Side elevation.
	Figs. 4 and 5	Plans showing possible positions of movable staircases.
	Fig. 6	Section.

CHAPTER XXXI

COURTS OF FOUR CLASSES OF EDIFICES, EACH COMPRISING FIVE TO SEVEN VARIETIES, FOR OFFERINGS, FAMILY MEMBERS, BEAUTY, AND DEFENCE

Plate no.	Figure	Description
C	First type	For Jāti class of buildings, comprising five courts called Antarmaṇḍala, Antahārā, Madhyahārā, Prākāra, and Mahāmaryādā respectively.
	Second type	For Chhanda class of buildings, comprising five courts of the five epithets.
		Not illustrated
	Third type	For Vikalpa class of buildings, comprising five courts of the five epithets.
	Fourth type	For Ābhāsa class of buildings, comprising five courts of the five epithets.

N. B.—Beyond the fifth court there may be for defence the sixth and seventh varieties also (vide Translation, page 292).

CHAPTER XXXII

SHRINES OF ATTENDANT DEITIES IN VISHṆU, BUDDHA, JAIN AND OTHER TEMPLES

Plate no.	Figure	Description
CI	Shrines	Of Vishṇu temple, comprising groups of eight, sixteen, and thirty-two deities.
		Not illustrated
	Shrines	Of Buddha temple.
	Shrines	Of Jain temple.
	Shrines	Of Śiva and other temples.

CHAPTER XXXIII

GATEHOUSES OF FIFTEEN TYPES OF ONE TO SIXTEEN STOREYS AND WINDOWS OF EIGHT TYPES

Plate no.	Figure	Description
		GATEHOUSES
CII	First type	Dvāra-śobhā (beauty of the gate) of a single storey, of Antar-maṇḍala (innermost court), both for temples and residential buildings.
	Fig. 1	Plan.
	Fig. 2	Elevation.
	Fig. 3	Cross-section.
CIII	Second type	Dvāra-śālā (gatehouse) of two storeys, of Antanihāra (second court), both for temples and residential buildings.
	Fig. 1	Plan.
	Fig. 2	Elevation.
	Fig. 3	Cross-section.
CIV	Third type	Dvāra-prāśāda (gate-palace) of three storeys, of Madhyama-hārā (third court), both for temples and residential buildings.
	Fig. 1	Plan (of first floor).
	Fig. 2	Elevation.
	Fig. 3	Cross-section.

Plate no.	Figure	Description
CV	Fourth type	Dvāra-harmya (gate-edifice) of four storeys, of Prākāra (fourth court), both for temples and residential buildings.
	Fig. 1	Plan (of first floor).
	Fig. 2	Elevation.
	Fig. 3	Cross-section.
CVI	Fifth type	Mahāgopura (great gate-house) of five storeys, of Mahāmaryādā (extreme boundary), both for temples and residential buildings.
	Fig. 1	Plan (of first floor).
	Fig. 2	Elevation.
	Fig. 3	Cross-section.
		Not illustrated

N. B.—Each of the five types admits of three different sizes—small, intermediate and large, and may run up to sixteen storeys.

Plate no.	Figure	Description
		WINDOWS
CVII	First group	For Vaiśyas and Śūdras.
	Fig. 1	Elevation.
	Fig. 2	Section.
	Fig. 3	Plan.
	Second group	For temples of kings (kshatriyas) and Brahmans.
	Fig. 4	Elevation.
	Fig. 5	Section.
	Fig. 8	Plan.
	Fig. 6	Elevation.
	Fig. 7	Section.
	Fig. 9	Plan.
		Not illustrated
	First type	Nāga-bandha (snake-band).
	Second type	Valli-bandha (creeper-band).
	Third type	Govāksha (resembling cow's eye).
	Fourth type	Kuñjarāksha (resembling elephant's eye).
	Fifth type	Svastika (cross-shaped).
	Sixth type	Sarvatobhadra (*vide* plate no. XVI).
	Seventh type	Nandyāvarta (*vide* plate no. XVII).
	Eighth type	Pushpa-bandha (flower-band).
	Third group	Dormer-windows in roofs.

CHAPTER XXXIV

AVILIONS OF SOME HUNDRED TYPES, CLASSIFIED AS BELONGING TO TEMPLES AND RESIDENTIAL BUILDINGS OF BRAHMANS, KINGS, VAIŚYAS AND ŚŪDRAS AND IN ACCORDANCE WITH SHAPES, NUMBER OF FACES AND NUMBER OF COLUMNS

Plate no.	Figure	Description
CVIII	First type	Himaja, with four parts square, both for temples and residential buildings, used as an ordinary bath-room.
	Second type	Nishadaja, with six parts square, both for temples and residential buildings, used as a reading-room.
	Third type	Vindhyaja, with seven parts square, both for temples and residential buildings, used as a special bath-room.
	Eighth type	Meruja, with 11 by 4 parts, both for temples and residential buildings, used as the stock-room of a library.
CIX	Eleventh type	Padmaka, with five parts square, for temples, used as refectory or kitchen for gods.
	Fourteenth type	Bhadra, with five parts square, both for temples and residential buildings, used as water-store and granary.
	Sixteenth type	Nṛitta, with 5 by 7 parts, both for temples and residential buildings, used as a music hall.
CX	Eighteenth type	Āsthāna-maṇḍapa, assembly hall, with nine parts square and with 100 columns.
	Fig. 1	Part section.
	Fig. 2	Plan.
	Fig. 4	Elevation.
	Twenty-fourth type	Kula-dhāraṇa, with 24 by 12 parts, both for temples and residential buildings, used as a cow-shed.
	Fig. 3	Plan.
CXI	Twenty-ninth type	Dhanādhipa, with plough-shaped walls, of several varieties, generally for the gods and the Brahmans, but also used as the shaving pavilion for the kings and the twice born, as well as the treasury for jewels of the Kshatriyas and Vaiśyas.

Plate no.	Figure	Description
CXI	Thirty-seventh type	Droṇa, with 15 by 7 parts, used as a place for ram-fighting, also as the sports-pavilion for gods, as also the chapel in king's palace and for practising archery and wrestling.
	Ninth type	Vijaya, with 4 by 2 parts, used as the wedding pavilion and also as a place dedicated to gods for free distribution of water.
	Thirtieth type	Dhānyāgāra, with 10 by 3 parts, for Śūdras, used as a dwelling-house.
	Fig. 5	Treasury, with 5 by 3 parts, for Kshatriyas and others.
CXII	Nineteenth type	Deva, with a thousand columns, used as council hall of gods and kings.
	Fig. 1	Elevation.
	Fig. 2	Section.
	Fig. 3	Plan with nine parts square, excluding porches.
		Not illustrated
	Fourth type	Mālyaja, used as a chapel with the image of a deity therein.
	Fifth type	Pāriyātra, used as a temple where a deity is installed.
	Sixth type	Gandha-mādana, used as a place for pilgrimage.
	Seventh type	Hema-kūṭa, used as a place for dancing and singing.
	Tenth type	Siddha-yoga, of 192 columns.
	Twelfth type	Sicha, used as an ordinary kitchen.
	Thirteenth type	Pushpa, used as a place for collecting flowers or as a bower.
	Fifteenth type	Śiva, used as a room for unhusking corn.
	Seventeenth type	Jālaka, used as a treasury for clothes, ornaments, jewels and other valuables.
	Twentieth type	Śālā, used as a residence.
	Twenty-first type	Kṛita used as a dwelling-house.
	Twenty-second type	Darbha, used as a stable for elephants.
	Twenty-third type	Kauśika, used as a stable for horses.
	Twenty-fifth type	Sukhāṅga, used as a guest-house.

...ate no.	Figure	Description
	Twenty-sixth type	Saukhyaka, built on the bank of a river, lake, or sea, and used as a place for pilgrimage.
	Twenty-seventh type	Mālikā, also called Mālikākṛiti, shaped like a garland, and used as the spring residence of gods, kings, and others.
	Twenty-eighth type	Dhanada, specially for Brahmans, used as a dwelling-house.
	Thirty-first type	Bhūshaṇa with several varieties, used as a place for the silence (worship) of the gods, for the Puṁsavana ceremonies of the Brahmans, and also as the kitchen for the Śūdras.
	Thirty-second type	Subhūshaṇa, used as a hall for the Upanayana (sacred thread) ceremonies of the Brahmans, Kshatriyas and Vaiśyas.
	Thirty-third type	Harmya, with several varieties, used as the kitchen of the gods, the Brahmans and the kings, and also as the place (lying-in room) to see the newly-born baby in.
	Thirty-fourth type	Śṛiṅgāra, used as the bed chamber of the gods and others.
	Thirty-fifth type	Sugata, fit for all castes in all provinces for all purposes.
	Thirty-sixth tpye	Prāgata, suitable for all sorts of work.
	Thirty-eighth type	Kharvaṭa, of several varieties, used as the dining hall of the kings, also as the coronation hall.
	Thirty-ninth type	Śrīrūpa, generally for temples, used as the coronation hall of the kings.
	Fortieth type	Maṅgala, specially for palaces of kings, used as the place for balancing the kings (against gold which is distributed).
	Forty-first type	Kānta, used as the place to see sports from, for the Crown Prince.
	Forty-second type	Śrīviśāla, used as the residence for the queen.
	Forty-third type	Somārka, of several varieties, used as the kitchen for the Brahmans, Kshatriyas, and Vaiśyas.
	Forty-fourth type	Jāti, style of pavilions for the gods and the Brahmans.
	Forty-fifth type	Chhanda, style of pavilions for the Kshatriyas.

Plate no.	Figure	Description
	Forty-sixth type	Vikalpa, style of pavilions for the Vaiśyas.
	Forty-seventh type	Ābhāsa, style of pavilions for the Sūdras.
	Forty-eighth type	Daṇḍaka, group of pavilions with two faces.
	Forty-ninth type	Svastika, group of pavilions with three faces and shaped like the plough.
	Fiftieth type	Nandyāvarta, group of pavilions with four faces.
	Fifty-first type	Maulika, group of pavilions with six faces.
	Fifty-second type	Sarvatobhadra, group of pavilions with eight faces.
	Fifty-third type	Grāma-maṇḍapa, pavilions for villages, square or rectangular in shape, with even or odd number of walls.
	Fifty-fourth type	Sabhā, for villages, used as the assembly hall.
	Fifty-fifth type	Nagara-maṇḍapa, pavilions for the cities.
	Fifty-sixth type	Pattana-maṇḍapa, pavilions for towns on the bank of a river or sea.
	Fifty-seventh type	Kharvaṭa-maṇḍapa, pavilions in small towns for the Śūdras.
	Fifty-eighth type	Yātrā-mārga-maṇḍapa, pavilions or sheds on the road-side, used as the rest-house for travellers.
		Pavilions also mentioned in other chapters and used as stated below:
	Fifty-ninth type	For besmearing oil in (*vide* Translation, p. 401).
	Sixtieth type	For cock-fight in palaces (p. 430).
	Sixty-first type	In front of mansions (p. 382).
	Sixty-second type	For installation of the bull (p. 593).
	Sixty-third type	For keeping clothes in (p. 296).
	Sixty-fourth type	For preparing dishes in (p. 296).
	Sixty-fifth type	For gathering flowers in (p. 296).
	Sixty-sixth type	For keeping jewels in (p. 297).
	Sixty-seventh type	For music (p. 402).
	Sixty-eighth type	For keeping perfumes, etc. (p. 297).
	Sixty-ninth type	For making flower garlands in (p. 297).
	Seventieth type	For keeping ornaments of gods (pp. 297-8).
	Seventy-first type	For keeping umbrellas and chowries (p. 298).

Plate no.	Figure	Description
	Seventy-second type	For seeing the military march from (p. 431).
	Seventy-third type	For unhusking rice (p. 402).
	Seventy-fourth type	For wedding (p. 401), a secord variety.
	Seventy-fifth type	For performing sacrifice, built in front or sides of temples, square in shape, with twelve or sixteen columns, one pinnacle, a shed-yard, four doors and arches, and an altar in.

CHAPTER XXXV

STOREYED MANSIONS OF SIX TYPES, EACH COMPRISING SEVERAL VARIETIES, RUNNING UP TO TWELVE STOREYS, BUILT FOR THE SAKE OF BEAUTY, HEALTH AND ENJOYMENT OF THE GODS, KINGS, AND OTHERS

Plate no.	Figure	Description
CXIII	First type	Daṇḍaka, an isolated mansion comprising a single row of buildings, used generally by the Pārshṇika, the Maṇḍaleśa and the inferior classes of kings.
	Fig. 1	First variety (Dandaka-śālā).
	Fig. 2	Third variety (Daṇḍaka-kānta).
	Figs. 3 to 6	Plans showing various positions of doors.
	Fig. 7	Second variety (Paṇḍi-sālā).
	Fig. 8	Fourth variety (Daṇḍaka-śālā).
	Fig. 9	Fifth variety (Daṇḍaka-śālā).
CXIV	Second type	Svastika, plough-shaped, comprising two rows of buildings, used generally by the Paṭṭadhara and other inferior classes of kings.
	Fig. 2	Plan of the ground floor.
	Third type	Maulika, shaped like the winnowing basket, comprising three rows of buildings, used generally by the Maṇḍaleśa (Pārshṇika) and other inferior classes of kings.
	Fig. 1	Plan of the ground floor.
CXV	Fourth type	Chaturmukha, comprising four rows of buildings, used generally by the Narendra and other inferior classes of kings.

Plate no.	Figure	Description
	Fig. 1	Plan of the ground floor.
	Fifth type	Sarvatobhadra, comprising seven rows of buildings, used generally by the Adhirāja (Mahārāja) and other inferior classes of kings.
	Fig. 2	Plan of the ground floor.
CXVI	Sixth type	Vardhamāna, comprising ten rows of buildings, used generally by the Chakravartin and other inferior classes of kings.
	Fig. 1	First variety (plan of the ground floor).
	Fig. 2	Third variety (plan of the ground floor).

CHAPTER XXXVI

SITUATION, ETC., OF DWELLING-HOUSES

Not illustrated

CHAPTER XXXVII

SITUATION OF DOORS IN TEMPLES AND RESIDENTIAL BUILDINGS

Not illustrated

CHAPTER XXXIX

DOORS OF VARIOUS TYPES

Plate no.	Figure	Description
CXVII	First type	Small size, of rectangular shape.
	Fig. 1	Elevation.
	Fig. 2	Section.
	Fig. 3	Plan.
CXVIII	Second type	Intermediate size, of rectangular shape.
	Fig. 1	Elevation.
	Fig. 2	Section.
	Fig. 3	Plan.
CXIX	Third type	Large size, of rectangular shape.
	Fig. 1	Elevation
	Fig. 2	Section.
	Fig. 3	Plan.

Plate no.	Figure	Description
		Not illustrated
	Fourth type	Square shape, of various sizes Translation, p. 417).
	Fifth tpye	Gutter, of circular and oth r shapes, of various sizes (p. 232).
	Sixth type	Horse pattern, of various sizes (p. 359).
	Other types	Of houses for all (pp. 402, 404, 410), of temples (p. 410), of Jain temples (p. 564), of main building (p. 407), in mansions (pp. 376, 396), in different storeys (pp. 230, 231, 243, 252, 270, etc.), of pavilions (pp. 234, 235, 342, 410, 642, etc.), in auxiliary temples (p. 292), of courts (p. 410), according to castes (p. 292), in palaces (pp. 410, 427), at roofs (p. 410), at the wall (p. 325), for swings (p. 507), of temples (p. 600), of tiger cages (p. 512), with panels (pp. 216, 231), with single panel (p. 512), with leaf (pp. 419-421), etc.

CHAPTER XL

ROYAL PALACES OF NINE TYPES, EACH COMPRISING NINE VARIETIES

Plate no.	Figure	Description
CXX	First type	For Astra-grāha kings, Plan of the ground floor
CXXI	Fourth type	For Maṇḍaleśa kings, Plan of the ground floor.
CXXII	Sixth type	For Pārshṇika kings, Plan of the ground floor.
CXXIII	Eighth type	For Mahārāja kings, Plan of the ground floor.
CXXIV	Ninth type	For Chakravartin kings, Plan of the ground floor.
		Not illustrated
		Elevations of the above types.
	Second type	For Prāhāraka kings.
	Third type	For Paṭṭabhāj kings.
	Fifth type	For Paṭṭadhara kings.
	Seventh type	For Narendra kings.

CHAPTER XLIII

CARS AND CHARIOTS OF SEVEN MAIN TYPES AND FIVE STYLES, COMPRISING SEVERAL VARIETIES AND RUNNING UP TO NINE STOREYS, FOR GODS, BRAHMANS, AND KINGS, FOR BATTLE, MOCK-FIGHTING, DAILY RIDES, USE DURING FESTIVALS, ETC.

Plate no	Figure	Description
CXXV	Fig. 1	Of single-storey, Plan of the ground floor.
	Fig. 2	Outline section.
	Fig. 3	Front elevation
	Fig. 4	Side elevation.
CXXVI	Fig. 1	Two-storeyed, Plan of the ground floor.
	Fig. 2	Outline section.
	Fig. 3	Front elevation.
	Fig. 4	Side elevation.
		Not illustrated
		Cars and chariots of three, four, five, six, seven, eight, and nine storeys.
	First type	Nabhasvān-bhadraka, of circular shape, furnished with square porticos and other features.
	Second type	Prabhañjana-bhadraka, of elliptical shape, furnished with hexagonal porticos and other features.
	Third type	Nivāta-bhadraka, of square shape, furnished with two-sided porticos and other features.
	Fourth type	Pavana-bhadraka, of rectangular shape, furnished with three-sided porticos and other features.
	Fifth type	Pṛishata-bhadraka, of octagonal shape, furnished with decagonal porticos and other features.
	Sixth type	Indraka-bhadraka, of hexagonal shape, furnished with decagonal porticos and other features.
	Seventh type	Anila-bhadraka, of oval shape, furnished with twelve-sided porticos and other features.
	Eighth variety	Nāgara style, of square shape.
	Ninth variety	Drāviḍa style, of octagonal shape.
	Tenth variety	Vesara style, of circular shape.
	Eleventh variety	Āndhra style, of hexagonal shape.

Plate no.	Figure	Description
	Twelfth variety	Kāliṅgaka style, of equiangular shape.
	Thirteenth variety	Divine cars, with one, two, or three storeys.
	Fourteenth variety	Royal cars, with one to nine storeys.
	Fifteenth variety	Battle-chariots, with three platforms.
	Sixteenth variety	Chariots for Mock-fight, with two platforms.
	Seventeenth variety	Chariots for daily ride, with one, two, or three platforms.
	Eighteenth variety	Chariots for special use, with three to nine platforms.
	Nineteenth variety	Chariots for Sārvabhauma kings, with one to nine platforms.
	Twentieth variety	Chariots for Mahārāja kings, with one to seven platforms.
	Twenty-first variety	Chariots for Narendra kings, with one to five platforms.
	Twenty-second variety	Chariots for Pārshṇika kings, with one to four platforms.
	Twenty-third variety	Chariots for Vishṇu, with one to nine platforms.
	Twenty-fourth variety	Chariots for Śiva, with one to nine platforms.
	Twenty-fifth variety	Chariots for Buddhists, with one to seven platforms.
	Twenty-sixth variety	Chariots for Jains, with one to seven platforms.
	Twenty-seventh variety	Chariots for other gods and goddesses, with one to four or five platforms.

CHAPTER XLIV

COUCHES, BEDSTEADS, AND SWINGS OF SEVERAL TYPES

Plate no.	Figure	Description
CXXVII	First type	Bedsteads for gods.
	Fig. 1	Elevation.
	Fig. 2	Section.
	Fig. 3	Plan.

Plate no.	Figure	Description
CXXVII	Second type	Bedsteads for children.
	Fig. 4	Elevation.
	Fig. 5	Part section.
	Fig. 8	Plan.
	Third type	Bedsteads for Brahmans.
	Fig. 6	Part elevation.
	Fig. 7	Part section.
	Fig. 9	Plan.

Not illustrated

Couches of quadrangular, rectangular, and circular cane patterns (Translation, p. 453).

Vajra-pāda and Padma-pāda types (p. 453), lion-legged for kings, other kinds for Kshatriyas and others covered with canopies (p. 501); Divan, Āsandi, sofa with arms to it, state chairs, cushioned chairs, chair raised on a pedestal, chair with many legs, cane-bottomed chair, leaning board, etc. (p. 501).

Swings—*vide* plate no. CXLIV.

CHAPTER XLV

THRONES (ARCHITECTURAL), FOR GODS AND KINGS, OF EIGHTEEN KINDS WITH TEN GENERAL TYPES, FOUR SPECIAL TYPES FOR GODS, AND FOUR SPECIAL TYPES FOR KINGS

Plate no.	Figure	Description
CXXVIII	First group	For gods, Śiva and Vishṇu.
	Fig. 1	Elevation (architectural, of Padmāsana type).
	Fig. 4	Plan (of the same).
	Fig. 2	Section (of Mahotsava type).
	Fig. 3	Elevation (of the same).
	Fig. 5	Plan (of the same).
CXXIX	Second group	For higher order of kings such as Chakravartin and others.
	Fig 1	Elevation.
	Fig. 2	Plan.
	Fig. 3	Section.

Plate no.	Figure	Description
CXXX	Third group	For lower order of kings such as Maṇḍaleśa and others.
	Fig. 1	Plan.
	Fig. 2	Elevation.
	Fig. 3	Section.
	Fourth group	Conopied seat.
	Fig. 4	Elevation.
	Fig. 5	Plan.
	Fig. 6	Section.

Not fully illustrated

	First type	Prathama thrones, for the first stage of coronation of the kings.
	Second type	Maṅgala thrones, for the second stage of coronation of the kings.
	Third type	Vira thrones, for the third stage of coronation of the kings.
	Fourth type	Vijaya thrones, for the concluding stage of coronation of the kings.
	Fifth type	Nityārchana thrones, for the daily worship of the gods.
	Sixth type	Nityotsava thrones, for the ordinary festival of the gods.
	Seventh type	Viśesha thrones, for the special use of the gods.
	Eighth type	Mahotsava thrones, for the great festival of the gods.
	Ninth type	Padmāsana, for gods Śiva and Vishṇu and the Chakravartin order of kings (for sculptural illustration (*vide* plate no. CXXXVI).
	Tenth type	Padma-keśara, for the gods and the Chakravartin and other kings (*vide* plate no. CXXXVII).
	Eleventh type	Padma-bhadra, for the Adhirāja class of kings.
	Twelfth type	Śrī-bhadra, for all purposes of the Adhirāja and Narendra classes of kings.
	Thirteenth type	Śrī-viśāla, for all purposes of the Narendra and Pārshṇika classes of kings.
	Fourteenth type	Śrī-bandha, for all purposes of the Pārshṇika and Paṭṭadhara classes of kings.

Plate no.	Figure	Description
	Fifteenth type	Śrī-mukha, for all purposes of the Maṇḍaleśa class of kings.
	Sixteenth type	Bhadrāsana, for all purposes of the Paṭṭabhāj class of kings.
	Seventeenth type	Padma-bhadra (bandha), for all purposes of the Prāhāraka class of kings.
	Eighteenth type	Pāda-bandha, without lion-legs, for all purposes of the Astrgrāha class of kings.

N.B.—For the sculptural illustration of Padmāsana and Padmakesara (*vide* plates nos. CXXXVI and CXXXVII).

CHAPTER XLVI

ARCHES OF NINE TYPES WITH SEVERAL VARIETIES FOR TEMPLES, PALACES, RESIDENTIAL BUILDINGS, PAVILIONS, THRONES, BALANCES, ETC.

Plate no.	Figure	Description
CXXXI	First group	Simple varieties based on geometrical patterns :
	Third type	Crescent-shaped.
	Fifth type	Bow-shaped.
	Fourth type	Triangular.
	First type	Circular.
	Second type	Hexagonal.
CXXXII	Second group	Decorative varieties based on special ornamentation :
	Seventh type	Pushpa-toraṇa or flower pattern.
	Sixth type	Patra-toraṇa or leaf pattern.
	Ninth type	Chitra-toraṇa or variegated pattern.
	Eighth type	Ratna-toraṇa or jewel pattern.
CXXXIII	Third group	Makara-toraṇa or shark pattern (from Suprabhedāgama).
	Fourth group	Kumbha-toraṇa or jug pattern (from Rāmāyaṇa).

CHAPTER XLVII

THE CENTRAL THEATRE

Plate no.	Figure	Description
CXXXIV	Theatre	Sectional elevation.
	Fig. 2	Plan (of the ground floor).

CHAPTER XLVIII

THE ORNAMENTAL TREE

Plate no.	Figure	Description
CXXXV	Tree	For decoration of thrones for gods and kings, and for the Jains (Translation, pp. 563, 565).

CHAPTER XLV

THRONES (SCULPTURAL), FOR GODS AND KINGS AND THEIR CONSORTS, OF EIGHTEEN KINDS VARYING IN SIZE, PLAN, AND ORNAMENTS

Plate no.	Figure	Description
CXXXVI	Ninth type	Padmāsana, for details *see* page 43 above.
CXXXVII	Tenth type	Padmakesara, for details *see* page 45 above.

N.B.—For descriptions of these eighteen thrones *see* pp. 45—46 above.

CHAPTER XLIX

CROWNS FOR GODS, KINGS AND THEIR CONSORTS, OF FOURTEEN KINDS VARYING IN SIZE, PLAN, AND ORNAMENTS

Plate no.	Figure	Description
CXXXVIII	First type	Jaṭā, triangular in plan, decorated with various ornaments, for Brahmā, Rudra, Love-goddess, Brahmāṇī, Chāmuṇḍī, and others.
CXXXIX	Second type	Mauli, of ear-like plan, decorated with various ornaments, for Mana-unmādinī (enchantress of the mind).
CXL	Sixth type	Kuntala, of triangular plan, decorated with various ornaments for Mana-unmādinī (enchantress of the mind), Sarasvatī, Sāvitrī, Earth-goddess, Love-goddess and the queen of the Chakravartin king.

Not illustrated

	Figure	Description
	Third type	Kirīṭa, of ear-like plan, decorated with various ornaments, for Nārāyaṇa, Vishṇu, the Chakravartin, Adhirāja, Mahārāja classes of kings and for Tārakā, Vārāhi, and Vaishṇavī.

Plate no.	Figure	Description
	Fourth type	Karaṇḍa, of peacock's beak-like plan, deco- ted with various ornaments, for inferior go for female deities (Durgā, Earth-godde Kaumārī, Lakshmī, Sarasvatī, Sāvitrī, etc.), mythical beings (Yakshas, Vidyādhar Gandarvas, Kinnaras, Rākshasas, Nīgrah etc.), for Dauvārika, Sugrīva, Pushpadan for Garuḍa and for the Chakravartin, Nare dra, Mahendra and other classes of kings.
	Fifth type	Śirastraka, of bubble plan, decorated with vario ornaments and gold pieces, for the Pārshni class of kings.
	Seventh type	Keśabandha, of triangular plan, decorat with various ornaments, for the goddess Sarasvatī, Sāvitrī, Durgā, Lakshmī, and f the Adhirāja and Narendra classes of kin and their queens.
	Eighth type	Dhammilla, of creeper plan, decorated wi various ornaments, for the queens of th Pārshṇika, Paṭṭadhara, Maṇḍaleśa and Paṭṭ- bhāj classes of kings.
	Ninth type	Alaka, of ear-like plan, decorated wi various ornaments, for Bhairavī, and f the queens of the Prāhāraka and Astragrāh classes of kings.
	Tenth type	Chūḍaka, of cock's crest-like plan, decorate with various ornaments, for the queens the Prāhāraka and Astragrāha classes of king
	Eleventh type	Mukuṭa, of triangular plan, marked with th crescent moon and the sun, decorated wit various ornaments and gold pieces, f Brahmā, Rudra, Nārāyaṇa, Śiva, Vishṇ for inferior gods (Dauvārika, etc.), for Man unmādini and all other female deities, fo the Chakravartin and other classes of king for the queens of Chakravartin, Pārshṇik Paṭṭadhara, Maṇḍaleśa and Paṭṭabhaj kings.
	Twelfth type	Patra-paṭṭa, of ploughshare shape, decorate with various ornaments and gold pieces, fo the Paṭṭadhara class of kings.
	Thirteenth type	Ratna-paṭṭa, of ploughshare shape, marked wit the nine gems and decorated with vario ornaments and gold pieces, for Pārshṇik and Maṇḍaleśa kings.

Plate no.	Figure	Description
	Fourteenth type	Pushpa-paṭṭa, of quadrangular or circular plan, decorated with various ornaments, gold pieces, and flowers, for the Paṭṭabhāj class of kings.

N.B.—Petty kings are not allowed to put on a real crown; they wear garlands in place of the crown.

CHAPTER L

ORNAMENTS OF FOUR GROUPS OF SOME THIRTY TYPES AND FURNITURE OF EIGHT GROUPS, COMPRISING SEVERAL VARIETIES

Plate no.	Figure	Description
		ORNAMENTS
CXLI	First type	Hāra (chain), of 108 or 64 strings, worn round the neck, suspending down to the heart.
CXLII	Special group	Suvarṇa-kañchuka (cuirass or bodice) worn round the breast (taken from the other texts).
		Not illustra ed
	First group	Patra-kalpa, adorned with leaves and creepers, for the gods and the Sārvabhauma class of kings.
	Second group	Chitra-kalpa, adorned with leaves, creepers, paintings, all jewels and calyxes, for the gods and the Chakravartin class of kings.
	Third group	Ratna-kalpa, adorned with flowers and jewels, for the gods and the Adhirāja and Narendra classes of kings.
	Fourth group	Miśra-kalpa, adorned with leaves and jewels, for the gods and the Adhirāja, Narendra and all other kings.
	Second type	Pendant, Skandhamālā-avalambana, suspended from the root of the arm and connected with the Keyura and Kaṭaka armlets.
	Third type	Mid-armlets, Keyura and Kaṭaka.
	Fourth type	Upper-armlets, Supurīma.
	Fifth type	String-armlets, Valaya-dāman.
	Sixth type	Wrist-bangle, Prakoshṭha-valaya.
	Seventh type	String-bracelets, Maṇibandha-kalāpaka.

Plate no.	Figure	Description
	Eighth type	Jewelled rings for fingers except the middle one.
	Ninth type	Breast-string (Brassiere), Stana-sūtra.
	Tenth type	Belly-band, Udara-bandha.
	Eleventh type	Chain, worn on the side of the sacred thread covering the breasts.
	Twelfth type	Front string, Pura-sūtra, suspended from where the sacred thread is tied down to the hip-chain.
	Thirteenth type	Hip-chain, Kaṭi-sūtra, worn round the waist.
	Fourteenth type	Armlet, Valaya, put around the root of the arm.
	Fifteenth type	String bracelet, Dāman, worn round the arm-pits.
	Sixteenth type	Belt, Paṭṭikā, put along the breadth of the hip-chain and round the knee-cap.
	Seventeenth type	Lion-face, put covering the sex-organ.
	Eighteenth type	Jewelled band, put covering the sex-organ.
	Nineteenth type	Five saphires, suspended with chains along the waist.
	Twentieth type	Net-ornaments, Jāla, for the feet.
	Twenty-first type	Silk-cloth, suspending down to the ankle.
	Twenty-second type	Skin, worn down to the knee.
	Twenty-third type	Bark, worn down to the knee.
	Twenty-fourth type	Skirt, worn down to the knee.
	Twenty-fifth type	Chinnavīra (or Chhannavīra), bodice, passing over both shoulders and hips, crossing and fastening in the middle of the breast and the back.
	Twenty-sixth type	Vana-mālā, garland worn round the neck.
	Twenty-seventh type	Serpent-belt, Kaṭaka, worn above the ankle.
	Twenty-eighth type	Anklets, Nūpura, for the feet.

Plate no.	Figure	Description
	Twenty-ninth type	Ear-rings, Makara, crocodile shaped.
	Thirteenth type	Gold rings, Tāṭaṅka, for the ears.
		FURNITURE
CXLIII	Fourth group	Mañjushā, basket, made of leaf, wood, etc., decorated with several ornaments, used as wardrobe, oil-tank, trunk, etc.
CXLIV	Fifth group	Dolā, swing or palanquin, consisting of pillars, walls, iron rings, transom, board, mirrors, portico, doors, etc., for the use of the gods and men.
		Not illustrated
	First group	Dīpa-daṇḍa, lamp-post, made of wood, metals, and stone, movable and stationary, erected in front of the house and elsewhere.
	Second group	Vyajana, fan, furnished with posts made of wood or iron, leather chain, ornaments, etc., surfaces decorated with images of gods and inscribed with colours and metallic substances, used in cars, chariots and elsewhere.
	Third group	Darpaṇa, mirror, generally circular or lotus pattern, made of wooden or metal post, brass board, handle and other members, varying, according to castes, used as an attribute of the goddess of learning (Sarasvatī) and an ornament for doors, for cars and chariots, for decoration of buildings, for porticos or swings, for royal umbrellas, and fixed on crowns, etc.
	Sixth group	Tulā, balance, made of wood and metals, consisting of scale beam, scale pans, tongue, pivot, bar-like chains and other members, used also for the kings to be weighed against gold to be distributed, varying according to the nine classes of kings.
	Seventh group	Patra, seal, of leaf-pattern, imprinted with the palm-print of the right hand of the kings and well marked with gold lines, including a pen for marking the commencement of the new year, and varying according to the (nine) ranks of kings.

Plate no.	Figure	Description
	Eighth group	Pañjara, cages and nests, movable and stationary, made of suitable materials and necessary members, for the use of the musk deer (cat), the parrot, the Chātaka bird, the Chakora bird, the duck, the pigeon, the peacock, the francoline partridge, the wagtail, the cock, the mongoose, the sparrow, the boar, the tiger, etc.

N.B—The bigger articles of furniture are separately described: cars and chariots (Chapter XLIII), bedsteads and couches (Chapter XLIV), and seats and thrones (Chapter XLV), of which the following are further varieties more fully described in other texts:

	Ninth group	Benches—To accommodate three persons.
	Tenth group	Couches—Covered with canopies.
	Eleventh group	Chairs—Rectangular, cushioned, cane-bottomed.
	Twelfth group	Sofa—Raised on a pedestal, with many legs, state, etc., with arms to it.
	Thirteenth group	Carpets—Of various tpyes, inwrought with gold or with silk.
	Fourteenth group	Rugs—Of various kinds, including horse-rugs and carriage-rugs, with long hair on one or both sides.
	Fifteenth group	Curtains—Of various patterns and materials.
	Sixteenth group	Counterpanes—Of many colours.
	Seventeenth group	Coverlets—With long fleece, woollen marked with thick flowers, cotton dyed with figures of animals.
	Eighteenth group	Matresses—Of various kinds.
	Nineteenth group	Pillows—Of the size of man's head and body.
	Twentieth group	Bolsters—Of five kinds as stuffed with wool, cotton, bark, grass, and leaves.
	Twenty-first group	Elephant housings—Richly decorated and of various kinds.
	Twenty-second group	Skins—Of panthers, antelope, etc.
	Twenty-third group	Cushions—Large, crimson and of other kinds.
	Twenty-fourth group	Mosquito-curtains—Of various sizes and colours.
	Twenty-fifth group	Spittoon—Of various kinds.

CHAPTER LI

THE TRIAD, COMPRISING BRAHMĀ, VISHṆU, AND ŚIVA

Plate no.	Figure	Description
CXLV	Brahmā	With consorts, Sarasvatī on the right and Śāvitrī on the left, measured in the large ten *tāla*, the consorts being in the middle ten *tāla*; placed on one pedestal in the erect posture, (may also be seated on a lotus throne or be in a recumbent posture); in the equipoise (single flexion, three-flexion or excessive flexion) pose; stationary (or movable) position; made with gold, silver, copper, stone, wood, stucco, grit, glass, or terra-cotta; in high relief, (middle relief or low relief); furnished with four faces, one neck, eight eyes, eight ears, two legs, four arms, the two lower hands being in boon-giving and refuge-offering attitudes, and the two upper hands holding attributes of the water-pot, and the rosary (or two sacrificial ladles); wearing crowns, the matted hair, ear-rings, various ornaments, the sacred thread, outer garment, whitish clothes, a strip of bark, an upper garment and golden complexion.

N.B.—For description of Sarasvatī see plate CXLVIII, p. 57, and of Sāvitrī see pp. 57-58 above.

Plate no.	Figure	Description
CXLVI	Vishṇu	With consorts, Lakshmī and Bhūdevī, alternately on the right and the left, measured in the large ten *tāla*, the consorts being in the middle ten *tāla*, made in the erect, (seated or recumbent) posture, on three lotus seats, in the equipoise (single flexion, three flexion or excessive flexion) pose; stationary (or movable) position; made with gold, silver, copper, stone, wood, stucco, grit, glass, or terra-cotta; in the high relief, (middle relief, or low relief); furnished with a single head, two ears, two legs, but four arms, one hand being in refuge-offering attitude and three others holding attributes of the (lotus), mace, discus and conch-shell; wearing the *kirīṭa* crown, the ornamental nimbus at the back of the head, the Śrīvatsa symbol on the chest, the sacred thread, yellow garment, bright blue complexion, smiling face, straight nose and elongated eyes.

N.B.—For description of Lakshmī, see plate CXLIX, pp. 57-58, and of Bhūdevī otherwise called Mahī, p. 59 above.

Plate no.	Figure	Description
CXLVII	Śiva	With the consort Pārvatī on the le measured in the large ten *tāla*, the conso being in the middle ten *tāla*, made in ere (seated or recumbent posture), on tw lotus seats, in the equipoise (single flexio three flexion or excessive flexion) pos stationary (or movable) position; made wi gold, silver, copper, stone, wood, stucco, gri glass, or terra-cotta; in high relief, (midd relief, or low relief); furnished with a singl head but a third eye on the forehead, the le side of the neck being marked with th *kālakūṭa* poison, bearing two ears, two leg four arms, two hands in the boon-giving an the refuge-offering attitudes, the attribute in the other two hands being an antelop and a tabor, wearing a crown marked wit the Ganges and the crescent moon, and th matted hair of an ascetic, the tiger-skin an a waist cloth, the sacred thread, ear-rings an various ornaments and reddish complexion.

***N.B.*—For description of Pārvatī, otherwise called Durgā, *see* p. 59 above.**

CHAPTER LII

THE PHALLUS OR SYMBOL OF THE TRIAD, COMPRISING SEVERAL TYPES

Plate no.	Figure	Description
		Not illustrated
	Liṅga (general)	Brahmā portion at the bottom being of quadrangular shape, Vishṇu portion at the middle of octagonal shape, and the Śiva portion at the top of circular shape, with flutes (or stream-mark) varying from sixteen to one thousand. These shapes are interchangeable, the topmost point being like a bud, leaf or umbrella. It includes the *Pīṭha* (pedestal) upon which it stands. It is carved singly or in group, varying according to castes, materials (gold, silver, copper, stone, wood, stucco, grit, glass, or terra-cotta), and sizes. It is used for personal and public worship.
	First type	Śaiva, with its characteristic features.

Plate no.	Figure	Description
	Second type	Pāśupata, with its characteristic features.
	Third type	Kālamukha, with its characteristic features.
	Fourth type	Mahāvrata, with its characteristic features.
	Fifth type	Vāma, with its characteristic features.
	Sixth type	Bhairava, with its characteristic features.
	Seventh type	Samakarṇa, with its characteristic features, the worship by the Brahmans.
	Eighth type	Vardhamāna, with its characteristic features, for worship by the Kshatriyas.
	Ninth type	Śivāṅka, with its characteristic features, for worship by the Vaiśyas.
	Tenth type	Svastika, with its cross-like shape and other characteristic features, for worship by the Śūdras.
	Eleventh type	Jāti, with its characteristic height.
	Twelfth type	Chhanda, with its characteristic height.
	Thirteenth type	Vikalpa, with its characteristic height.
	Fourteenth type	Ābhāsa, with its characteristic height.
	Fifteenth type	Nāgara, with its characteristic width and square form.
	Sixteenth type	Drāviḍa, with its characteristic width and octagonal or hexagonal form.
	Seventeenth type	Vesara, with its characteristic width and round form.
	Eighteenth type	Daivika, self-revealed, with its characteristic features, for divine purposes.
	Nineteenth type	Mānusha, self-revealed, with its characteristic features, for human purposes, on the terrace of a mountain.
	Twentieth type	Gāṇava, self-revealed, with its characteristic features, for the Gaṇas.
	Twenty-first type	Ārsha, self-revealed, with its characteristic features, for the seers or sages.
	Twenty-second type	Ātmārtha, with its characteristic features, for personal worship.
	Twenty-third type	Parārtha, with its characteristic features, for public worship.
	Twenty-fourth type	Kshaṇika, with its characteristic features, for temporary worship.

Plate no.	Figure	Description
	Twenty-fifth type	Sthāyin, with its characteristic features, for permanent use.
	Twenty-sixth type	Ekaliṅga, carved singly and independently, with its characteristic features.
	Twenty-seventh type	Bahu-liṅga, carved in groups, with its characteristic features.

N.B.—There are several other minor varieties.

CHAPTER LIII

ALTARS OR SYMBOLS OF SATĪ (ŚIVA'S CONSORT), COMPRISING EIGHT TYPES AND FIFTY ONE INDEPENDENT VARIETIES

Not illustrated

Plate no.	Figure	Description
	Pīṭha (general)	Erected both independently of the Liṅga and as a component part thereof and conforming to the shape of the Liṅga, but of a different material; installed both inside and outside the main temple, in the central plot (*Brahma-pīṭha*) of villages and the palaces, on the top of a mountain and the bank of a river, etc., on the fifty-one sacred spots (*Pīṭha-sthāna*), of white colour for the Brahmans, of red colour for the Kshatriyas, of yellow colour for the Vaiśyas, and of black colour for the Śūdras.
	First type	Bhadrapīṭha, with its characteristic features.
	Second type	Śrībhadra, with its characteristic features.
	Third type	Śrīviśāla, with its characteristic features.
	Fourth type	Upapīṭha, with its characteristic features.
	Fifth type	Nāgara, with its characteristic features and quadrangular form.
	Sixth type	Drāviḍa, with its characteristic features and octagonal form.
	Seventh type	Vesara, with its characteristic features and round form.
	Eighth type	Āndhra, with its characteristic features and hexagonal form.

N.B.—There are fifty-one independent varieties with slightly different features, but bearing as many epithets.

CHAPTER LIV

FEMALE DEITIES, COMPRISING THIRTEEN GODDESSES

Plate no.	Figure	Description
CXLVIII	First type	Sarasvatī, goddess of learning, carved both independently (and as consort of Brahmā), measured in the (middle) ten *tāla*, placed on a lotus pedestal as seated in a *padmāsana* (cross-legged) posture, in the equipoised pose, and in a stationary position; made of gold, silver, copper, stone, wood, stucco, grit, glass, or terra-cotta; furnished with a cheerful face, two eyes, two ears, two legs, four arms, holding the mirror (or lute) in the upper right hand, a book in the upper left hand, the rosary garland in the lower right hand, and a pot in the lower left hand. Her complexion is crystal white (or gold). She wears yellow clothes and a knotted garment, jewel scarf, etc. She puts on the *keśa-bandha*, *karanda* or *kuntala* crown together with the crest jewel, a bee mark on pearl fillet on the forehead, crocodile shaped rings, flowers and pearl garlands on the ears, a chain and pearl strings over the neck and shoulders, breast-bands or brassier round the breasts and garlands for the arms, the *keyura* and *kataka* armlets, bracelets or bangles on the wrists, pearl bands on the root of the arms, rings of precious stones on all fingers except the middle one, serpent-shaped net ornaments on the legs, anklets, jewel rings on the toes, and all other ornaments. There is a second variety of Sarasvatī with two arms, the right hand being in boon-giving attitude, and the left holding a lotus; seated or erect on the right of Brahmā, with same complexion but slightly different ornaments.
CXLIX	Third type	Lakshmī, goddess of prosperity, of two types, great and ordinary, carved both independently and as a consort of Vishnu, measured in the (middle) ten *tāla*, placed on a red lotus as seated in a *padmāsana* (cross-legged) posture, in the equipoised pose and in a stationary position; made

Plate no.	Figure	Description
		of gold, silver, copper, stone, wood, stucco, grit, glass, or terra-cotta; furnished with plump and full breasts, a cheerful face with large and broad eyes smiling, having two ears, two legs, four arms, the upper right hand being in the refuge-offering attitude, the upper left hand holding a small drum, the lower right hand holding a lotus (or rosary garland), and the lower left hand holding a blue or red lotus. She bears a pure gold complexion and is clad in yellow clothes or a red garment, jewel *chhannavīra* jacket and gold or jewel scarf. She puts on the *kuntala* type of crown and there is a (bee-mark or) jewel fillet on the forehead. She is adorned with gold rings or crocodile rings with gold strings or garlands on the ears, a pretty chain and strings over the neck, jewels or gold fillets on the nipples and around the breasts, gold *keyura*, and *kaṭaka* upper armlets, jewel bracelets on the wrists and bangles on the wrist-joints, jewel strings round the buttock and jewel garlands, etc., three pendants adorned with all gems, serpent-shaped bracelets with jewel bands and anklets on the feet, and jewel rings on the toes, and all other ornaments.
		There is an ordinary type, furnished with two arms, two eyes, two elephants on the two sides and slightly different ornaments.
		There is a third type, placed on the right side of Vishṇu, in an erect or sitting posture, furnished with two eyes and two arms holding a lotus with the uplifted hand and the right hand being in the boon-giving posture or hanging downwards, and furnished with slightly different ornaments.
		Not illustrated
	Second type	Śāvitri, carved both independently and as a consort of Brahmā, measured in the middle ten *tāla*, placed on a lotus pedestal in an erect or sitting posture, in one of the four poses, in stationary or movable position; made of one of the nine materials; furnished with white, red, or

Plate no.	Figure	Description
		bright blue complexion, two eyes, two arms, a peaceful face, a silk garment or yellow clothes, with a characteristic crown and various ornaments.
	Fourth type	Mahī or Bhūdevi, earth-goddess (mother country), carved both independently and as a consort of Vishṇu, measured in the middle ten *tāla*, placed on a seat, in an erect or sitting posture, in one of the four poses, in stationary or movable position; made of one of the nine materials; furnished with bright blue complexion, two arms, two eyes, a peaceful motherly face, fine silk clothes, with a characteristic crown, lotus attribute, and various ornaments.
	Fifth type	Durgā or Pārvatī, the Maid of Mountain, carved both independently and as a consort of Śiva or Phallus, measured in the middle ten *tāla*, placed on a seat, in an erect or sitting posture, in one of the four poses, in the attitude of a milk-maid, in stationary (or movable) position; made of one of the nine materials; furnished with light blue complexion, fine silk clothes or yellow garment, lotus attribute, long arms, large eyes, plump breasts with high slope, broad belly, well marked buttock, large hip and thighs, broad smiling face, high neck prominent mouth, charactaristic crown and various ornaments.
		There are two other varieties: Gaurī or the White, and Pārvatī or the Maid of Mountain with slightly different features and ornaments.
	Sixth type	Mana-unmādinī (enchantress of the mind) or Ratī, goddess of love, measured in the middle ten *tāla*, generally placed in Śiva temple, in an erect posture and characteristic pose, or seated on a bull, made with one of the nine materials; furnished with three eyes, four arms, water-lily and rosary attributes, reddish-white or bright blue complexion, fine silk clothes, characteristic crown and various ornaments, carved, when independent, with a young hare and a horse on the two sides.

Plate no.	Figure	Description
	Seventh type	Vārāhī, measured in the nine *tāla*, placed on the Bhadra pedestal, in a suitable posture, pose and position; made of one of the nine materials; furnished with four arms bearing the plough and other attributes, hog's face with snout, bright blue complexion, characteristic crown and various ornaments.
	Eighth type	Kaumārī, measured in the nine *tāla*, placed on the Bhadra pedestal, in a suitable posture, pose and position; made of one of the nine materials; furnished with four arms, three eyes, the *karaṇḍa* crown, red complexion, bright blue clothes, characteristic attributes and various ornaments.
	Ninth type	Chāmuṇḍī, measured in the nine *tāla*, placed on the Bhadra pedestal, in a suitable posture, pose and position; made of one of the nine materials; furnished with three eyes, four arms, the *jaṭā* crown, arrow attribute, dark-bluish complexion, garland on the head, conch leaf and rings on the ears, and various other ornaments.
	Tenth type	Bhairavī, measured in the nine *tāla*, placed on the Bhadra pedestal, in a suitable posture, pose and position; made of one of the nine materials; furnished with three eyes, four arms, arrow attribute, red complexion, black clothes, characteristic crown, attributes, and various ornaments. There is a second type, Rudrāṇī, with slightly different features and ornaments.
	Eleventh type	Māhendrī, measured in the nine *tāla*, placed on the Bhadra pedestal in a suitable posture, pose and position; made of one of the nine materials; furnished with three eyes, four arms, bearing characteristic attributes, crown, complexion, clothes, and various ornaments.
	Twelfth type	Vaishṇavī, measured in the nine *tāla*, placed on the Bhadra pedestal, in a suitable posture, pose and position; made of one of the nine materials; furnished with four arms, three eyes, bright blue complexion, yellow clothes, characteristic attributes, crown, and various ornaments.

Plate no	Figure	Description
	Thirteenth type	Brahmāṇī, measured in the nine *tāla*, placed on the Bhadra pedestal, in a suitable posture, pose and position; made of one of the nine materials; furnished with four arms, three eyes, four faces, the *jaṭā* crown, pot and rosary attributes, white complexion, red clothes, and various ornaments.

N.B.—There are references to other minor varieties of female deities also.

CHAPTER LV

JAIN IMAGES, COMPRISING FIVE GROUPS AND TWENTY-FOUR TĪRTHANKARAS

Plate no.	Figure	Description
CL	Third group	Jina, measured in the large ten *tāla*, in a straight, erect or sitting posture in the equipoised pose, stationary (or movable) position; made with gold, silver, copper, stone, wood, stucco, grit, glass, or terra-cotta; in high relief; furnished with two arms and two eyes; the head being clean-shaven but furnished with the top knot (nimbus); the legs uniformly straight, two long hands, suspending, two feet on the lotus throne with a pinnacle, the crocodile arch, ornamental tree, royal elephants, etc., in a straight pose; the whole body being in a stiff attitude; bearing a meditative look on the supreme soul; placed below the fourth or third heaven; wearing no robes or ornaments; marked with the *śrīvatsa* symbol in gold on the chest; crystal complexion; accompanied by sages, demigods and goddesses in a praying mood: Nārada with his musical instrument, Yaksha and Yaksheśvara on the sides with raised chowries, Vidyādharas and minor kings.
		There is a sitting variety, placed on the lotus seat, with two hands placed upwards over the face.
		Not illustrated
	First group	Siddhas, measured in the large ten *tāla*, in an erect or sitting posture, in equipoised pose,

Plate no.	Figure	Description
		stationary or movable position; in high, middle or low relief; made of one of the nine materials, and with characteristic features slightly different from those of the Jinas.
	Second group	Sugandhas, measured in the large ten *tāla*, in an erect or sitting posture, in equipoised pose, in stationary or movable position; in high, middle or low relief; made of one of the nine materials, and with characteristic features slightly different from those of the Jinas.
	Fourth group	Arhatas, measured in the large ten *tāla*, in an erect or sitting posture, in equipoised pose, in stationary or movable position; in high, middle or low relief; made of one of the nine materials, and with characteristic features slightly different from those of the Jinas.
	Fifth group	Pārśvakas, measured in the large ten *tāla*, in an erect or sitting posture, in equipoised pose, stationary or movable position; in high, middle or low relief; made of one of the nine materials, and with characteristic features slightly different from those of the Jinas.
	Tīrthaṅkaras	Comprising twenty-four types, also measured in the large ten *tāla*, carved in an erect or sitting posture; in suitable pose and position, with one of the nine materials, generally in high relief, with slightly different characteristic features:
	First type	Ādinātha, with his distinctive sign of the bull.
	Second type	Ajitanātha, with his distinctive sign of the elephant.
	Third type	Śambhunātha, with his distinctive sign of the horse.
	Fourth type	Abhayānandanātha, with his distinctive sign of the monkey.
	Fifth type	Sumatinātha, with his distinctive sign of the red goose.

Plate no.	Figure	Description
	Sixth type	Supadmanātha, with his distinctive sign of the lotus.
	Seventh type	Supārśvanātha, with his distinctive sign of the Svastika.
	Eighth type	Chandraprabha, with his distinctive sign of the crescent moon.
	Ninth type	Pushpadanta, with his distinctive sign of the crocodile.
	Tenth type	Śītalanātha, with his distinctive sign of the tree or flower.
	Eleventh type	Aṁśanātha, with his distinctive sign of the rhinoceros.
	Twelfth type	Vasupadya, with his distinctive sign of the buffalo.
	Thirteenth type	Vimalanātha, with his distinctive sign of the boar.
	Fourteenth type	Anantanātha, with his distinctive sign of the porcupine.
	Fifteenth type	Dharmanātha, with his distinctive sign of the thunderbolt.
	Sixteenth type	Śāntanātha, with his distinctive sign of the antelope.
	Seventeenth type	Kunthanātha, with his distinctive sign of the goat.
	Eighteenth type	Aranātha, with his distinctive sign of the fish.
	Nineteenth type	Mallinātha, with his distinctive sign of the pinnacle.
	Twentieth type	Munisuvı his distinctive sign of the tortoise.
	Twenty-first type	Naminātha, with distinctive sign of the lotus with stalk.
	Twenty-second type	Neminātha, with his distinctive sign of the shell.
	Twenty-third type	Pārśvanātha, with his distinctive sign of the snake.
	Twenty-fourth type	Vardhamāna or Māhāvira, with his distinctive sign of the lion.

CHAPTER LVI

BUDDHIST IMAGES, COMPRISING SEVERAL TYPES

Plate no.	Figure	Description
CLI	Buddha	Measured in the large ten *tāla*, made of wood stone, or metallic substances (gold, silver, or copper), in sitting (or erect) posture, equipoised pose, stationary (or movable) position; in high, (middle, or low relief, or on a tablet or wall) with terra-cotta or grit; placed on a throne decorated with arches, holy fig tree and ornamental tree; furnished with a full face, long nose, smiling eyes, elongated ears, fleshy body, broad chest, round belly, long arms, white complexion, yellow clothes, the *ushṇisha* (protuberance of the skull), and carved in a praying attitude. There are other types, generally in an erect posture and with slightly different characteristic features.

CHAPTER LVII

SAGES, COMPRISING SEVEN GREAT PATRIARCHS

Plate no.	Figure	Description
CLII	Second type	Kāśyapa, measured in the eight *tāla*, carved in an erect (or sitting) posture, in stationary (or movable) position; in high relief; made with gold, silver, copper, wood, stone, stucco, grit, glass, or terra-cotta; furnished with yellow complexion, yellow clothes, two arms, two eyes, matted hair, sacred thread, upper garment, holding a book in the left hand and a staff in the right.
		Not illustrated
	First type	Agastya, measured in the seven *tāla*, carved in erect or sitting posture, in a praying attitude, and stationary or movable position; in high, middle, or low relief; made with one of the nine materials; furnished with bright-green complexion, yellow garments, two arms, two eyes, large belly, brownish complexion, full and crooked form, *jaṭā* and *juṭa* matted hair, sacred thread and upper garment, holding a book in one hand and a staff in the other,

Plate no.	Figure	Description
	Third type	Bhṛigu, measured in the eight *tāla*, carved in an erect or sitting posture, in a praying attitude, and stationary or movable position; in high, middle, or low relief: made with one of the nine materials; furnished with dark complexion, yellow clothes, two arms, two eyes, matted hair, sacred thread, upper garment, and holding a book in one hand and a staff in the other.
	Fourth type	Vaśishṭha, measured in the nine *tāla*, carved in an erect or sitting posture, in a praying attitude, in stationary or movable position; in high, middle, or low relief; made with one of the nine materials; furnished with red complexion, yellow clothes, matted hair, sacred thread, upper garment, holding a book in one hand and a staff in the other.
	Fifth type	Bhārgava, measured in the nine *tāla*, carved in an erect or sitting posture, in a praying attitude, and stationary or movable position; in high, middle, or low relief; made with one of the nine materials; furnished with brownish (tawny) complexion, yellow clothes, two arms, two eyes, matted hair, sacred thread, upper garment, holding a book in one hand and a staff in the other.
	Sixth type	Viśvāmitra, measured in the nine *tāla*, carved in an erect or sitting posture, in a praying attitude, and stationary or movable position; in high, middle, or low relief; made of one of the nine materials; furnished with reddish complexion, yellow clothes, matted hair, sacred thread, upper garment, two eyes, two arms, holding a book in one hand and a staff in the other.
	Seventh type	Bharadvāja, measured in the nine *tāla*, carved in an erect or sitting posture, in a praying attitude, and stationary or movable position; in high, middle, or low relief; made of one of the nine materials; furnished with greenish (turmeric) complexion, yellow clothes, matted hair, sacred thread, upper garment, two eyes, two arms, holding a book in one hand and a staff in the other.

CHAPTER LVIII

MYTHICAL BEINGS, COMPRISING SIX TYPES

Plate no.	Figure	Description
CLIII	Second type	Vidyādhara, chowry-bearer of the gods and a kind of fairy possessed of magical powers; measured in the nine *tāla*; made of one of the nine materials; furnished with two arms, two eyes, the *karaṇḍa* crown, demon shape, dark-red and yellow complexion, hands kept touching the knees, and raised towards the gateway, plough-shaped legs turned backwards, the right leg being in the *svastika* pose and the left bent (alternately), one hand holding up chowries and the other kept touching the ground; carved in a sitting posture and figured on arches, palaces and storeyed buildings.
		Not illustrated
	First type	Yaksha, attendant to the gods, Jain deities, bearer of chowries, measured in the nine *tāla*; made of one of the nine materials; furnished with two arms, two eyes, the *karaṇḍa* crown, legs clad in clothes, demon shape, bright-blue and yellow complexion, plough-shaped legs turned towards the back, the right leg being in the *svastika* pose and the left bent, hands kept touching the knees and raised towards the gateway, one hand holding up chowries and the other kept touching the ground; carved on arches thrones, palaces and storeyed buildings.
	Third type	Rākshasa, evil spirit of an offensive disposition, carved with characteristic features, measure, materials, look, etc.
	Fourth type	Nigraha, supernatural being of a benevolent disposition, carved with characteristic features, measure, materials, look, etc.
	Fifth type	Gandharva, celestial choir and musician, carved with suitable measure and materials; furnished with red complexion, two arms, two eyes, demon shape, singing or dancing pose, holding a lute and other musical instruments, and decorated with various ornaments.

Plate no.	Figure	Description
	Sixth type	Kinnara, a kind of hybrid being : legs being like those of an animal (horse), upper body like that of a man, face like of Garuḍa, and arms being provided with wings, holding a lute, possessing the beautiful hue of a flower, wearing the lotus crown, measured in the nine *tāla ;* made of one of the nine materials ; furnished with various ornaments ; figured on arches, chariots, etc.

CHAPTER LIX

DEVOTEES, COMPRISING FOUR CLASSES

Plate no	Figure	Description
CLIV	Fourth type	Sāyujya class, in intimate union with the god, measured in the large ten *tāla,* in an erect posture, and praying attitude ; furnished with characteristic features and ornaments ; figured on storeyed buildings.
		Not illustrated
	First type	Sālokya class, dwelling in the same place as the god, measured in the large nine *tāla* ; furnished with characteristic features and ornaments ; figured on storeyed buildings.
	Second type	Sāmīpya class, dwelling in the vicinity of the god, measured in the small ten *tāla* ; furnished with characteristic features and ornaments ; figured on storeyed buildings.
	Third type	Sārūpya class, in close identity with the god, measured in the middle ten *tāla* ; furnished with characteristic features and ornaments ; figured on storeyed buildings.

CHAPTER LX

THE GOOSE, VEHICLE OF BRAHMĀ

Not illustrated

Plate no.	Figure	Description
	Goose	Riding animal of Brahmā, measured in the two *tāla* ; furnished with plough-shaped wing-joint, circular thigh-root, white complexion

Plate no	Figure	Description
		all over the limbs, legs being reddish-white, beak goldish, variegated feathers, crest and tail; carved in rows in all buildings, foot-mark on the dome, figured on the entablature, architrave, finial, recess, and neck of various buildings.

CHAPTER LXI

GARUḌA, VEHICLE OF VISHṆU

Plate no.	Figure	Description
CLV	Garuda	Mythical being, riding animal of Vishṇu, measured in the nine *tāla*, carved in a sitting (erect or walking) posture, in stationary (or movable) position; furnished with the lion-feet, face smiling at end of the eyes, mind expressed on the face, two arms, two wings, alternately parrot beak and goose foot, face with fangs, bird-wings, eight-hooded snake, terrific look, various ornaments including the *karaṇḍa* crown, five colours (yellow, white, dark-blue, red and black); bright green from hair to ear, blue edge, five-coloured wings with spotted bodice, yellow from the heart (part to the hips and hands, red knee, whitish feet, alternately bent face, hands and legs, body gold; alternately five-coloured lion-head, red pointed tail; made of stone, earth wood, planked grit, etc.; carved in a sitting (or erect) posture, alternately with joined palms meditating on Vishṇu; installed in and at the gate of Vishṇu temple; figured in storeyed buildings.

CHAPTER LXII

THE BULL, VEHICLE OF ŚIVA AND LOVE-GODDESS

Not illustrated

Plate no.	Figure	Description
	Bull	Riding animal of Śiva and Love-goddess, carved in various (*tāla*) measures, in recumbent or erect posture, and walking pose, installed on a pedestal facing the Śiva temple both inside the shrine and in a

late no.	Figure	Description
		pavilion in front of the temple, or at the door; white all over, the four legs, hoofs and two ears being red; wearing a tiger-skin, garlands at the neck and foot-rings or anklets; made solid or hollow, of gold, silver, copper, stone, wood, glass, stucco, earth and planked grit or baked clay; furnished with various other ornaments; figured on the entablature, etc.

CHAPTER LXIII

THE LION, VEHICLE OF PĀRVATĪ

Not illustrated

Plate no	Figure	Description
	Lion	Riding animal of Pārvatī and others, carved in suitable measure, the tail being generally equal to the height; in erect, sitting, or recumbent posture, the four legs being like those of the tiger; furnished with white complexion, with red mane, crescent-shaped nails and teeth; figured on arches, thrones, pillars, etc.

CHAPTER LXV

TĀLAS, COMPRISING TWELVE TYPES

Plate no.	Figure	Description
CLVI	First type	Large ten *tāla*, in which measures of one hundred and fifty-four parts (limbs) of the body is given. It is used in measuring superhuman deities, including Buddha, Jina, etc
	Second type	Nine *tāla*, used in measuring goddesses, sages, demons, etc.
	Third type	Eight *tāla*, used in measuring sages, devotees ordinary human beings, etc
	Fourth type	Seven *tāla*, used in measuring sages, demigods, females, etc.
	Fifth type	Six *tāla*, used in measuring the tiger, etc.

Plate no.	Figure	Description
	Sixth type	Five *tāla*, used in measuring Gaṇeśa with elephant's head and human body.
	Seventh type	Four *tāla*, used in measuring goblins, etc.
	Eighth type	Three *tāla*, used in measuring Kinnara with horse's head and human body, etc.
	Ninth type	Two *tāla*, used in measuring birds.
	Tenth type	One *tāla*, used in measuring Vandukas Kabandhas (headless body), etc.
		Not illustrated
	Eleventh type	Eleven *tāla*, used in measuring certain gods
	Twelfth type	Twelve *tāla*, used in measuring Rākshasas, etc.

N.B.—Each of the *tāla* system admits of three varieties, large, middle, and small; ordinarily in the ten *tāla*, the whole height of an image is ten times its face, in nine *tāla* it is nine times, in eight *tāla* it is eight times, and so forth.

CHAPTER LXVII

PLUMB LINES, ELEVEN IN NUMBER

Plate no.	Figure	Description
CLVII	First type	Plumb-lines shown on the front of the image.
	Second type	Plumb-lines shown on the side of the image.

N.B.—There are eleven lines drawn through the body of an image in order to find out accurately the perpendicular and the horizontal measurement of, and the distance between different parts of the body, varying in accordance with the three postures (erect, seated, and recumbent) and the four poses (equipoise, slight flexion, three flexions, and excessive flexions).

ALLAHABAD UNIVERSITY,
February 6, 1933.

P. K. ACHARYA.

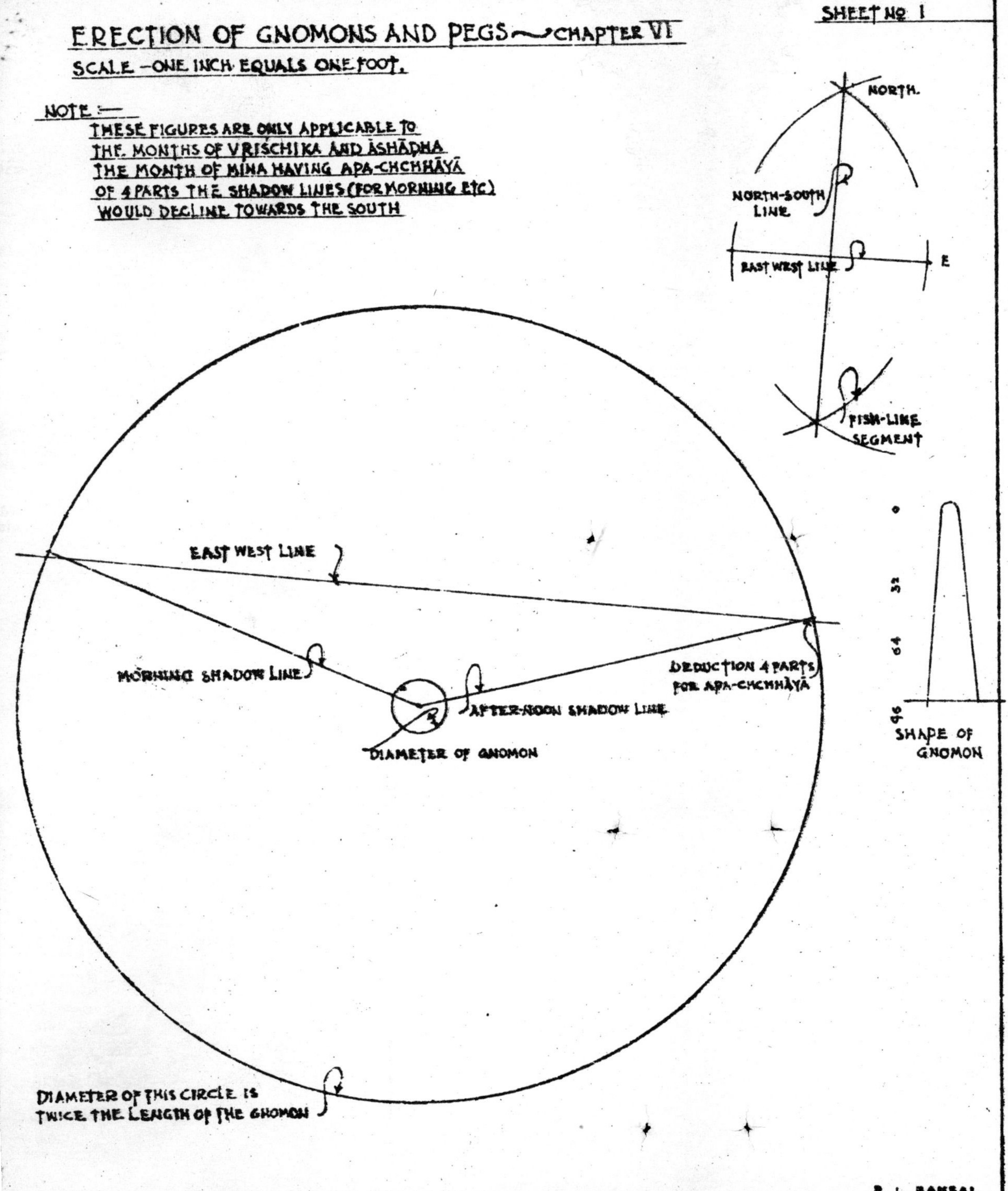
SHEET NO 1
ERECTION OF GNOMONS AND PEGS — CHAPTER VI
SCALE – ONE INCH EQUALS ONE FOOT.
NOTE :—
THESE FIGURES ARE ONLY APPLICABLE TO
THE MONTHS OF VRISCHIKA AND ASHĀDHA
THE MONTH OF MINA HAVING APA-CHCHHĀYĀ
OF 4 PARTS THE SHADOW LINES (FOR MORNING ETC)
WOULD DECLINE TOWARDS THE SOUTH
NORTH.
NORTH-SOUTH LINE
EAST WEST LINE
E
FISH-LIKE SEGMENT
EAST WEST LINE
MORNING SHADOW LINE
DEDUCTION 4 PARTS FOR APA-CHCHHĀYĀ
AFTER-NOON SHADOW LINE
DIAMETER OF GNOMON
0
32
64
96
SHAPE OF GNOMON
DIAMETER OF THIS CIRCLE IS TWICE THE LENGTH OF THE GNOMON
R. L. BANSAL.

SHEET NO. III

THE SITE PLANS ~ CHAPTER VII

FIG 1. SAKALA OF 1 PLOT.
FIG 2. PECHAKA — 4 —
FIG 3. PĪTHA — 9 —

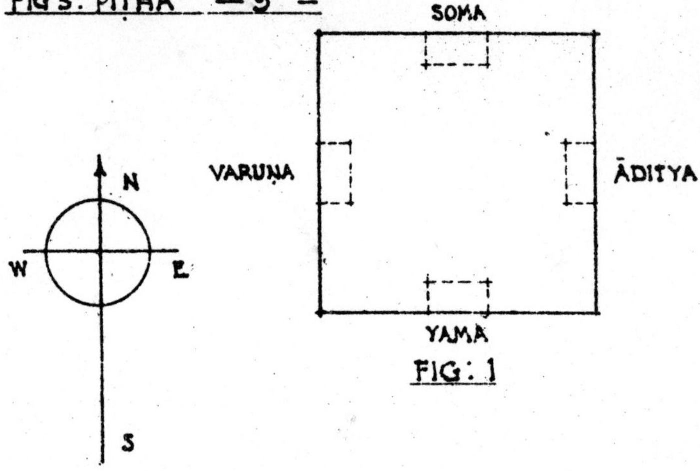

FIG: 1

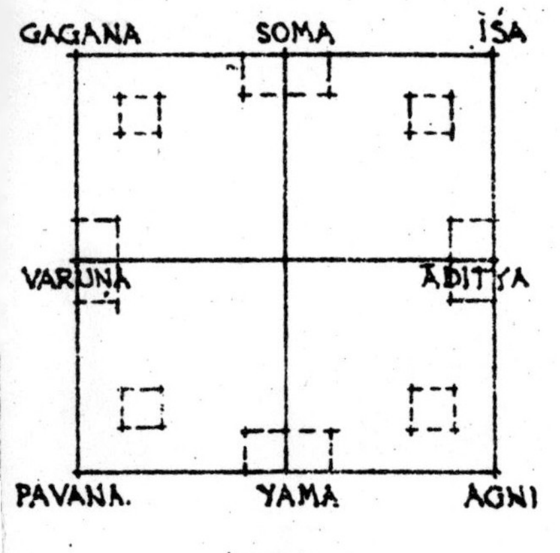

FIG: 2

PAVANA	SOMA	ĪŚA
VARUNA	PRITHVĪ	ĀDITYA
GAGANA	YAMA	AGNI

FIG 3

R. L. BANSAL.

THE SITE PLANS — CHAPTER VII

FIG.1. MAHĀPIṬHA OF 16 PLOTS.

FIG.1A — ARRANGED DIFFERENTLY

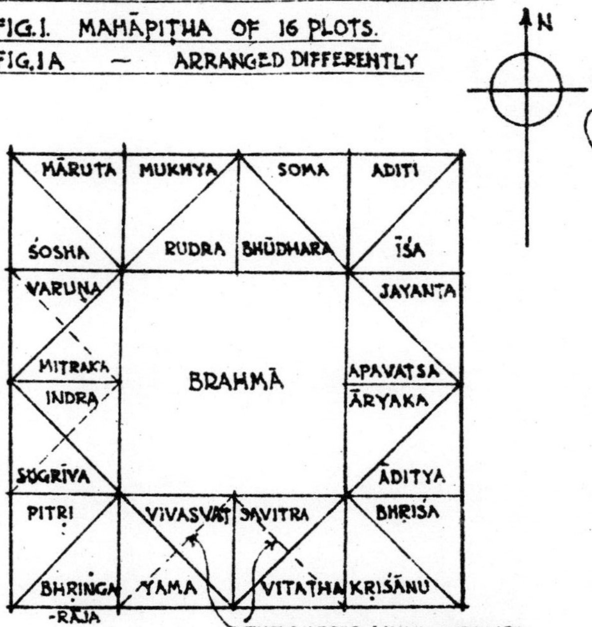

N

MĀRUTA
MUKHYA
SOMA
ADITI
ŚOSHA
RUDRA
BHŪDHARA
ĪŚA
VARUṆA
JAYANTA
MITRAKA
BRAHMĀ
APAVATSA
INDRA
ĀRYAKA
SUGRĪVA
ĀDITYA
PITṚI
VIVASVAT
SAVITRA
BHṚIŚA
BHṚINGA-RĀJA
YAMA
VITATHA
KṚIŚĀNU

THE DOTTED LINES INDICATE ANOTHER POSSIBLE ARRANGEMENT OF THOSE FOUR PLOTS

FIG.1

REPEAT THOSE NAMES FROM IDENTICAL PLOTS IN FIG.1

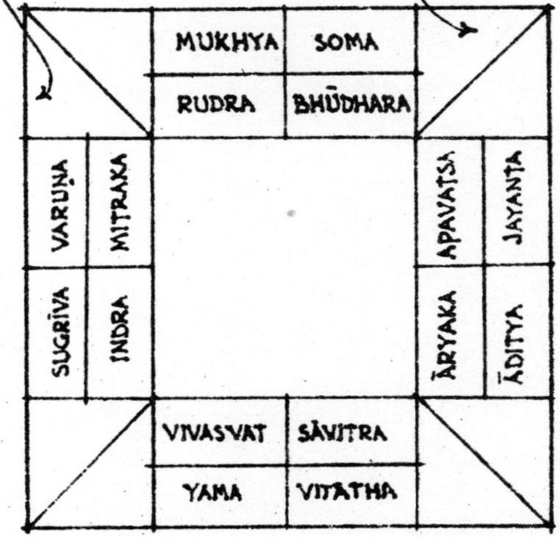

MUKHYA
SOMA
RUDRA
BHŪDHARA
VARUṆA
MITRAKA
APAVATSA
JAYANTA
SUGRĪVA
INDRA
ĀRYAKA
ĀDITYA
VIVASVAT
SĀVITRA
YAMA
VITATHA

FIG.1A

R. L. BANSAL.

SHEET NO. V

THE SITE PLANS ~ CHAPTER VII

UPA-PĪṬHA PLAN OF 25 PLOTS

MARUT	MUKHYA	SOMA	ADITI	ĪŚA
ŚOSHA	RUDRA	BHŪDHARA	APAVATSA	JAYANTA
VARUṆA	MITRA	BRAHMĀ	ĀRYAKA	ĀDITYA
SUGRĪVA	INDRA	VIVASVAT	SAVITRA	BHṚIŚA
PITRI	BHṚIṄGA-RĀJA	YAMA	VITATHA	AGNI

NOTE:-

DETAIL ALLOTMENTS FOR THIS TYPE HAVE BEEN OBTAINED FROM THE FOOTNOTE, PAGE 37

R. L. BANSA.

SHEET NO. VI

N

THE SITE PLANS ~ CHAPTER VII

UGRAPĪTHA PLAN OF 36 PLOTS

VĀYU	MUKHYA	SOMA	ADITI	ĪŚA
ŚOSHA	RUDRA	BHŪDHARA	APAVATSA	JAYANTA
VARUNA	MITRA	BRAHMA	ĀRYAKA	ĀDITYA
SUGRĪVA	INDRA	VIVASVAT	SAVITRA	BHRISA
PITRI.	BHRIṄGA- -RĀJA	YAMA	VITATHA	AGNI

NOTE :-

THIS IS AN AMPLIFICATION OF THE UPA PITHA TYPE

R. L. BANSAL.

SHEET NO. VII

THE SITE PLANS — CHAPTER VII

STHAṆḌILA PLAN OF 49 PLOTS

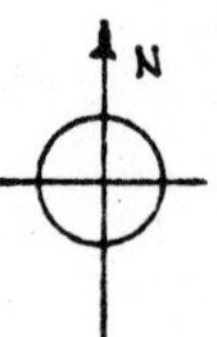

VĀYU	MUKHYA	SOMA	ADITI	ĪŚA
ŚOSHA	RUDRA	BHŪDHARA	APAVATSA	JAYANTA
VARUṆA	MITRA	BRAHMĀ	ĀRYAKA	ĀDITYA
SUGRĪVA	INDRA	VIVASVAT	SAVITRA	BHRIŚA
PITṚI	BHṚINGA-RĀJA	YAMA	VITATHA	AGNI

NOTE :-

THIS IS AN AMPLIFICATION OF THE UGRA PĪṬHA TYPE

R. L. BANSAL.

SHEET No. VIII

THE SITE PLANS — CHAPTER VII

CHAṆḌITA PLAN OF 64 PLOTS

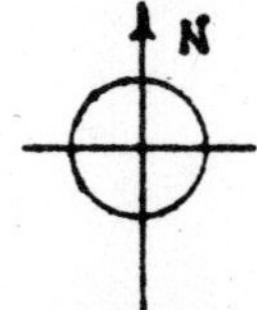

NĀGA / VĀYU	UDITA	BHALLĀTA	SOMA	BHṚIṄGA-RĀJA	ADITI	JAYANTA	ĪŚĀNA / PARJANYA
MUKHYA	RUDRAJAYA / RUDRA	BHALLĀTA	SOMA	BHṚIṄGA-RĀJA	ADITI	ĀPAVATSA / ĀPAVATSA	ANTA-RIKSHA
ROGA			BHŪDHARA			MAHENDRA	
ŚOSHA		MITRA	BRAHMĀ		ĀRYAKA	DINAKA	
VARUṆA						SATYA	
PUSHPA-DANTA			VIVASVAT			BHṚIŚA	
GODHĀ	INDRA-JAYA / INDRA	MṚIŚA	GANDHARVA	YAMA	RĀKSHASA	SĀVITRA / SĀVITRA	VITATHA
DAUVĀRIKA / PITṚI	SUGRĪVA					MṚIGA	AGNI / PŪSHAN

NOTE :-

1. THE DOTTED LINES ON THE FOUR CORNERS OF THE BRAHMĀ PLOT INDICATE ANOTHER ARRANGEMENT OF THOSE FOUR PLOTS (ĀRYAKA ETC.)
2. ANOTHER ALTERNATIVE ARRANGE-MENT IS POSSIBLE BY STARTING WITH ĀRYAKA FROM THE DUE NORTH-EASTERN PLOT OF BRAHMĀ.

R. L. BANSAL.

SHEET NO IX

THE SITE PLANS — CHAPTER VII

CHANDITA PLAN OF 64 PLOTS

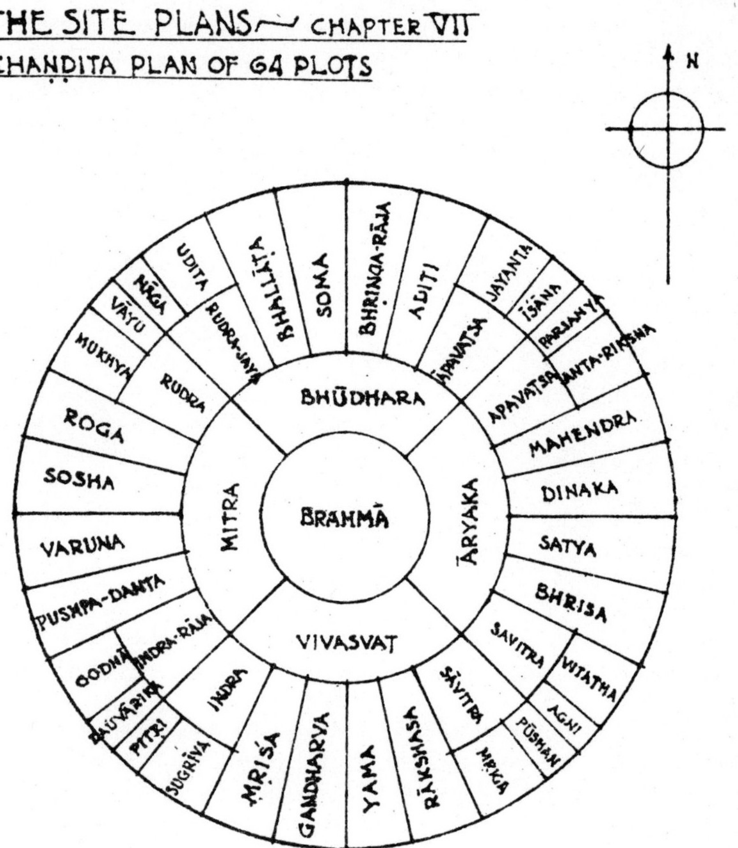

NOTE :-
THE IDEA OF CIRCULAR PLANS HAS BEEN TAKEN FROM BRIHAT-SAMHITĀ. SEE FOOT-NOTES ON PAGES 44 AND 45.

R. L. BANSAL

SHEET No. X

THE SITE PLANS ~ CHAPTER VII

PARAMA-ŚĀYIKA PLAN OF 81 PLOTS

MARUT	NĀGA	MUKHYA	BHALLĀṬA	SOMA	MṚIGA	ADITI	UDITA	ĪŚA
ROGA	RUDRA	RUDRA-JAYA	BHŪDHARA			ĀPAVATSA	ĀPAVATSYA	PARJANYA
ŚOSHA								JAYANTA
ASURA	MITRA		BRAHMĀ			ĀRYAKA		MAHENDRA
VARUṆA								BHĀNU
PUSHPA-DANTA								SATYA
SUGRĪVA	INDRA-JAYA	INDRA	VIVASVAT			SĀVITRA	SAVITRA	BHṚIŚA
DAUVĀRIKA								ANTA-RIKSHA
PITṚI	MṚIŚA	BHṚINGA-RĀJA	GANDHARVA	YAMA	GṚIHA-KSHATA	VITATHA	PŪSHAN	AGNI

INDRA-JAYA

INDRA

VIVASVAT

THE OTHER THREE CORNERS OF BRAHMĀ PLOT MAY LIKE-WISE BE ARRANGED DIFFERENTLY

ALTERNATIVE ARRANGEMENT

R. L. BANSAL.

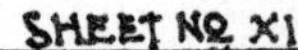

THE SITE PLANS ~ CHAPTER VII

PARAMA-ŚĀYIKA PLAN OF 81 PLOTS

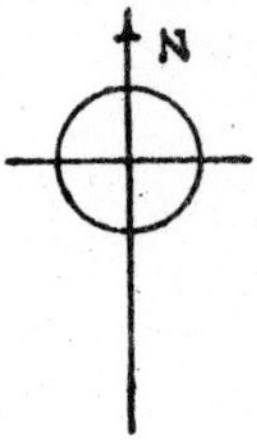

N

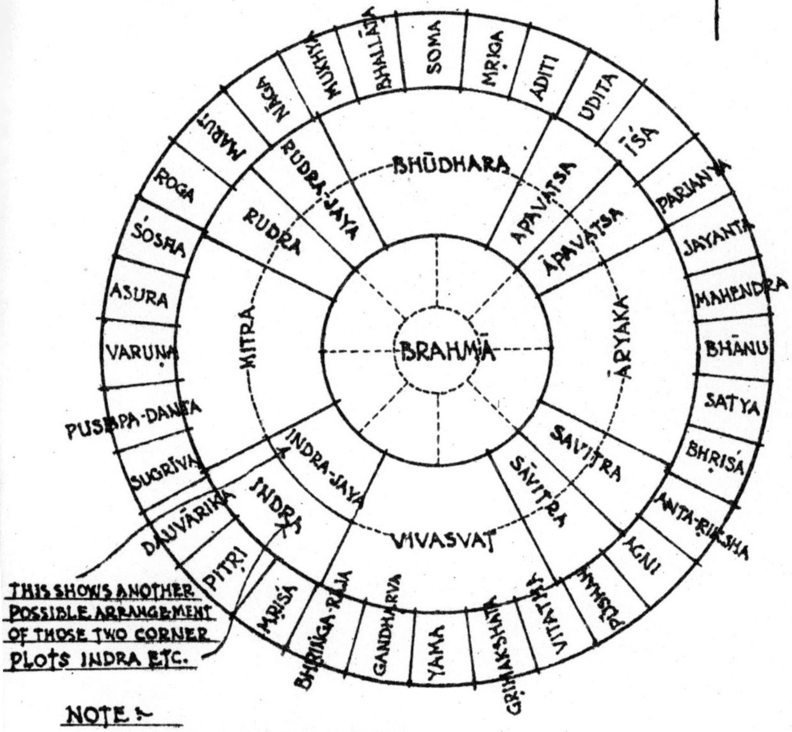

SOMA
MṚIGA
ADITI
UDITA
ĪŚA
PARJANYA
JAYANTA
MAHENDRA
BHĀNU
SATYA
BHṚIŚA
ANTA-RIKSHA
AGNI
PUSHAN
VITATHA
GṚIHAKSHATA
YAMA
GANDHARVA
BHṚIṄGA-RĀJA
MṚIŚĀ
PITṚI
DAUVĀRIKA
SUGRĪVA
PUSHPA-DANTA
VARUṆA
ASURA
ŚOSHA
ROGA
MARUT
NĀGA
MUKHYA
BHALLĀṬA

BHŪDHARA
APAVATSA
ĀPAVATSA
ĀRYAKA
SAVITRA
SĀVITRA
VIVASVAT
INDRA-JAYA
INDRA
MITRA
RUDRA
RUDRA-JAYA
BRAHMĀ

THIS SHOWS ANOTHER POSSIBLE ARRANGEMENT OF THOSE TWO CORNER PLOTS INDRA ETC.

NOTE :-

THE IDEA OF CIRCULAR PLANS HAS BEEN TAKEN FROM BṚIHAT-SAMHITĀ. SEE FOOT-NOTES ON PAGES 44 AND 45.

R. L. BANSAL.

THE SITE PLANS — CHAPTER VII

PARAMA-ŚĀYIKA PLAN OF 81 PLOTS.

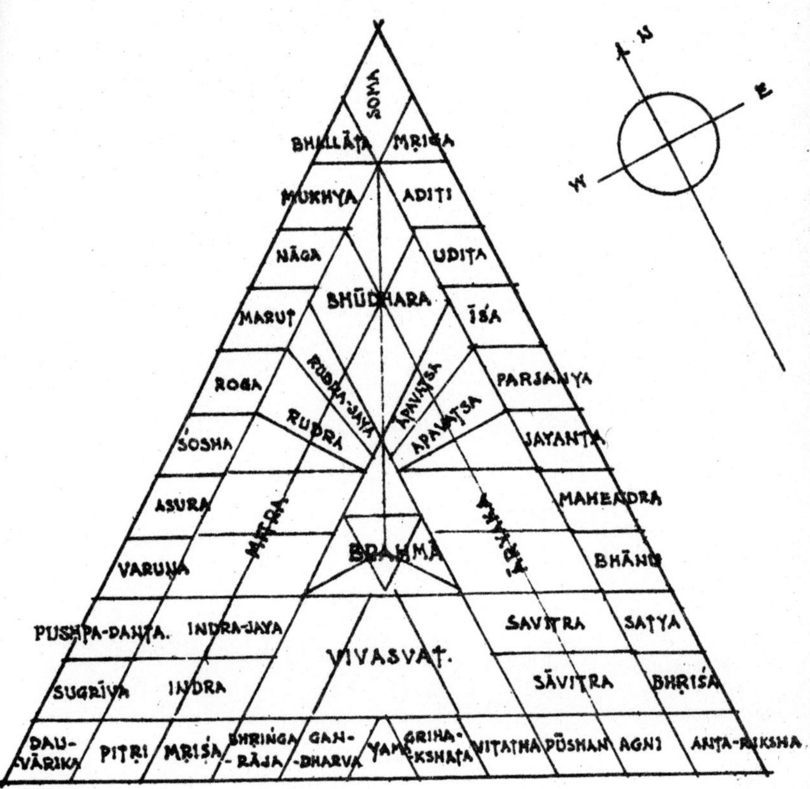

NOTE :—

THE IDEA OF TRIANGULAR PLAN HAS BEEN OBTAINED FROM UTPALA SEE FOOTNOTES ON PAGES 44 AND 45.

R. L. BANSAL.

SHEET NO. XIII

THE SITE PLANS ~ CHAPTER VII

ĀSANA PLAN OF 100 PLOTS

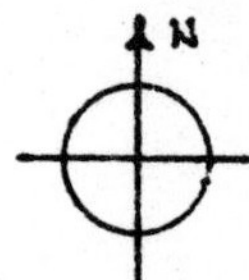

VAYU / ROGA — NĀGA — MUKHYA — BHALLATA — SOMA — MRIGA — ADITI — UDITA / ĪSA

ŚOSHA — RUDRAJAYA — BHŪDHARA — APAVATSA — PARJANYA

RUDRA — ĀPAVATSA

ASURA — JAYANTA

VARUNA — MITRA — BRAHMĀ — ĀRYAMAN — MAHENDRA

PUSHPA-DANTA — ĀDITYA

SUGRĪVA — SATYA

DAUVĀRIKA — INDRA-JAYA — VIVASVAT — SAVITRA — BHRIŚA

INDRA — SĀVITRA

PITRI / MRIŚĀ — BHRINGARĀJA — GAN-DHARVA — YAMA — GRIHA-KSHATA — VITATHA — PŪSHAN — ANTARIKSHA / AGNI

NOTE :–

THE DETAILS OF THIS PLAN HAVE BEEN OBTAINED FROM ŚILPA-RATNA ETC. SEE FOOTNOTE ON PAGE 46.

R. L. BANSAL.

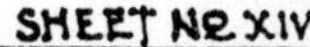

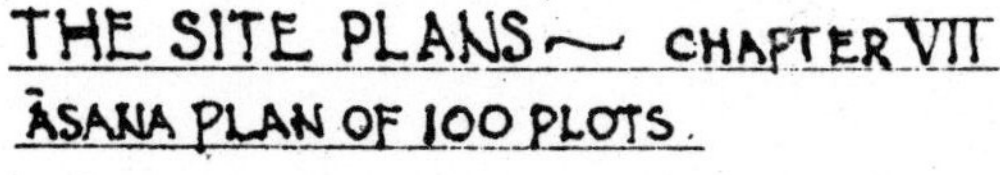

SHEET No. XIV

THE SITE PLANS — CHAPTER VII

ĀSANA PLAN OF 100 PLOTS.

N
BRAHMĀ
BHŪDHARA
VIVASVAT
MITRA
ĀRYAMAN
RUDRA-JAYA
RUDRA
ĀPAVATSA
ĀPAVATSA
SAVITRA
SĀVITRA
INDRA
INDRA-JAYA
NĀGA
MUKHYA
BHALLĀTA
SOMA
MṚIGA
ADITI
UDITA
ĪSA
PARJANYA
JAYANTA
MAHENDRA
ĀDITYA
SATYA
BHṚISĀ
ANTA-RIKSHA
AGNI
PŪSHAN
VITATHA
GṚIHAKSHATA
YAMA
GANDARVA
BHṚINGA-RĀJA
MṚISĀ
PITṚI
DAUVĀRIKA
SUGRĪVA
PUSHPA-DANTA
VARUNA
ASURA
SOSHA
ROGA
VĀYU

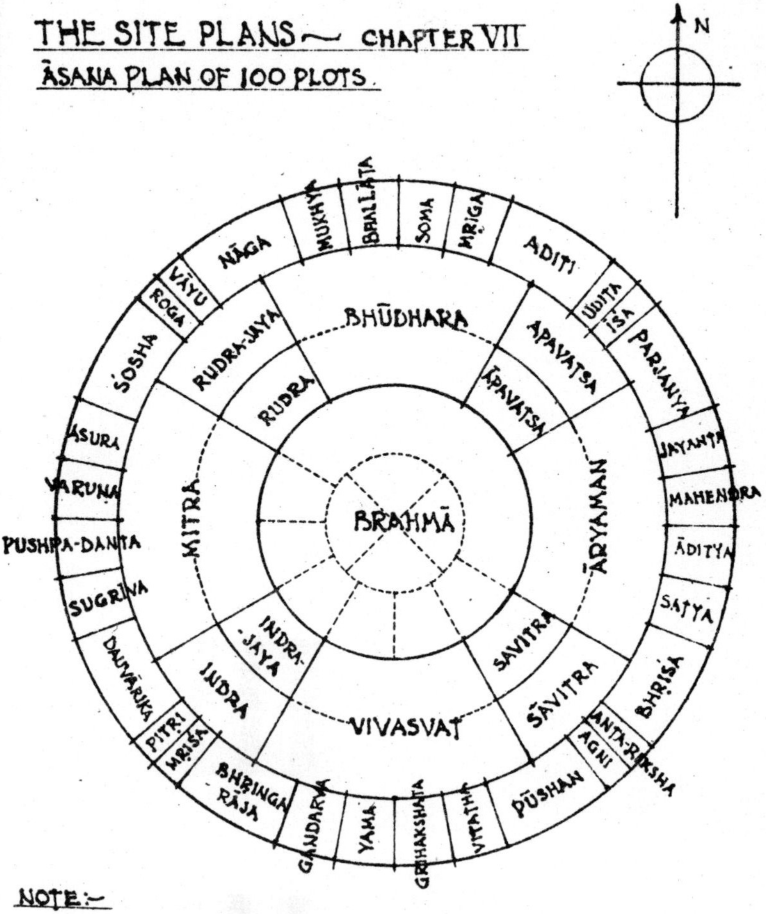

NOTE:—

THE IDEA OF CIRCULAR PLANS HAS BEEN OBTAINED FROM BRIHAT-SAMHITĀ AND SILPA-RATNA SUPPLIES DETAILS. SEE FOOTNOTES ON PAGES 44, 45 AND 46

R. L. BANSAL.

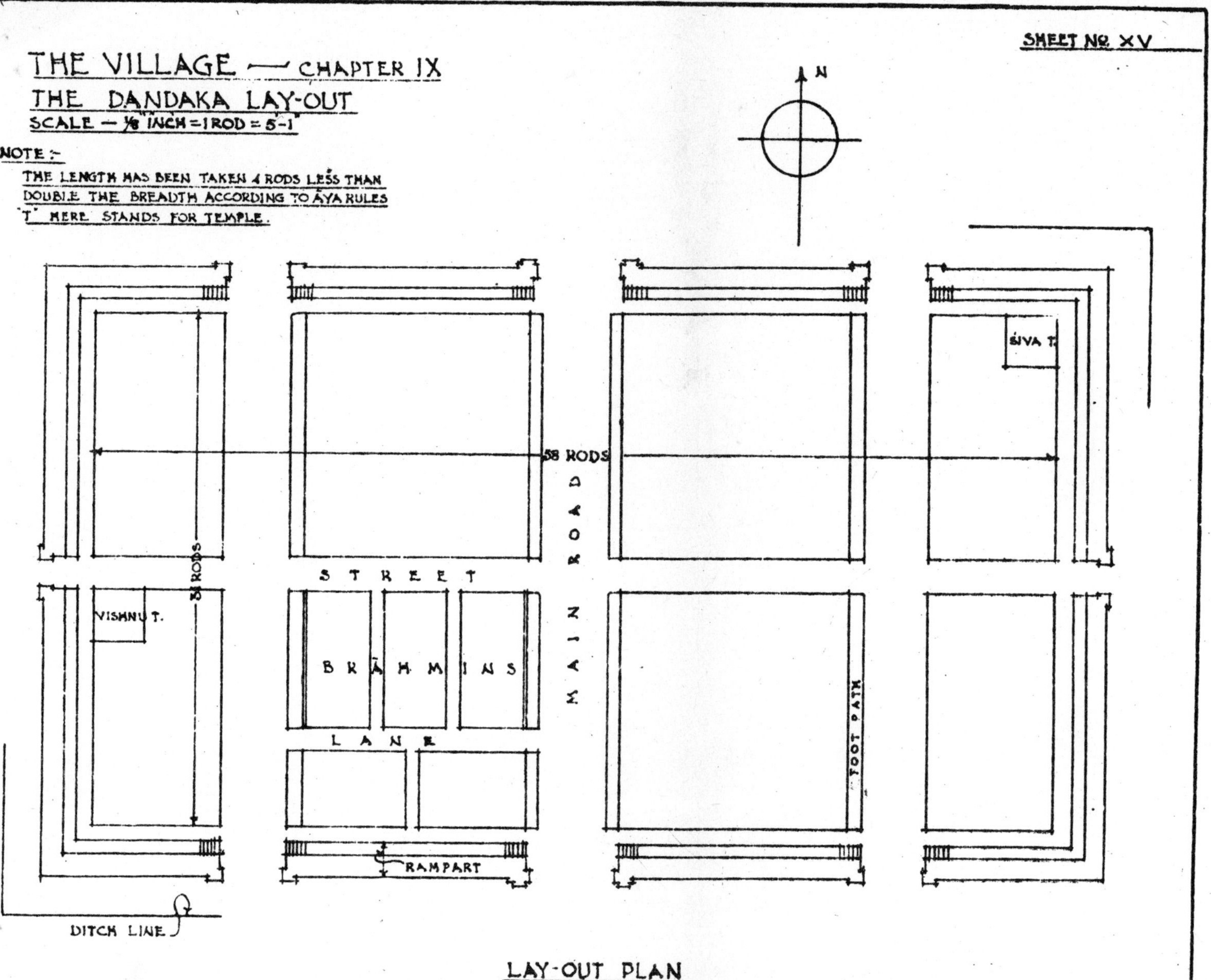
SHEET No. XV
THE VILLAGE — CHAPTER IX
THE DANDAKA LAY-OUT
SCALE — 1/8" INCH = 1 ROD = 5'-1"
NOTE :-
THE LENGTH HAS BEEN TAKEN 4 RODS LESS THAN
DOUBLE THE BREADTH ACCORDING TO ĀYA RULES
"T" HERE STANDS FOR TEMPLE.
N
SIVA T.
58 RODS
VISHNU T.
31 RODS
STREET
MAIN ROAD
BRĀHMINS
LANE
FOOT PATH
RAMPART
DITCH LINE
LAY-OUT PLAN
S. C. MUKHERJI.

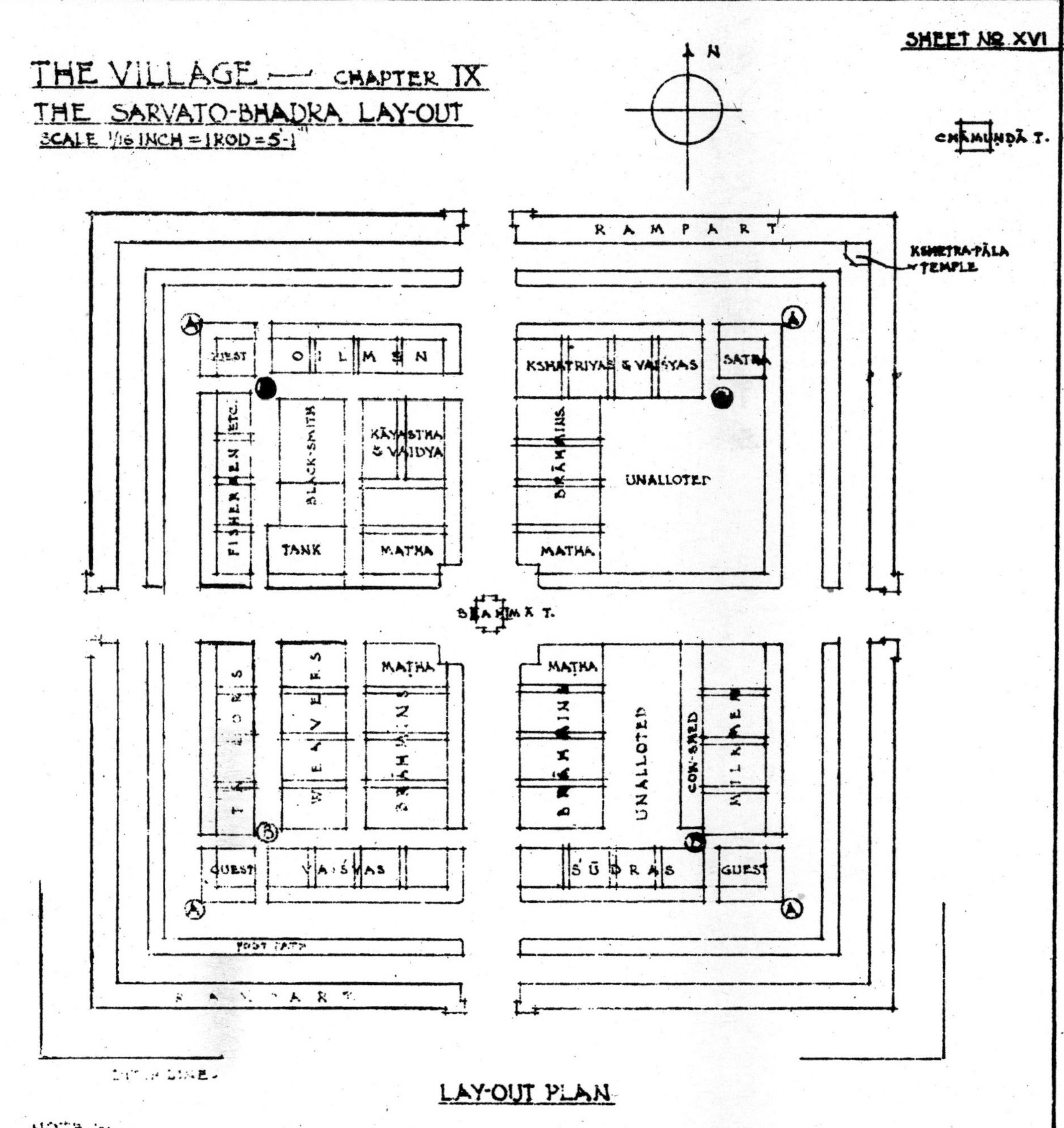

SHEET NO XVI
THE VILLAGE — CHAPTER IX
THE SARVATO-BHADRA LAY-OUT
SCALE 1/16 INCH = 1 ROD = 5'-1"
N
CHĀMUṆḌĀ T.
RAMPART
KSHETRA-PĀLA TEMPLE
GUEST
OILMEN
KSHATRIYAS & VAIŚYAS
SATRA
FISHERMEN ETC.
BLACK-SMITH
KĀYASTHA & VAIDYA
BRĀHMAṆS
UNALLOTED
TANK
MATHA
MATHA
BRAHMA T.
WEAVERS
MATHA
BRĀHMAṆS
MATHA
BRĀHMAṆS
UNALLOTED
COW-SHED
MILKMEN
GUEST
VAIŚYAS
ŚŪDRAS
GUEST
FOOT PATH
RAMPART
LAY-OUT PLAN
NOTE:-
THE SURROUNDING PLOT BETWEEN (A) AND (B) IS THE LAST OR PAISĀCHA ROUND
"T" STANDS FOR "TEMPLE".
S. C. MUKHERJI.

THE VILLAGE — CHAPTER IX

THE NANDYĀVARTA LAY-OUT

SCALE — 1/8 INCH = 5 RODS = 25'-5"

NOTE:-

THE SURROUNDING STRIP OF PLOT BETWEEN (C) AND (B) ROUGHLY INDICATES THE PAIŚĀCHA AND BETWEEN (B) AND (A) THE MĀNUSHA ROUNDS. CENTRAL PORTION IS THE DAIVA PLOT.

"T" STANDS FOR TEMPLE.

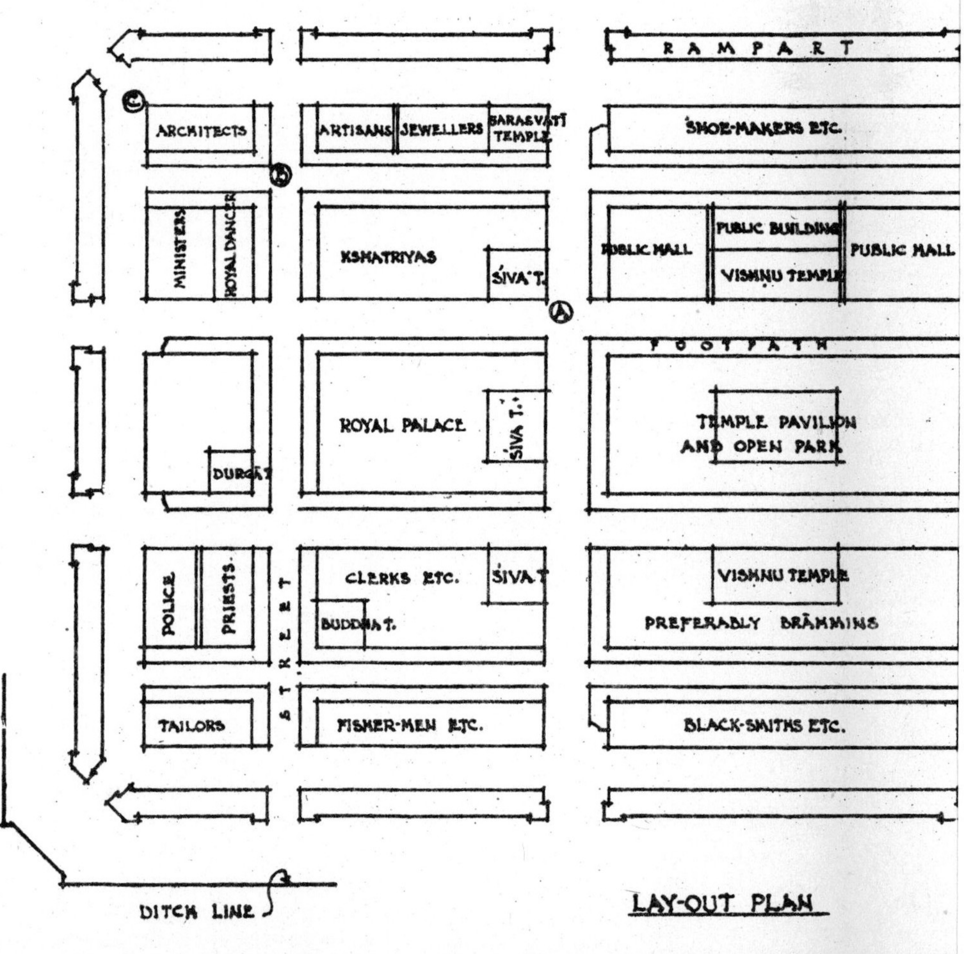

LAY-OUT PLAN

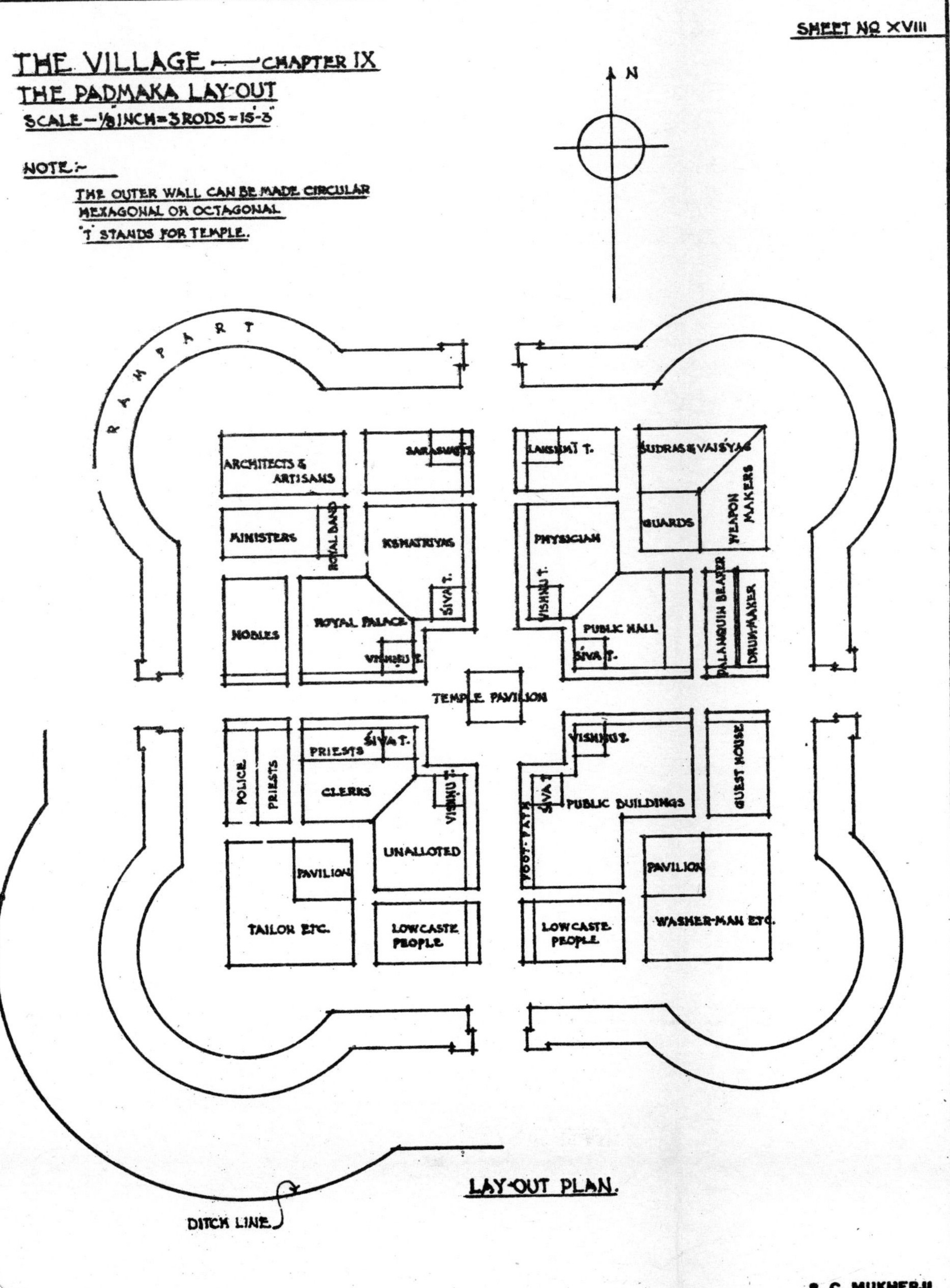
SHEET NO XVIII
THE VILLAGE — CHAPTER IX
THE PADMAKA LAY-OUT
SCALE – 1/8" INCH = 3 RODS = 15'-3"
NOTE:-
THE OUTER WALL CAN BE MADE CIRCULAR
HEXAGONAL OR OCTAGONAL
"T" STANDS FOR TEMPLE.
N
RAMPART
ARCHITECTS & ARTISANS
SUDRAS & VAISYAS
MINISTERS
ROYAL BAND
KSHATRIYAS
PHYSICIAN
GUARDS
WEAPON MAKERS
NOBLES
ROYAL PALACE
SIVA T.
VISHNU T.
PUBLIC HALL
PALANQUIN BEARER
DRUM-MAKER
TEMPLE PAVILION
POLICE
PRIESTS
CLERKS
UNALLOTED
PUBLIC BUILDINGS
GUEST HOUSE
PAVILION
TAILOR ETC.
LOWCASTE PEOPLE
WASHER-MAN ETC.
LAY-OUT PLAN.
DITCH LINE
S. C. MUKHERJI.

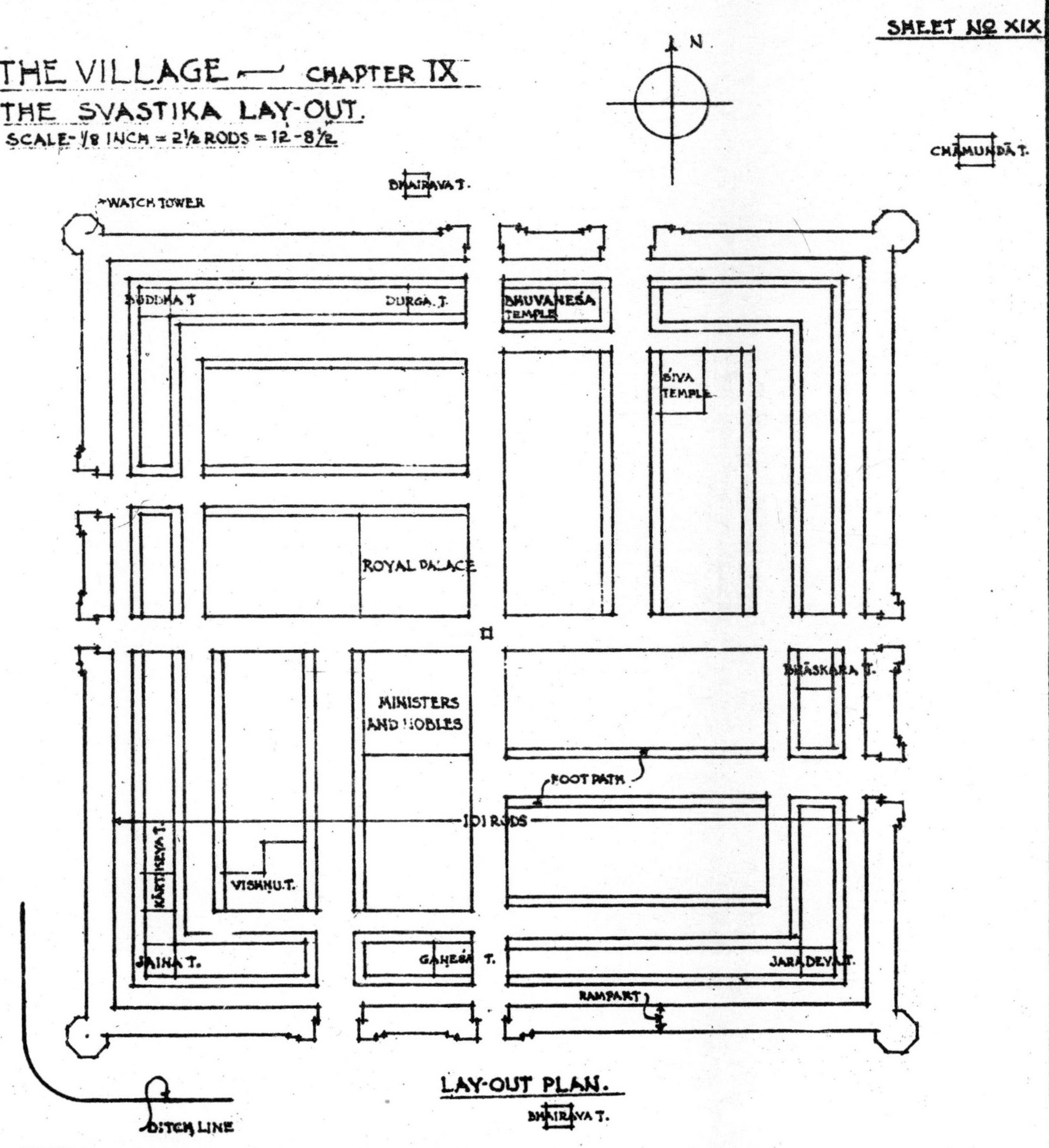

NOTE :-

ONLY THE ALLOT-MENT OF PALACES FOR KINGS AND NOBLES AS WELL AS OF TEMPLES FOR GODS HAS BEEN GIVEN IN THE TEXT

'T' STANDS FOR TEMPLE.

S. C. MUKHERJI.

THE VILLAGE — CHAPTER IX

THE PRASTARA LAY-OUT

SCALE 1/8 INCH = 10 RODS = 50-10

SHEET NO. XX

NOTE:-

THE SURROUNDING STRIP OF PLOT BETWEEN (C) AND (B) ROUGHLY INDICATES THE PAIŚĀCHA AND BETWEEN (B) AND (A) THE MANUSHA ROUNDS. CENTRAL PORTION IS THE DAIVA PLOT.

T STANDS FOR TEMPLE

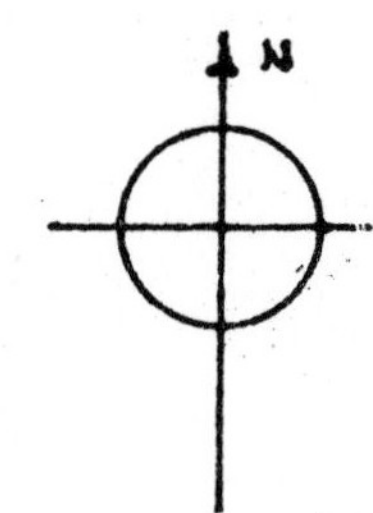

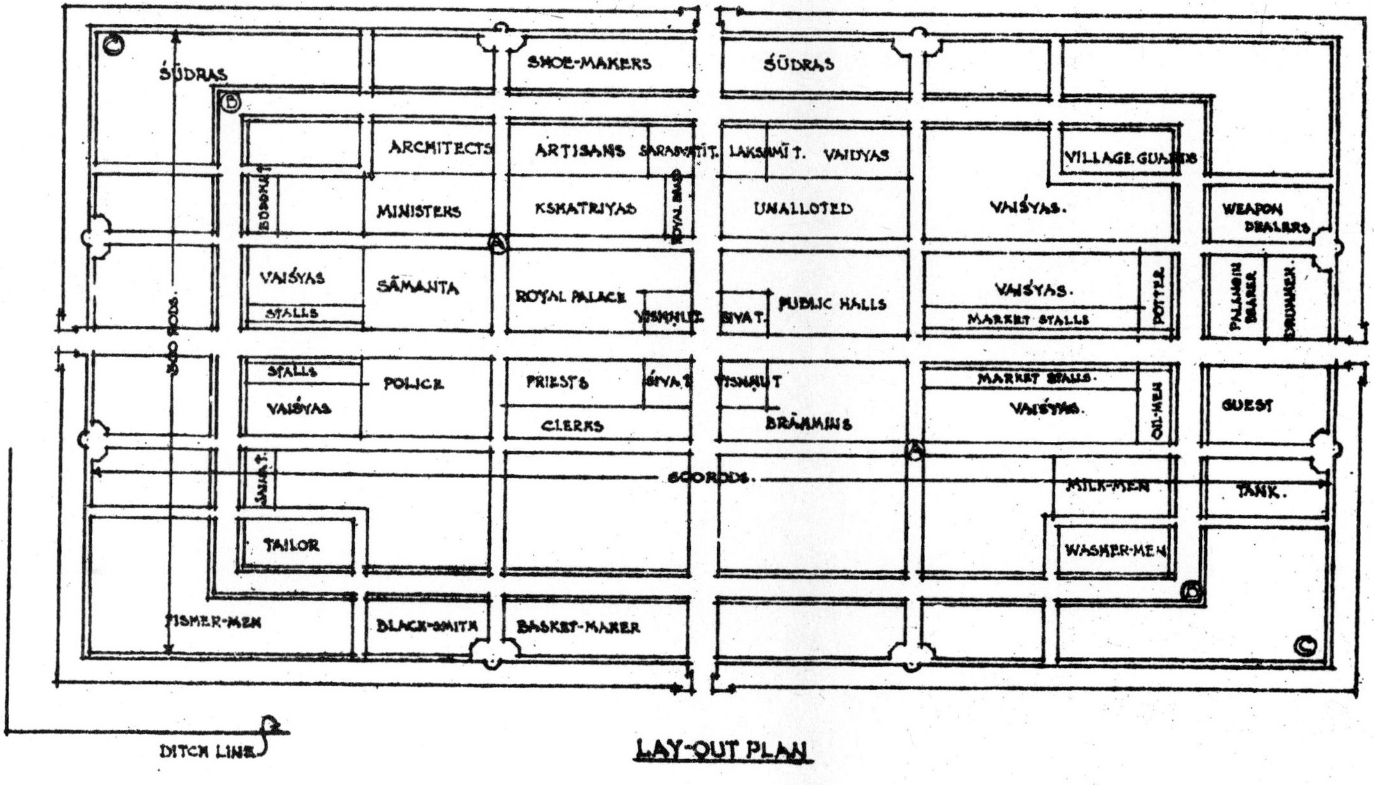

ŚŪDRAS
SHOE-MAKERS
ŚŪDRAS
ARCHITECTS
ARTISANS
SARASVATI T.
LAKSHMĪ T.
VAIDYAS
VILLAGE GUARDS
BODDHA T.
MINISTERS
KSHATRIYAS
ROYAL BAND
UNALLOTED
VAIŚYAS.
WEAPON DEALERS
VAIŚYAS
STALLS
SĀMANTA
ROYAL PALACE
VISHNU T.
ŚIVA T.
PUBLIC HALLS
VAIŚYAS.
MARKET STALLS
POTTER
PALANQUIN BEARER
DRUMMER
300 RODS
STALLS
VAIŚYAS
POLICE
PRIESTS
ŚIVA T.
VISHNU T
CLERKS
BRĀHMINS
MARKET STALLS.
VAIŚYAS.
OIL-MEN
GUEST
SANI T.
600 RODS.
MILK-MEN
TANK.
TAILOR
WASHER-MEN
FISHER-MEN
BLACK-SMITH
BASKET-MAKER
DITCH LINE

LAY-OUT PLAN

S. C. MUKHERJI.

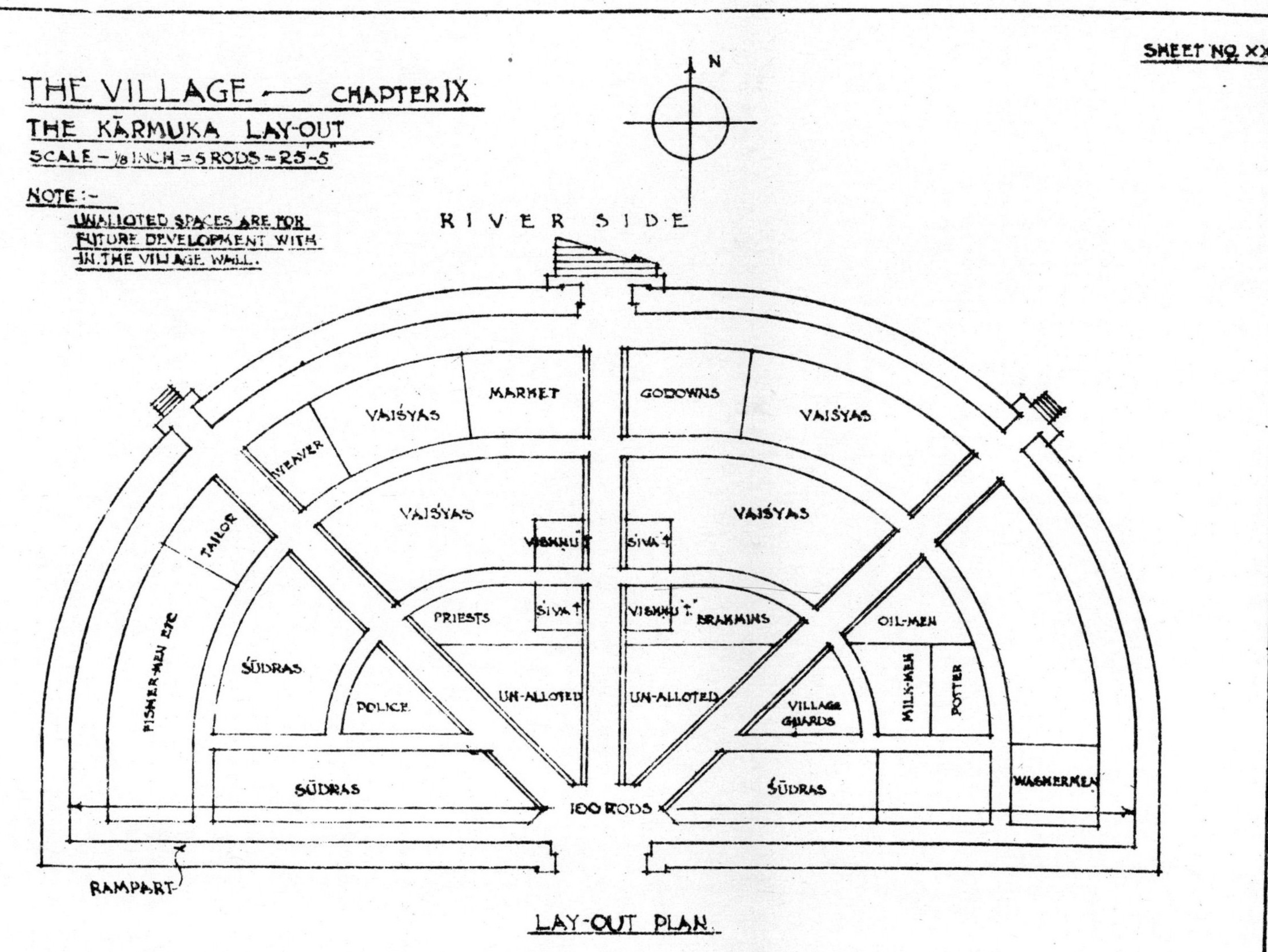
SHEET NO. XXI
THE VILLAGE — CHAPTER IX
THE KĀRMUKA LAY-OUT
SCALE – 1/8 INCH = 5 RODS = 25'-5"
NOTE :-
UNALLOTED SPACES ARE FOR FUTURE DEVELOPMENT WITH-IN THE VILLAGE WALL.
N
RIVER SIDE
MARKET
GODOWNS
VAIŚYAS
VAIŚYAS
WEAVER
VAIŚYAS
VAIŚYAS
TAILOR
VISHNU
SIVA
SIVA
VISHNU
PRIESTS
BRAHMINS
OIL-MEN
FISHER-MEN ETC
ŚŪDRAS
POLICE
UN-ALLOTED
UN-ALLOTED
VILLAGE GUARDS
MILK-MEN
POTTER
ŚŪDRAS
ŚŪDRAS
WASHERMEN
100 RODS
RAMPART
LAY-OUT PLAN
S. C. MUKHERJI.

THE VILLAGE — CHAPTER IX

THE CHATUR-MUKHA LAY-OUT

SCALE — 1/8 INCH = 3 RODS = 15'-3"

NOTE:-

THE SURROUNDING STRIP OF PLOT BETWEEN (C) AND (B) ROUGHLY INDICATES THE PAISĀCHA AND BETWEEN (B) AND (A) THE MĀNUSHA ROUNDS. CENTRAL PORTION IS THE DAIVA PLOT.

"T" STANDS FOR TEMPLE.

THIS VILLAGE IS FOR THE VAISYAS MAINLY.

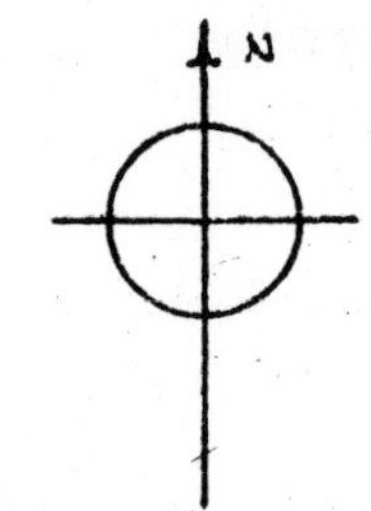

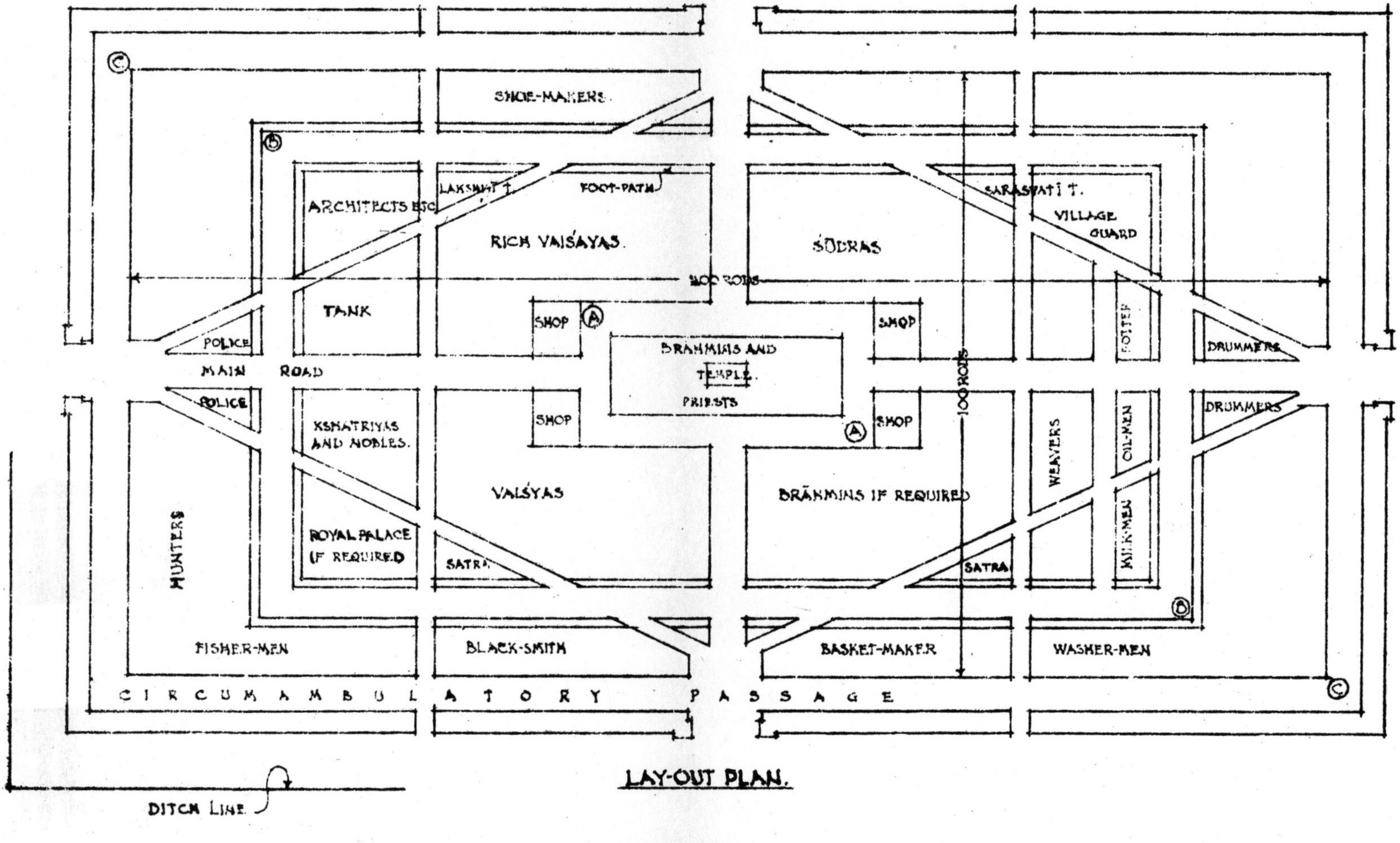

C
SHOE-MAKERS
B
ARCHITECTS ETC.
LAKSHMI T.
FOOT-PATH
RICH VAIŚAYAS.
ŚŪDRAS
SARASVATI T.
VILLAGE GUARD
100 RODS
TANK
SHOP
A
SHOP
POTTER
DRUMMERS
POLICE
MAIN ROAD
BRĀHMINS AND PRIESTS
TEMPLE
POLICE
SHOP
A
SHOP
100 RODS
DRUMMERS
KSHATRIYAS AND NOBLES.
VAIŚYAS
BRĀHMINS IF REQUIRED
WEAVERS
OIL-MEN
MILK-MEN
HUNTERS
ROYAL PALACE IF REQUIRED
SATRA
SATRA
B
FISHER-MEN
BLACK-SMITH
BASKET-MAKER
WASHER-MEN
C
CIRCUMAMBULATORY PASSAGE
DITCH LINE

LAY-OUT PLAN.

S. C. MUKHERJI.

TOWNS AND FORTS — CHAPTER X

SHEET No. XXIII

RĀJADHĀNĪYA LAY-OUT — SCALE 1/8 INCH = 15 RODS = 76'-3"

FOR CHAKRA-VARTIN KINGS.

NOTE:—

THE DETAILS FOR ALLOTMENT HAVE MAINLY BEEN TAKEN FROM CHAPTER IX.

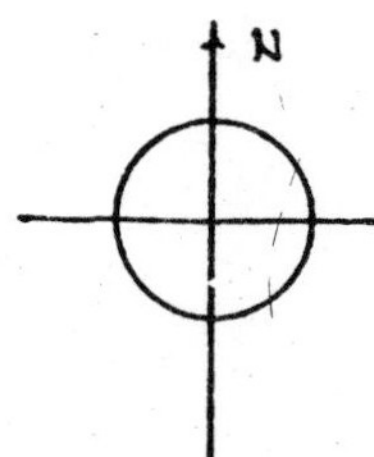

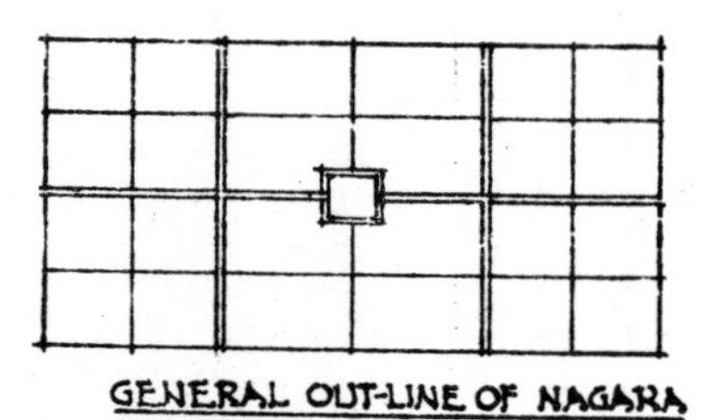

GENERAL OUT-LINE OF NAGARA
NOT TO SCALE

NOTE:—

NAGARA IS A SMALLER TOWN THAN RĀJDHĀNĪYA, SO A GENERAL OUT-LINE HAS BEEN SHOWN. KEVALA & NAGARA VARY ONLY IN MINOR DETAILS

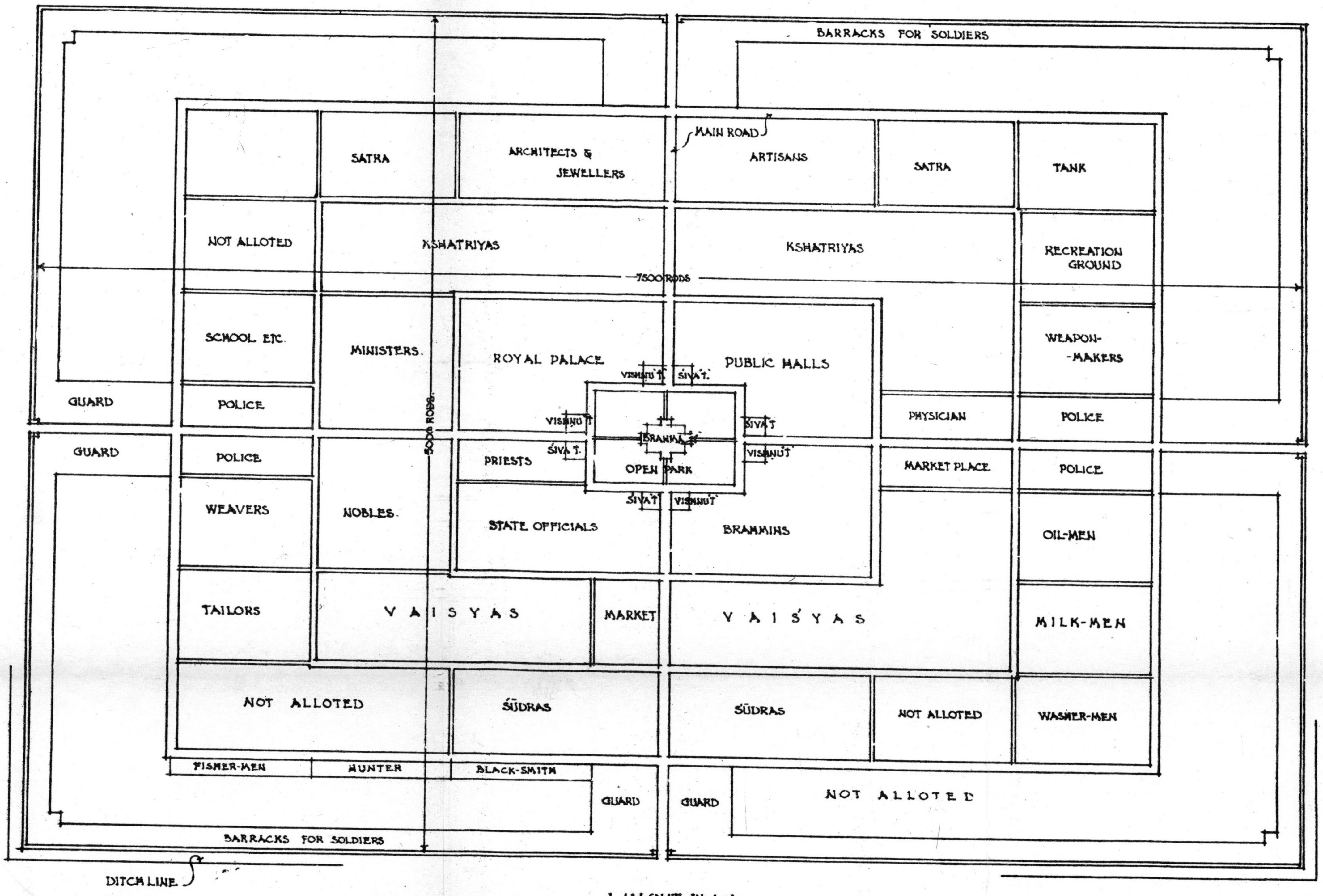

BARRACKS FOR SOLDIERS

MAIN ROAD

SATRA

ARCHITECTS & JEWELLERS

ARTISANS

SATRA

TANK

NOT ALLOTED

KSHATRIYAS

KSHATRIYAS

RECREATION GROUND

7500 RODS

SCHOOL ETC.

MINISTERS.

ROYAL PALACE

PUBLIC HALLS

WEAPON-MAKERS

GUARD

POLICE

VISHNU T.

SIVA T.

VISHNU T.

SIVA T.

PHYSICIAN

POLICE

GUARD

POLICE

5000 RODS

PRIESTS

SIVA T.

BRAHMA

OPEN PARK

VISHNU T.

MARKET PLACE

POLICE

SIVA T.

VISHNU T.

WEAVERS

NOBLES.

STATE OFFICIALS

BRAHMINS

OIL-MEN

TAILORS

V A I S Y A S

MARKET

V A I S' Y A S

MILK-MEN

NOT ALLOTED

SŪDRAS

SŪDRAS

NOT ALLOTED

WASHER-MEN

FISHER-MEN

HUNTER

BLACK-SMITH

GUARD

GUARD

NOT ALLOTED

BARRACKS FOR SOLDIERS

DITCH LINE

LAY-OUT PLAN

S. C. MUKHERJI.

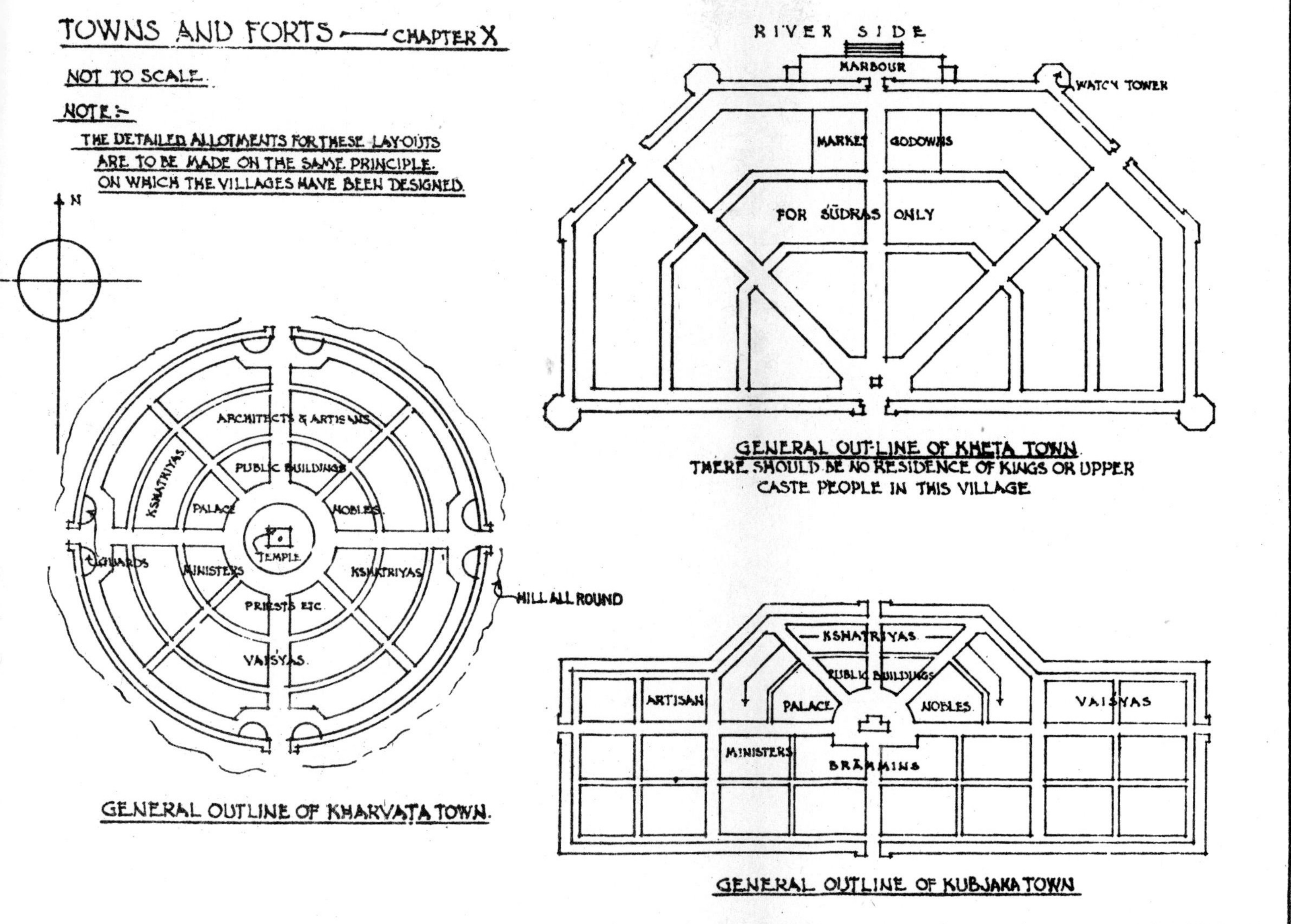

SHEET NO XXIV
TOWNS AND FORTS — CHAPTER X
NOT TO SCALE.
NOTE:-
THE DETAILED ALLOTMENTS FOR THESE LAY-OUTS ARE TO BE MADE ON THE SAME PRINCIPLE ON WHICH THE VILLAGES HAVE BEEN DESIGNED.
N
RIVER SIDE
HARBOUR
WATCH TOWER
MARKET
GODOWNS
FOR SŪDRAS ONLY
GENERAL OUT-LINE OF KHETA TOWN
THERE SHOULD BE NO RESIDENCE OF KINGS OR UPPER CASTE PEOPLE IN THIS VILLAGE
ARCHITECTS & ARTISANS
KSHATRIYAS
PUBLIC BUILDINGS
PALACE
NOBLES.
TEMPLE
GUARDS
MINISTERS
KSHATRIYAS
PRIESTS ETC.
VAISYAS.
HILL ALL ROUND
GENERAL OUTLINE OF KHARVATA TOWN.
KSHATRIYAS
PUBLIC BUILDINGS
ARTISAN
PALACE
NOBLES
VAISYAS
MINISTERS
BRĀHMINS
GENERAL OUTLINE OF KUBJAKA TOWN
S. C. MUKHERJI.

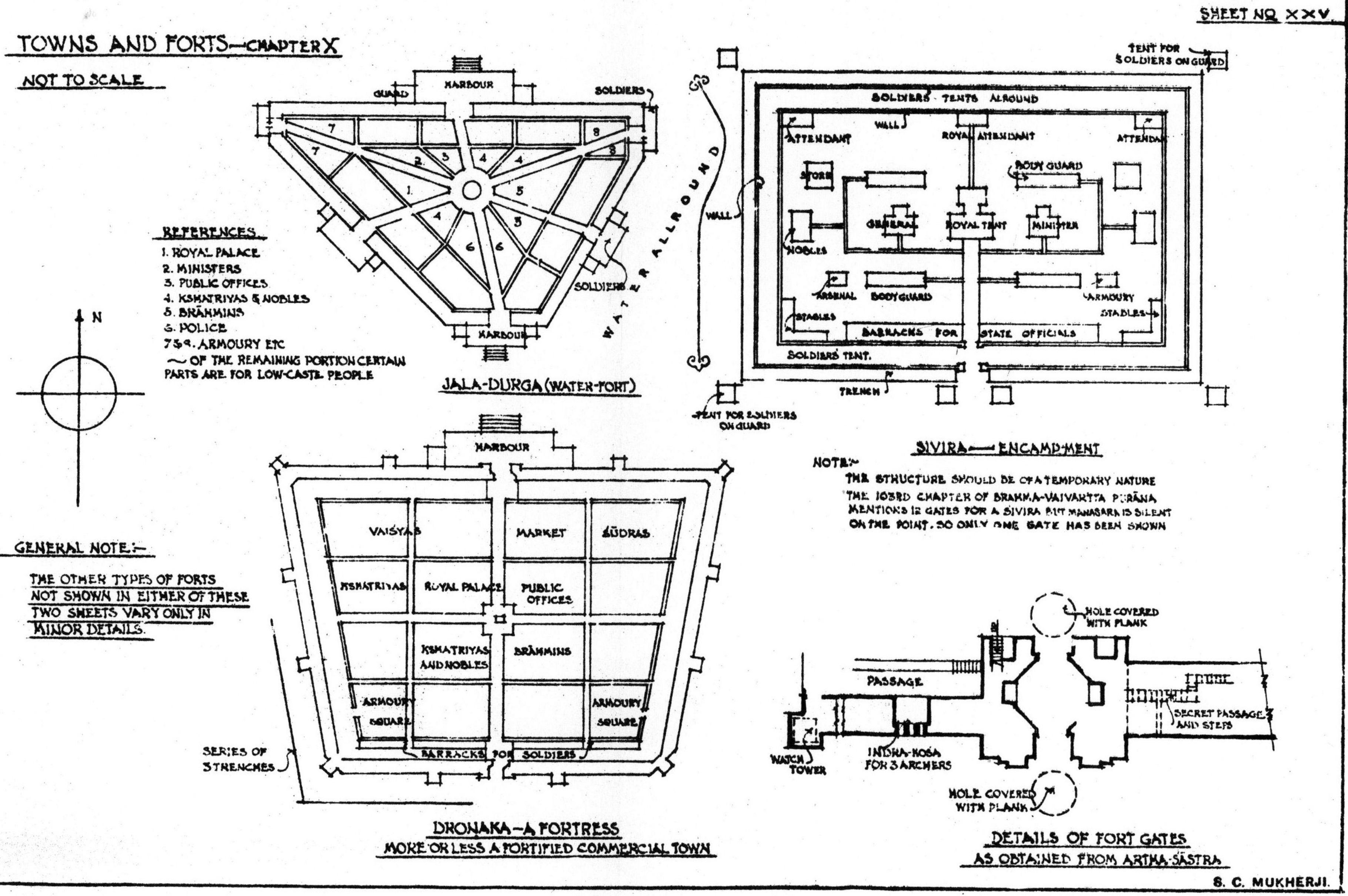
SHEET NO. XXV.
TOWNS AND FORTS—CHAPTER X
NOT TO SCALE
HARBOUR
GUARD
SOLDIERS
REFERENCES.
1. ROYAL PALACE
2. MINISTERS
3. PUBLIC OFFICES
4. KSHATRIYAS & NOBLES
5. BRĀHMINS
6. POLICE
7 & 8. ARMOURY ETC
— OF THE REMAINING PORTION CERTAIN PARTS ARE FOR LOW-CASTE PEOPLE
N
JALA-DURGA (WATER-FORT)
WATER ALLROUND
TENT FOR SOLDIERS ON GUARD
SOLDIERS TENTS ALLROUND
WALL
ATTENDANT
ROYAL ATTENDANT
STORE
BODY GUARD
GENERAL
ROYAL TENT
MINISTER
NOBLES
ARSENAL
BODYGUARD
ARMOURY
STABLES
BARRACKS FOR STATE OFFICIALS
SOLDIERS' TENT.
TRENCH
TENT FOR SOLDIERS ON GUARD
SIVIRA—ENCAMPMENT
NOTE:—
THE STRUCTURE SHOULD BE OF A TEMPORARY NATURE
THE 103RD CHAPTER OF BRAHMA-VAIVARTTA PURĀNA MENTIONS 12 GATES FOR A SIVIRA BUT MANASARA IS SILENT ON THE POINT. SO ONLY ONE GATE HAS BEEN SHOWN
GENERAL NOTE:—
THE OTHER TYPES OF FORTS NOT SHOWN IN EITHER OF THESE TWO SHEETS VARY ONLY IN MINOR DETAILS.
HARBOUR
VAISYAS
MARKET
SŪDRAS
KSHATRIYAS
ROYAL PALACE
PUBLIC OFFICES
KSHATRIYAS AND NOBLES
BRĀHMINS
ARMOURY SQUARE
ARMOURY SQUARE
BARRACKS FOR SOLDIERS
SERIES OF STRENCHES
DRONAKA—A FORTRESS
MORE OR LESS A FORTIFIED COMMERCIAL TOWN
HOLE COVERED WITH PLANK
PASSAGE
SECRET PASSAGE AND STEPS
WATCH TOWER
INDRA-KOSA FOR 3 ARCHERS
HOLE COVERED WITH PLANK
DETAILS OF FORT GATES
AS OBTAINED FROM ARTHA-SĀSTRA
S. C. MUKHERJI.

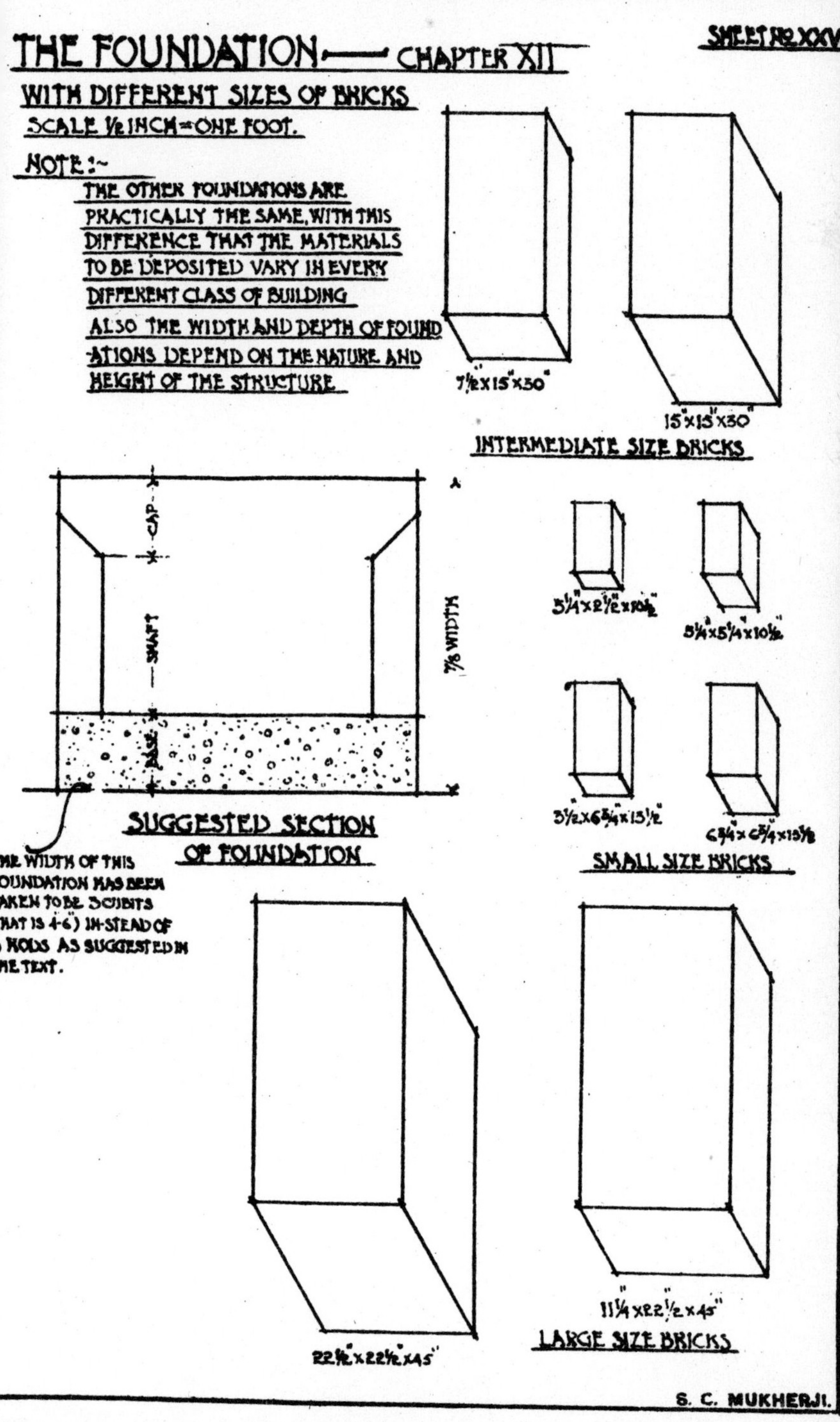

THE FOUNDATION — CHAPTER XII
SHEET No. XXVI
WITH DIFFERENT SIZES OF BRICKS
SCALE ½ INCH = ONE FOOT.
NOTE:~
THE OTHER FOUNDATIONS ARE PRACTICALLY THE SAME, WITH THIS DIFFERENCE THAT THE MATERIALS TO BE DEPOSITED VARY IN EVERY DIFFERENT CLASS OF BUILDING
ALSO THE WIDTH AND DEPTH OF FOUNDATIONS DEPEND ON THE NATURE AND HEIGHT OF THE STRUCTURE
7½"x15"x30"
15"x15"x30"
INTERMEDIATE SIZE BRICKS
CAP
SHAFT
BASE
⅞ WIDTH
5¼"x2½"x10½"
5¼"x5¼"x10½"
3½"x6¾"x13½"
6¾"x6¾"x13½"
SMALL SIZE BRICKS
SUGGESTED SECTION OF FOUNDATION
THE WIDTH OF THIS FOUNDATION HAS BEEN TAKEN TO BE 3 CUBITS (THAT IS 4'-6") IN-STEAD OF 3 HODS AS SUGGESTED IN THE TEXT.
22½"x22½"x45"
11¼"x22½"x45"
LARGE SIZE BRICKS
S. C. MUKHERJI.

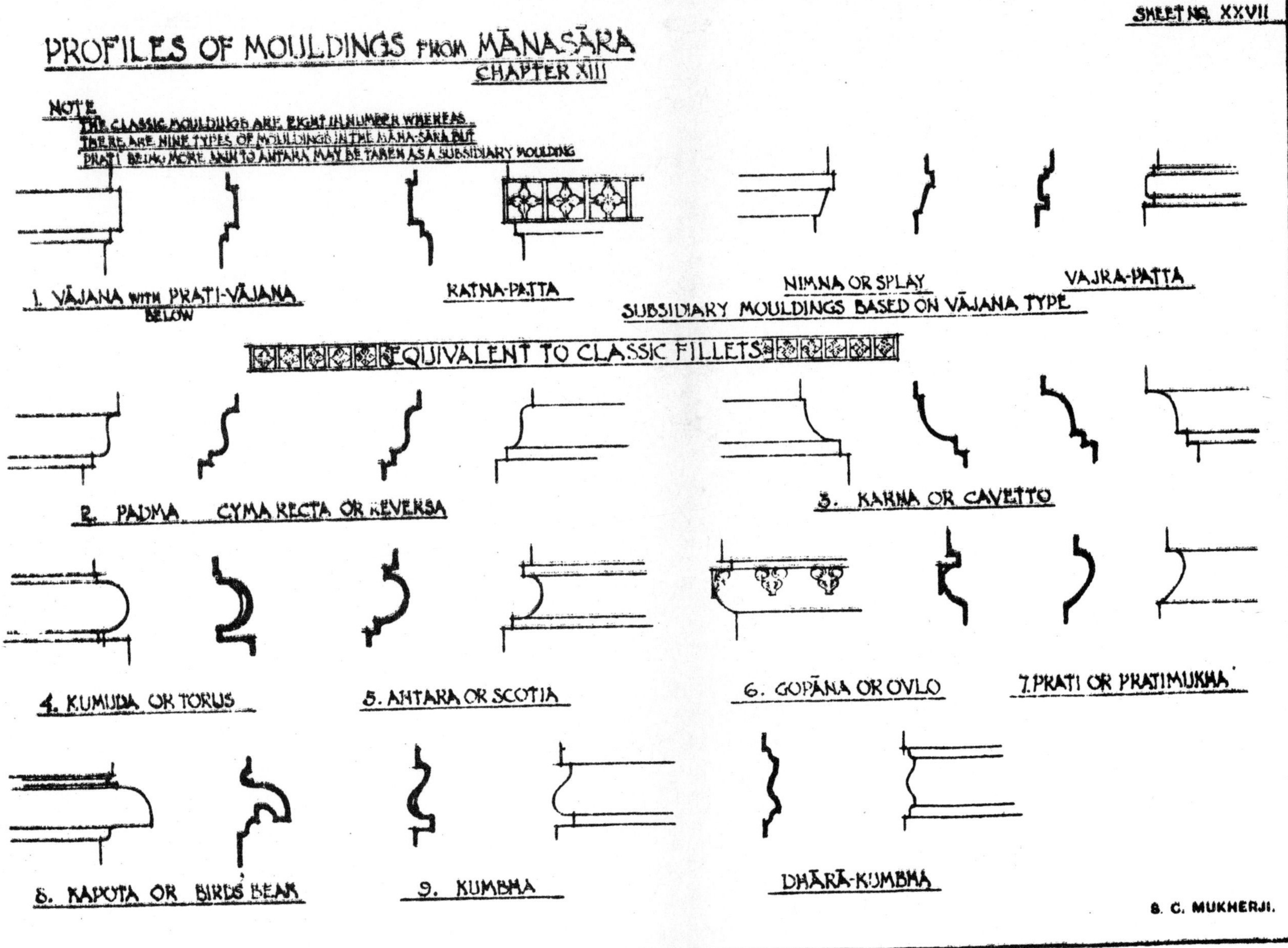
SHEET NO. XXVII
PROFILES OF MOULDINGS FROM MĀNASĀRA
CHAPTER XIII
NOTE
THE CLASSIC MOULDINGS ARE EIGHT IN NUMBER WHEREAS
THERE ARE NINE TYPES OF MOULDINGS IN THE MĀNA-SĀRA BUT
PRATI BEING MORE AKIN TO ANTARA MAY BE TAKEN AS A SUBSIDIARY MOULDING
1. VĀJANA WITH PRATI-VĀJANA BELOW
RATNA-PATTA
NIMNA OR SPLAY
VAJRA-PATTA
SUBSIDIARY MOULDINGS BASED ON VĀJANA TYPE
EQUIVALENT TO CLASSIC FILLETS
2. PADMA CYMA RECTA OR REVERSA
3. KARNA OR CAVETTO
4. KUMUDA OR TORUS
5. ANTARA OR SCOTIA
6. GOPĀNA OR OVLO
7. PRATI OR PRATIMUKHA
8. KAPOTA OR BIRDS BEAK
9. KUMBHA
DHĀRĀ-KUMBHA
S. C. MUKHERJI.

PEDESTALS OF COLUMNS

— CHAPTER XIII

VEDI-BHADRA CLASS

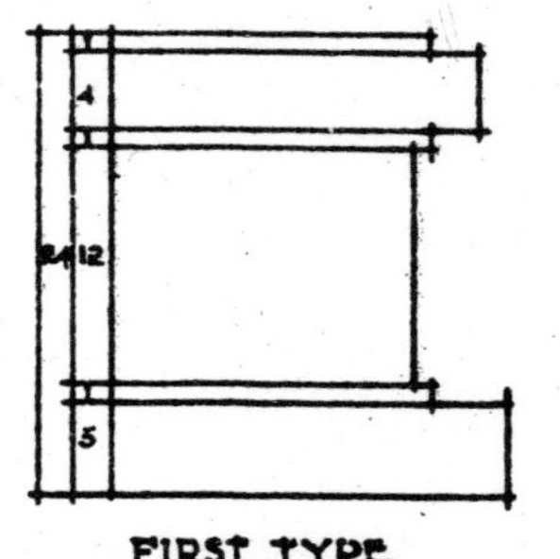

FIRST TYPE
OF 24 PARTS —

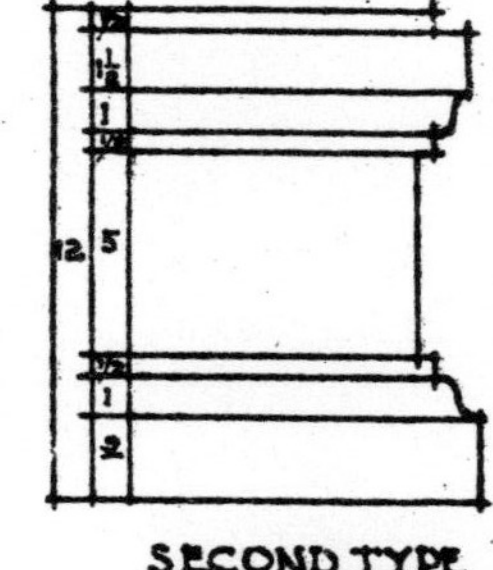

SECOND TYPE
OF 12 PARTS —

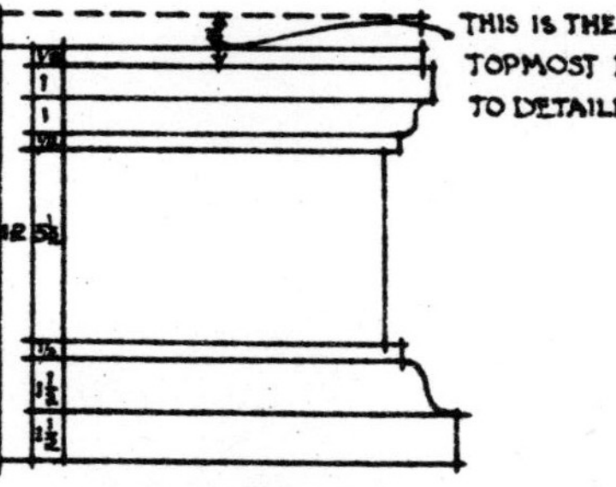

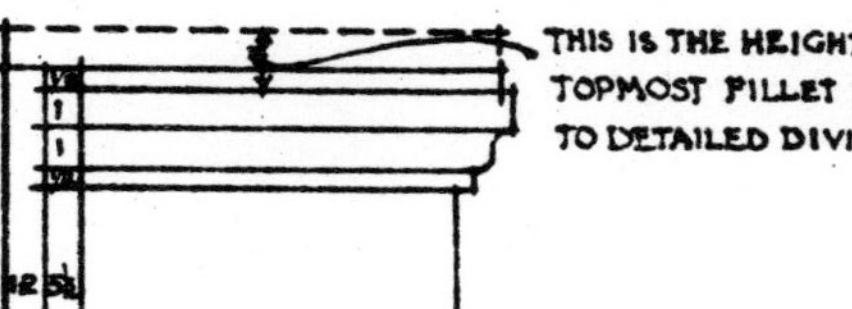

THIRD TYPE
OF 12 PARTS —

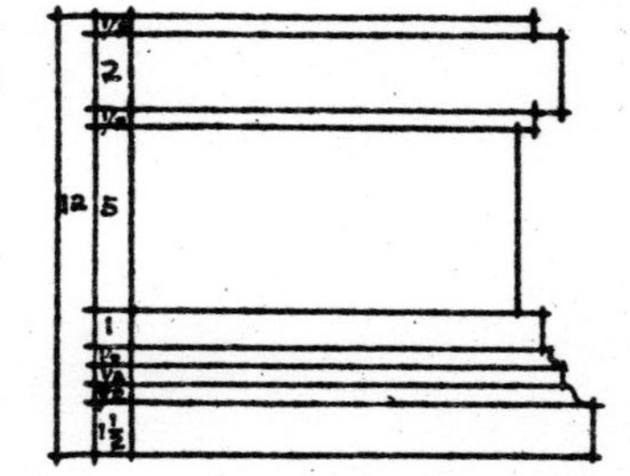

FOURTH TYPE
OF 12 PARTS —

S. C. MUKHERJI.

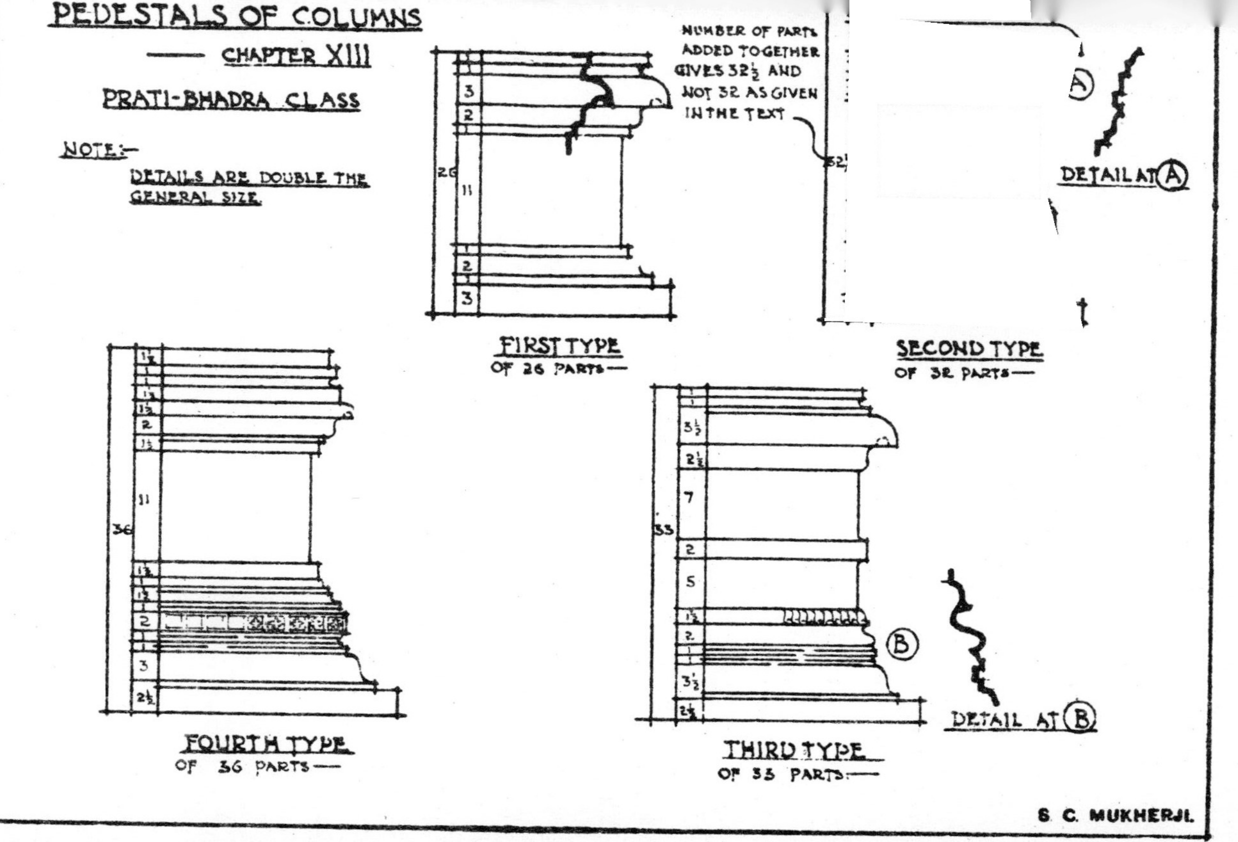
PEDESTALS OF COLUMNS
— CHAPTER XIII
PRATI-BHADRA CLASS
NOTE:—
DETAILS ARE DOUBLE THE GENERAL SIZE
NUMBER OF PARTS ADDED TOGETHER GIVES 32½ AND NOT 32 AS GIVEN IN THE TEXT
FIRST TYPE
OF 26 PARTS—
SECOND TYPE
OF 32 PARTS—
DETAIL AT (A)
THIRD TYPE
OF 33 PARTS—
DETAIL AT (B)
FOURTH TYPE
OF 36 PARTS—
S. C. MUKHERJI.

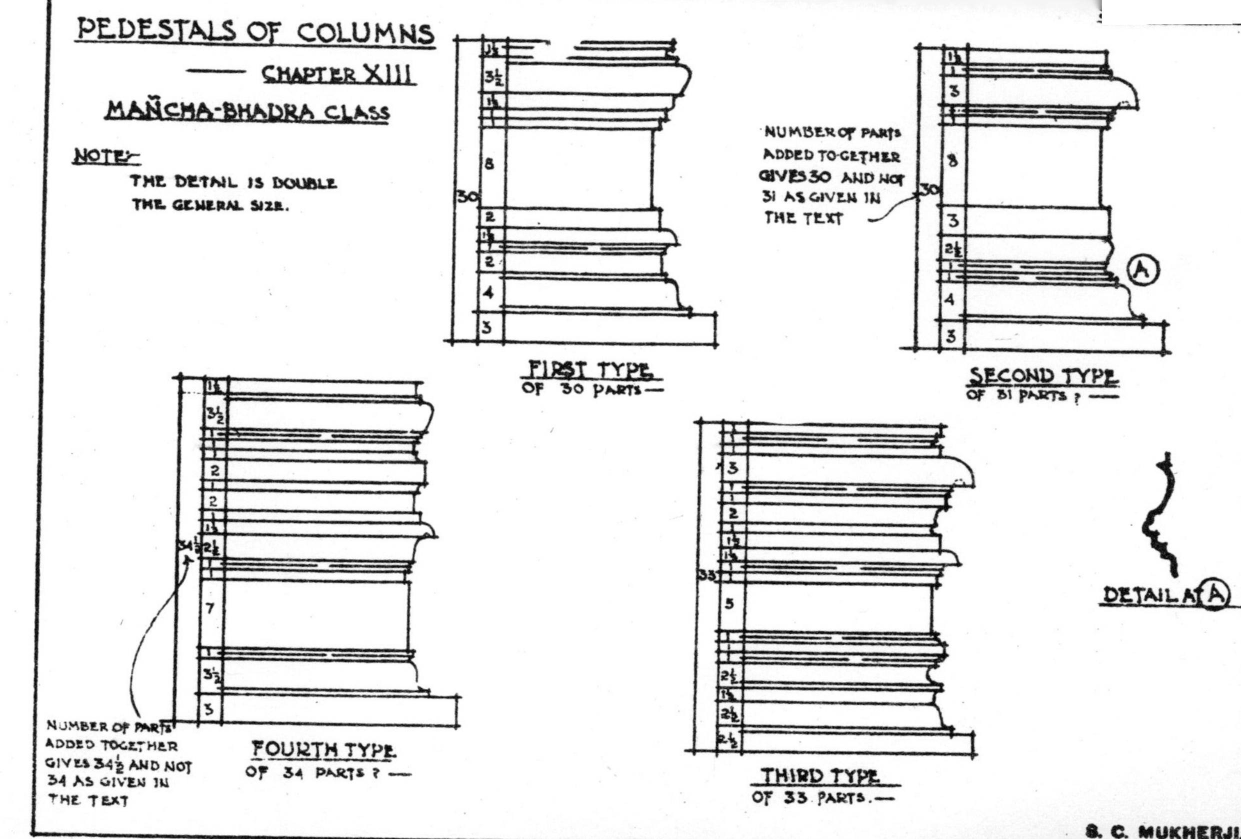
PEDESTALS OF COLUMNS
— CHAPTER XIII
MAÑCHA-BHADRA CLASS
NOTE:-
THE DETAIL IS DOUBLE THE GENERAL SIZE.
FIRST TYPE
OF 30 PARTS —
NUMBER OF PARTS ADDED TO-GETHER GIVES 30 AND NOT 31 AS GIVEN IN THE TEXT
SECOND TYPE
OF 31 PARTS ? —
DETAIL AT (A)
NUMBER OF PARTS ADDED TOGETHER GIVES 34½ AND NOT 34 AS GIVEN IN THE TEXT
FOURTH TYPE
OF 34 PARTS ? —
THIRD TYPE
OF 33 PARTS. —
S. C. MUKHERJI.

SHEET NO. XXXI

THE BASES OF COLUMNS

CHAPTER XIV

THE PĀDA-BANDHA CLASS

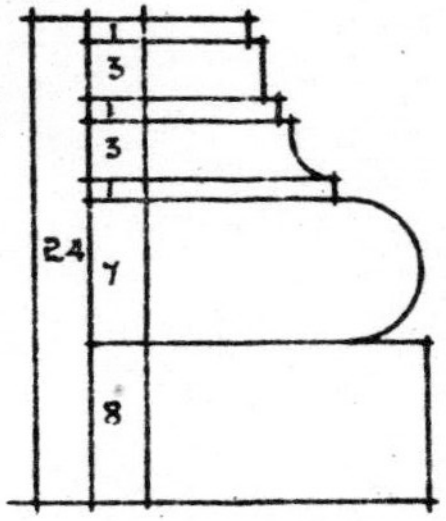

1
3
1
3
1
7
8
24

FIRST TYPE
OF 24 PARTS —

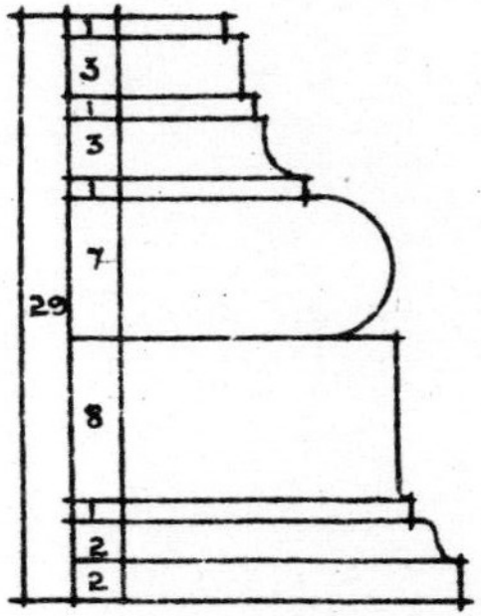

1
3
1
3
1
7
8
1
2
2
29

SECOND TYPE
OF 29 PARTS —

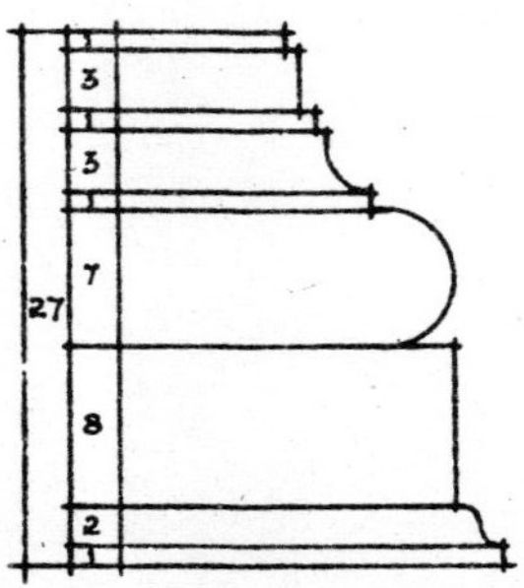

1
3
1
3
1
7
8
2
1
27

THIRD TYPE
OF 27 PARTS.—

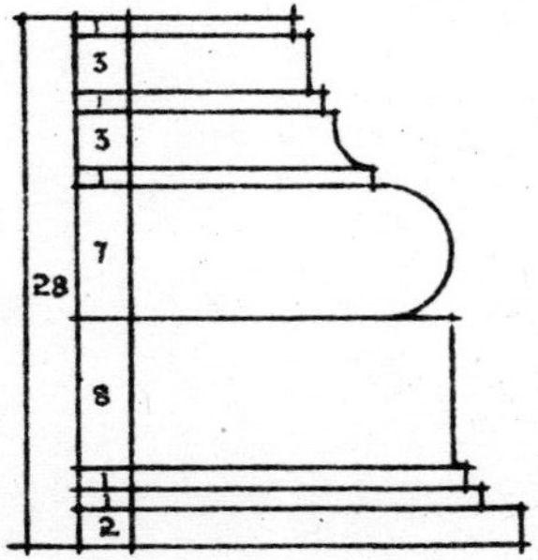

1
3
1
3
1
7
8
1
1
2
28

FOURTH TYPE
OF 28 PARTS. —

S. C. MUKHERJI

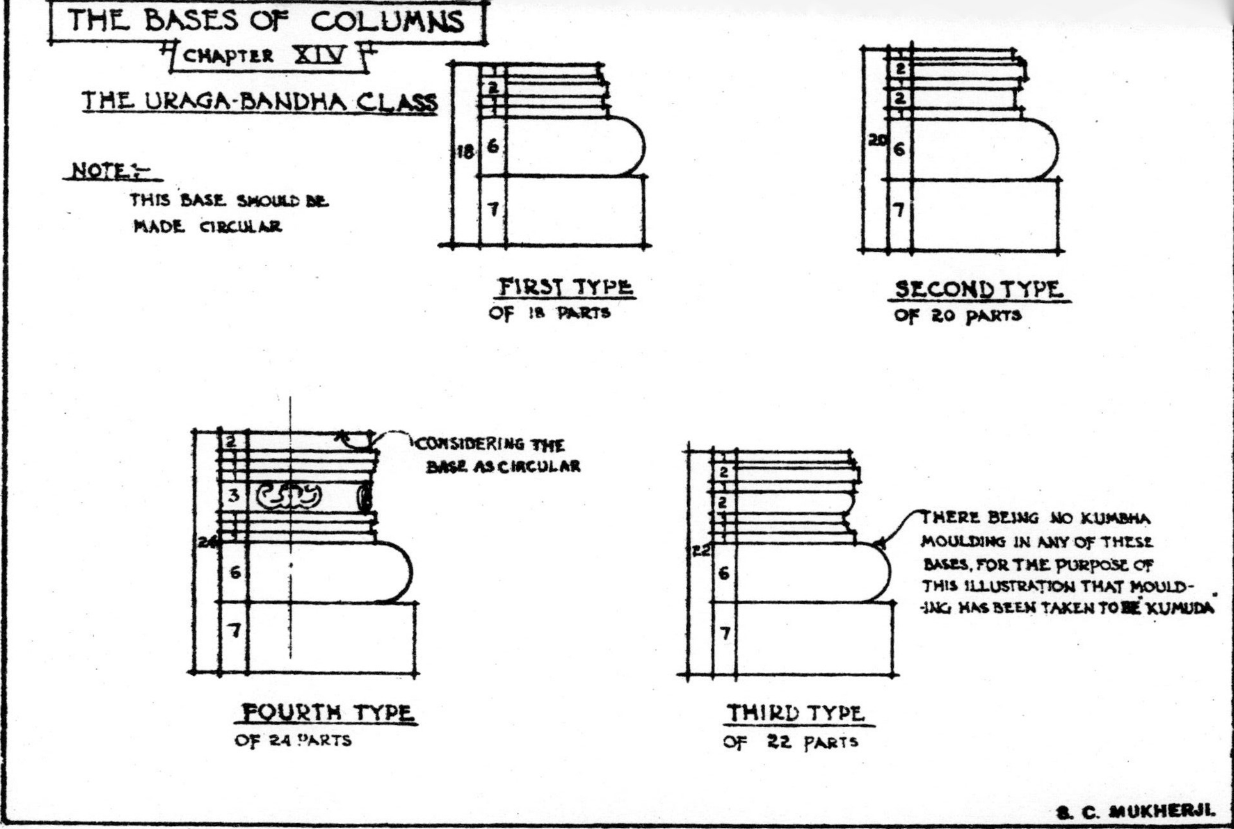
THE BASES OF COLUMNS
CHAPTER XIV
THE URAGA-BANDHA CLASS
NOTE:-
THIS BASE SHOULD BE MADE CIRCULAR
18
2
6
7
FIRST TYPE
OF 18 PARTS
20
2
2
6
7
SECOND TYPE
OF 20 PARTS
24
2
3
6
7
CONSIDERING THE BASE AS CIRCULAR
FOURTH TYPE
OF 24 PARTS
22
2
2
6
7
THERE BEING NO KUMBHA MOULDING IN ANY OF THESE BASES, FOR THE PURPOSE OF THIS ILLUSTRATION THAT MOULD-ING HAS BEEN TAKEN TO BE KUMUDA
THIRD TYPE
OF 22 PARTS
S. C. MUKHERJI.

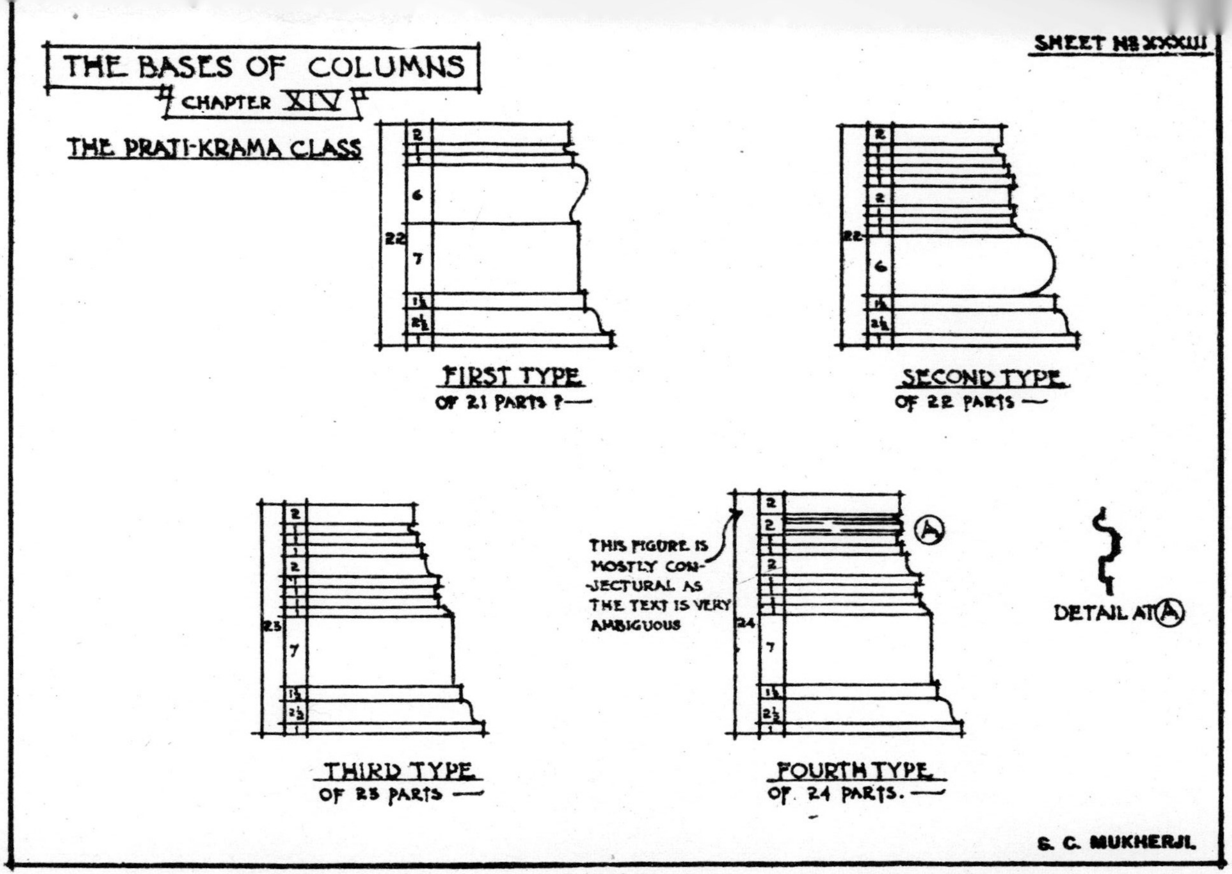

SHEET No XXXIII

THE BASES OF COLUMNS

CHAPTER XIV

THE PRATI-KRAMA CLASS

FIRST TYPE
OF 21 PARTS ?—

SECOND TYPE
OF 22 PARTS —

THIS FIGURE IS MOSTLY CONJECTURAL AS THE TEXT IS VERY AMBIGUOUS

DETAIL AT (A)

THIRD TYPE
OF 23 PARTS —

FOURTH TYPE
OF 24 PARTS. —

S. C. MUKHERJI

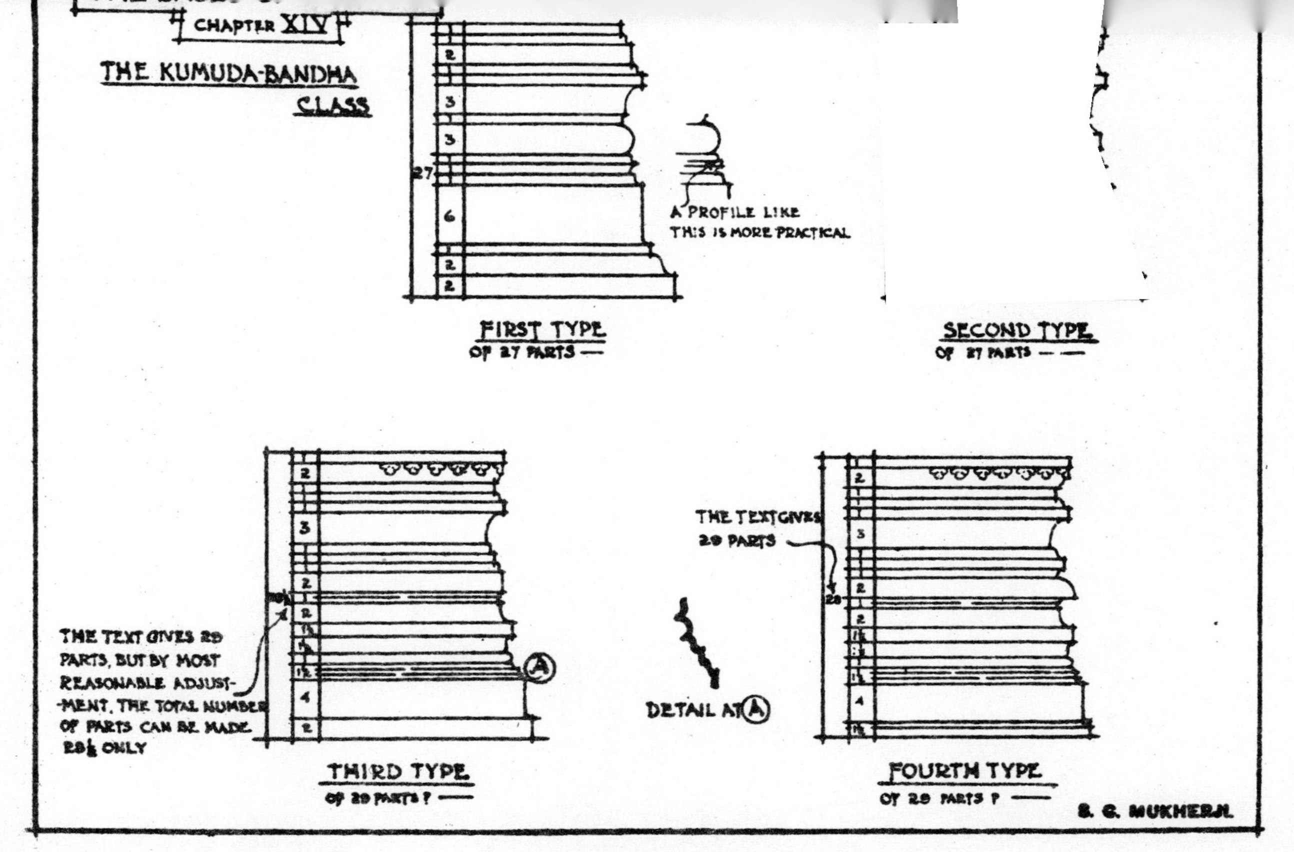
CHAPTER XIV
THE KUMUDA-BANDHA CLASS
27
2
3
3
6
2
2
A PROFILE LIKE THIS IS MORE PRACTICAL
FIRST TYPE
OF 27 PARTS —
SECOND TYPE
OF 27 PARTS — —
THE TEXT GIVES 29 PARTS, BUT BY MOST REASONABLE ADJUSTMENT, THE TOTAL NUMBER OF PARTS CAN BE MADE 28½ ONLY
A
THIRD TYPE
OF 29 PARTS ? —
THE TEXT GIVES 29 PARTS
28
DETAIL AT A
FOURTH TYPE
OF 29 PARTS ? —
S. G. MUKHERJI

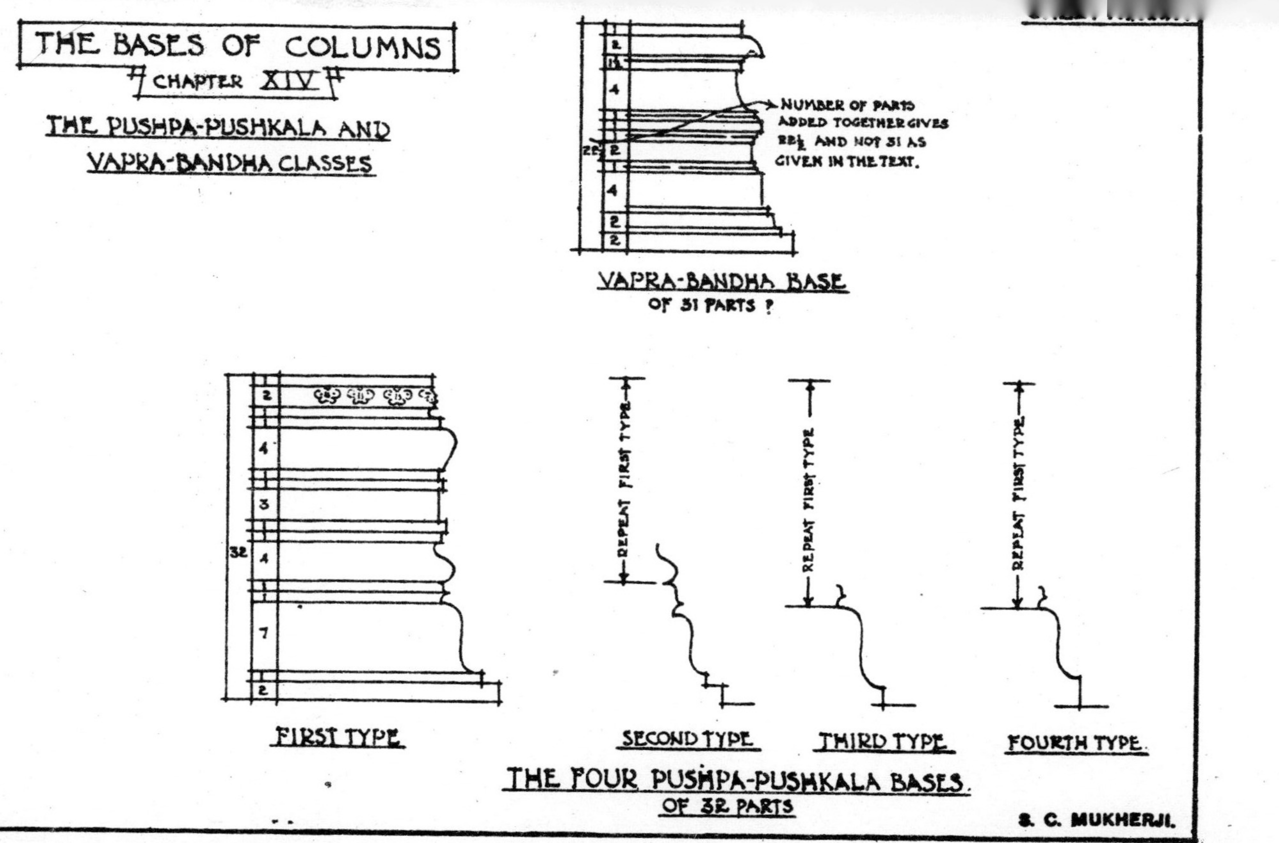
THE BASES OF COLUMNS
CHAPTER XIV
THE PUSHPA-PUSHKALA AND
VAPRA-BANDHA CLASSES
NUMBER OF PARTS ADDED TOGETHER GIVES 22½ AND NOT 31 AS GIVEN IN THE TEXT.
VAPRA-BANDHA BASE
OF 31 PARTS ?
REPEAT FIRST TYPE
REPEAT FIRST TYPE
REPEAT FIRST TYPE
FIRST TYPE
SECOND TYPE
THIRD TYPE
FOURTH TYPE.
THE FOUR PUSHPA-PUSHKALA BASES.
OF 32 PARTS
S. C. MUKHERJI.

THE BASES OF COLUMNS

CHAPTER XIV

THE ŚRĪ-BHOGA AND VAPRA-BANDHA CLASSES

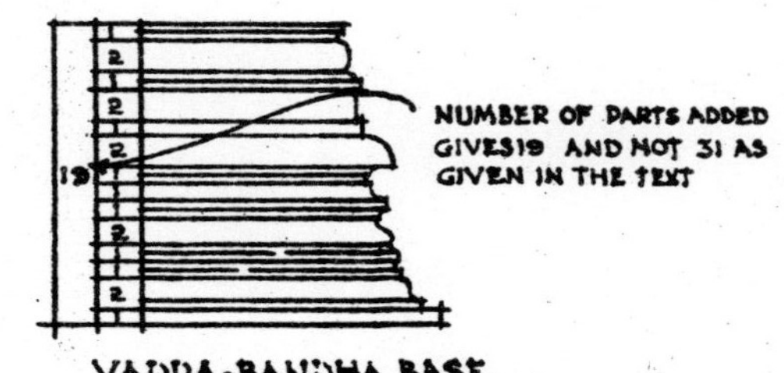

VAPRA-BANDHA BASE

OF 31 PARTS ?

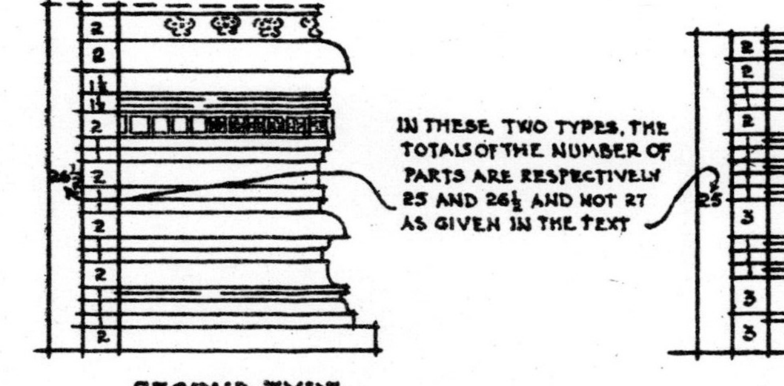

SECOND TYPE

FIRST TYPE

THE TWO ŚRĪ-BHOGA BASES.

OF 27 PARTS ?

S. C. MUKHERJI.

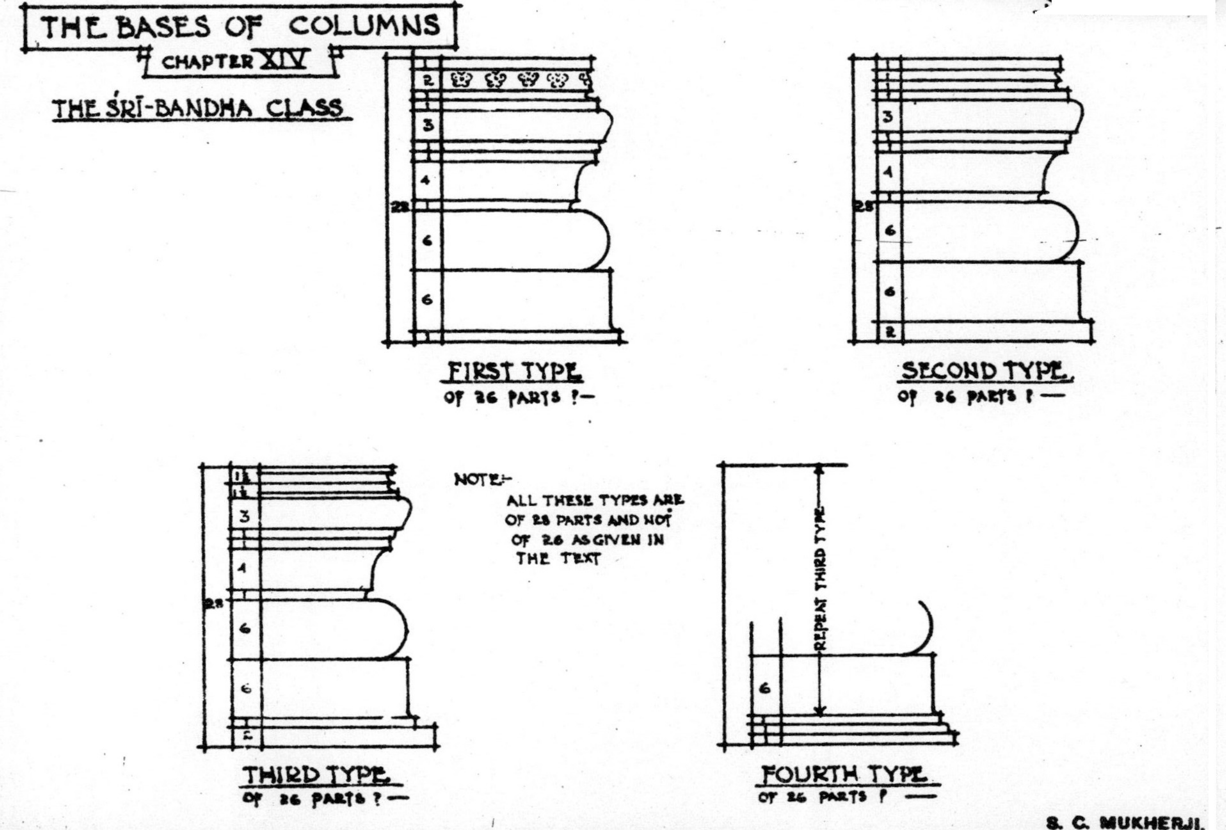
THE BASES OF COLUMNS
CHAPTER XIV
THE ŚRĪ-BANDHA CLASS
FIRST TYPE
OF 26 PARTS ?—
SECOND TYPE.
OF 26 PARTS ? —
THIRD TYPE
OF 26 PARTS ? —
FOURTH TYPE
OF 26 PARTS ? —
REPEAT THIRD TYPE
NOTE:-
ALL THESE TYPES ARE OF 28 PARTS AND NOT OF 26 AS GIVEN IN THE TEXT
S. C. MUKHERJI.

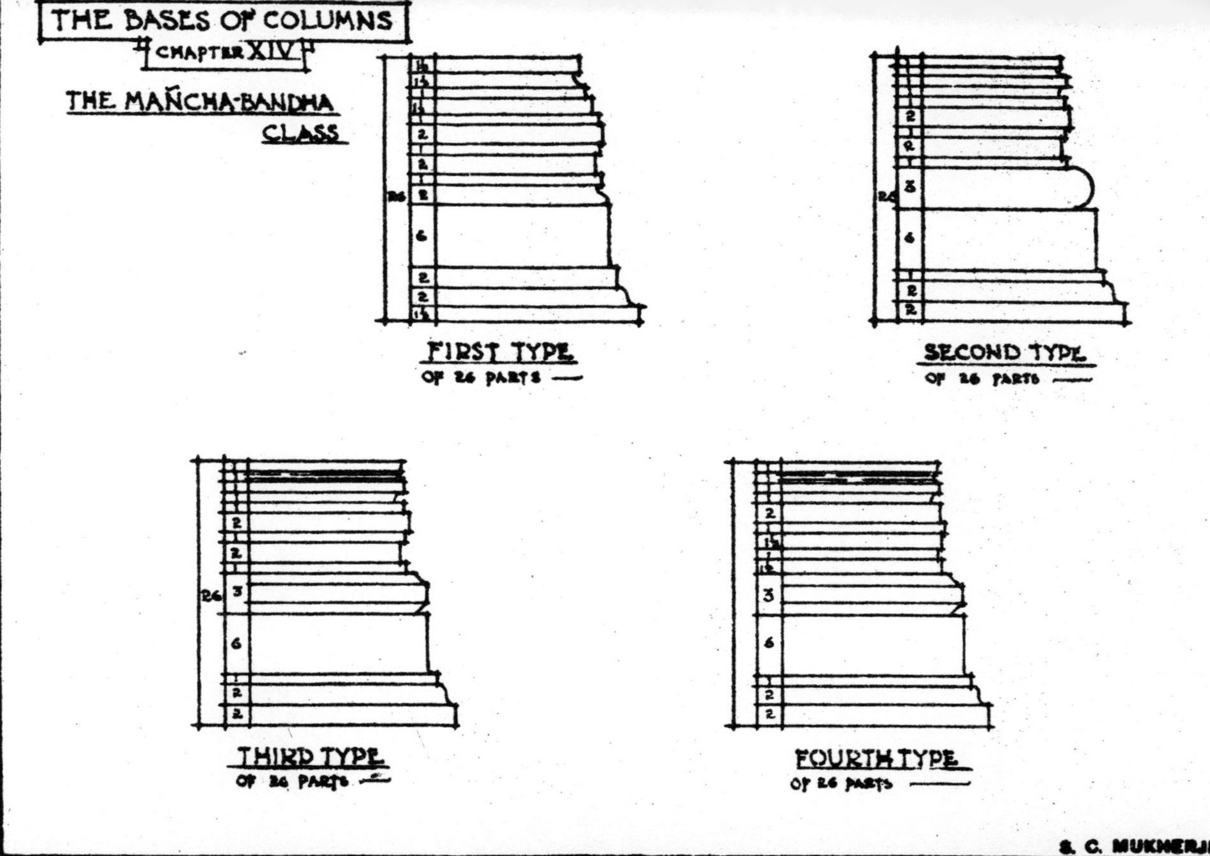
THE BASES OF COLUMNS
CHAPTER XIV
THE MAÑCHA-BANDHA
CLASS
FIRST TYPE
OF 26 PARTS —
SECOND TYPE
OF 26 PARTS —
THIRD TYPE
OF 26 PARTS —
FOURTH TYPE
OF 26 PARTS —
S. C. MUKHERJI.

THE BASES OF COLUMNS

CHAPTER XIV

THE ŚREṆI-BANDHA CLASS

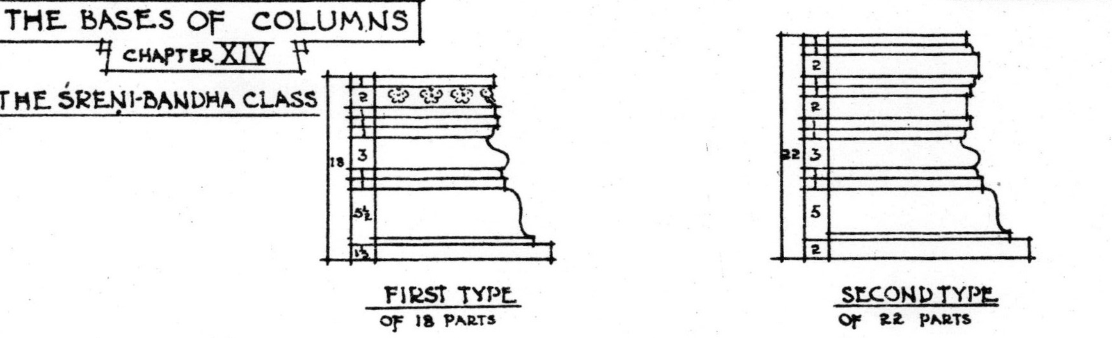

FIRST TYPE
OF 18 PARTS

SECOND TYPE
OF 22 PARTS

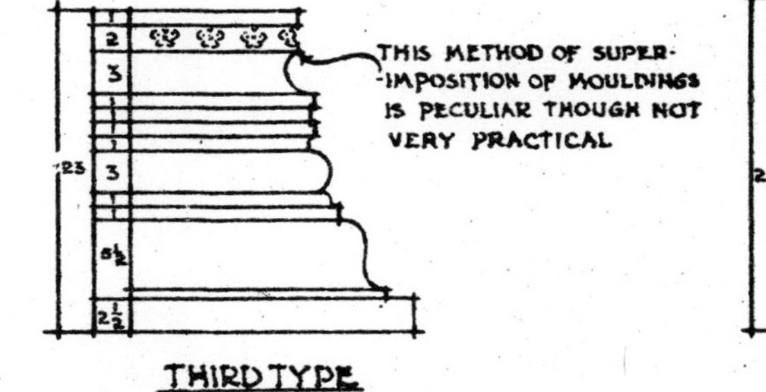

THIRD TYPE
OF 23 PARTS

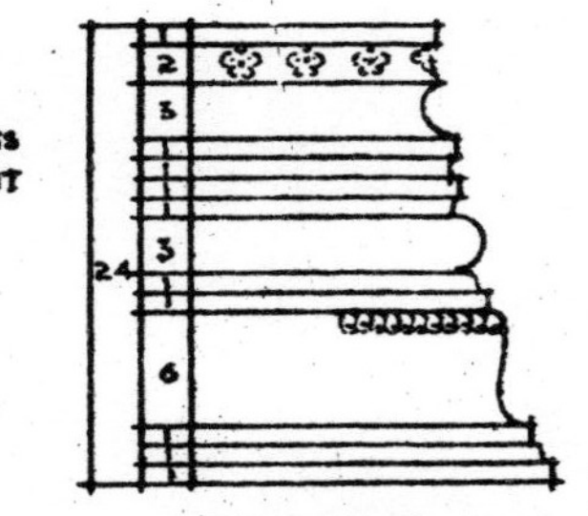

FOURTH TYPE
OF 24 PARTS

S. C. MUKHERJI.

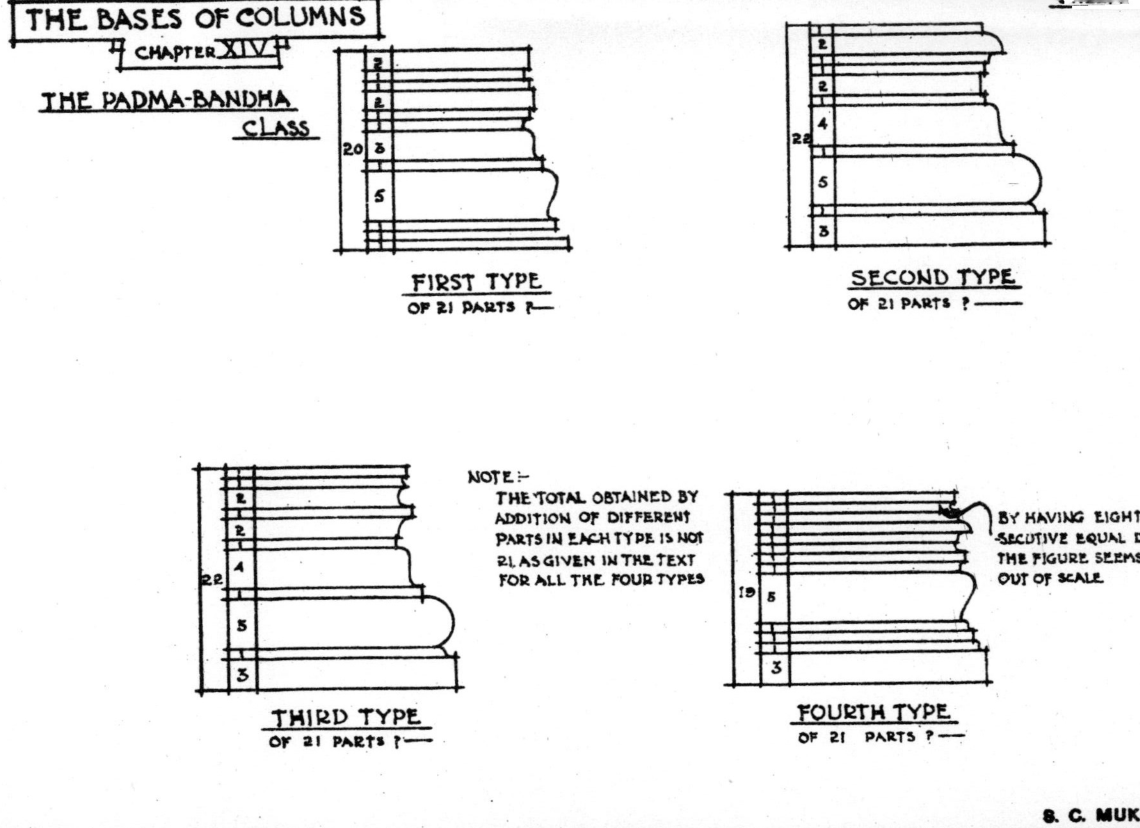
THE BASES OF COLUMNS
CHAPTER XIV
THE PADMA-BANDHA CLASS
2
2
20
3
5
FIRST TYPE
OF 21 PARTS ?—
2
2
4
22
5
3
SECOND TYPE
OF 21 PARTS ?—
2
2
4
22
5
3
THIRD TYPE
OF 21 PARTS ?—
NOTE:-
THE TOTAL OBTAINED BY ADDITION OF DIFFERENT PARTS IN EACH TYPE IS NOT 21, AS GIVEN IN THE TEXT FOR ALL THE FOUR TYPES
19
5
3
BY HAVING EIGHT CON-SECUTIVE EQUAL DIVISIONS THE FIGURE SEEMS TO BE OUT OF SCALE
FOURTH TYPE
OF 21 PARTS ?—
S. C. MUKHERJI.

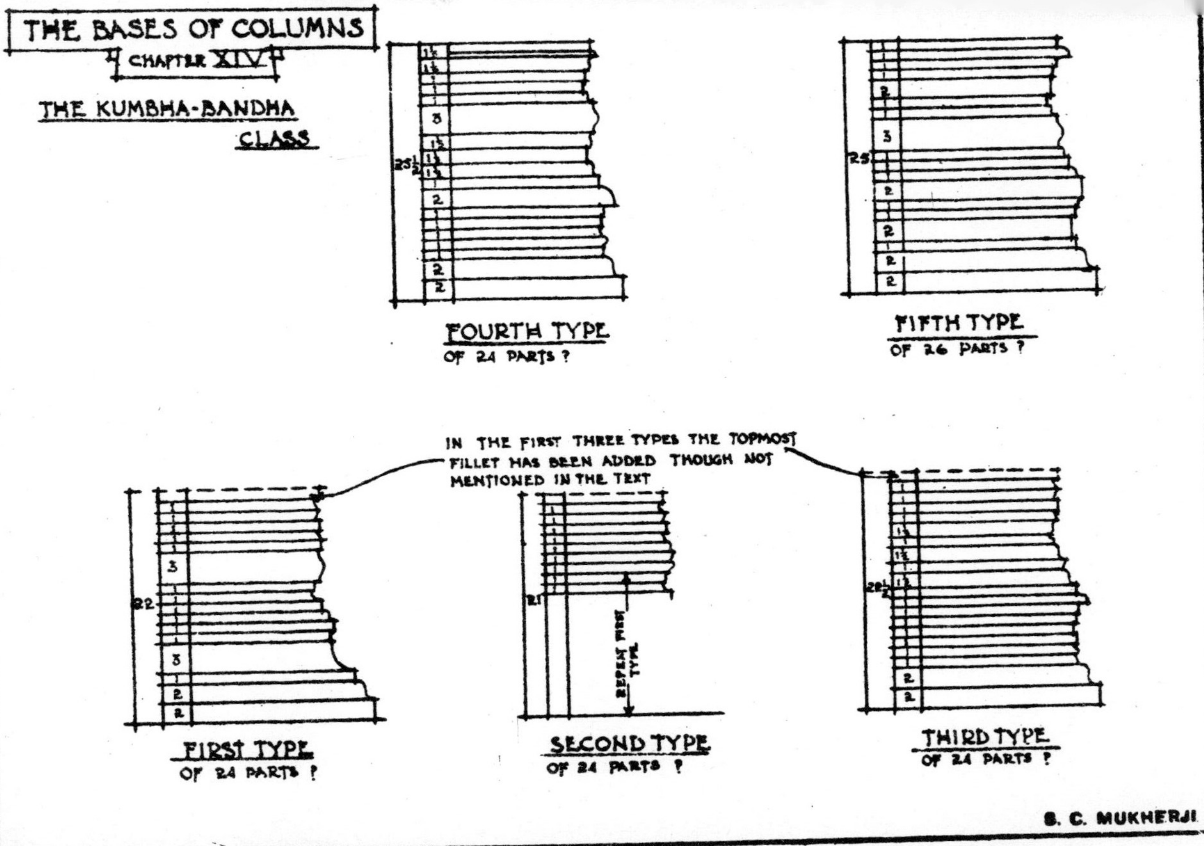
THE BASES OF COLUMNS
CHAPTER XIV
THE KUMBHA-BANDHA CLASS
FOURTH TYPE
OF 24 PARTS ?
FIFTH TYPE
OF 26 PARTS ?
IN THE FIRST THREE TYPES THE TOPMOST FILLET HAS BEEN ADDED THOUGH NOT MENTIONED IN THE TEXT
REPEAT FIRST TYPE
FIRST TYPE
OF 24 PARTS ?
SECOND TYPE
OF 24 PARTS ?
THIRD TYPE
OF 24 PARTS ?
S. C. MUKHERJI

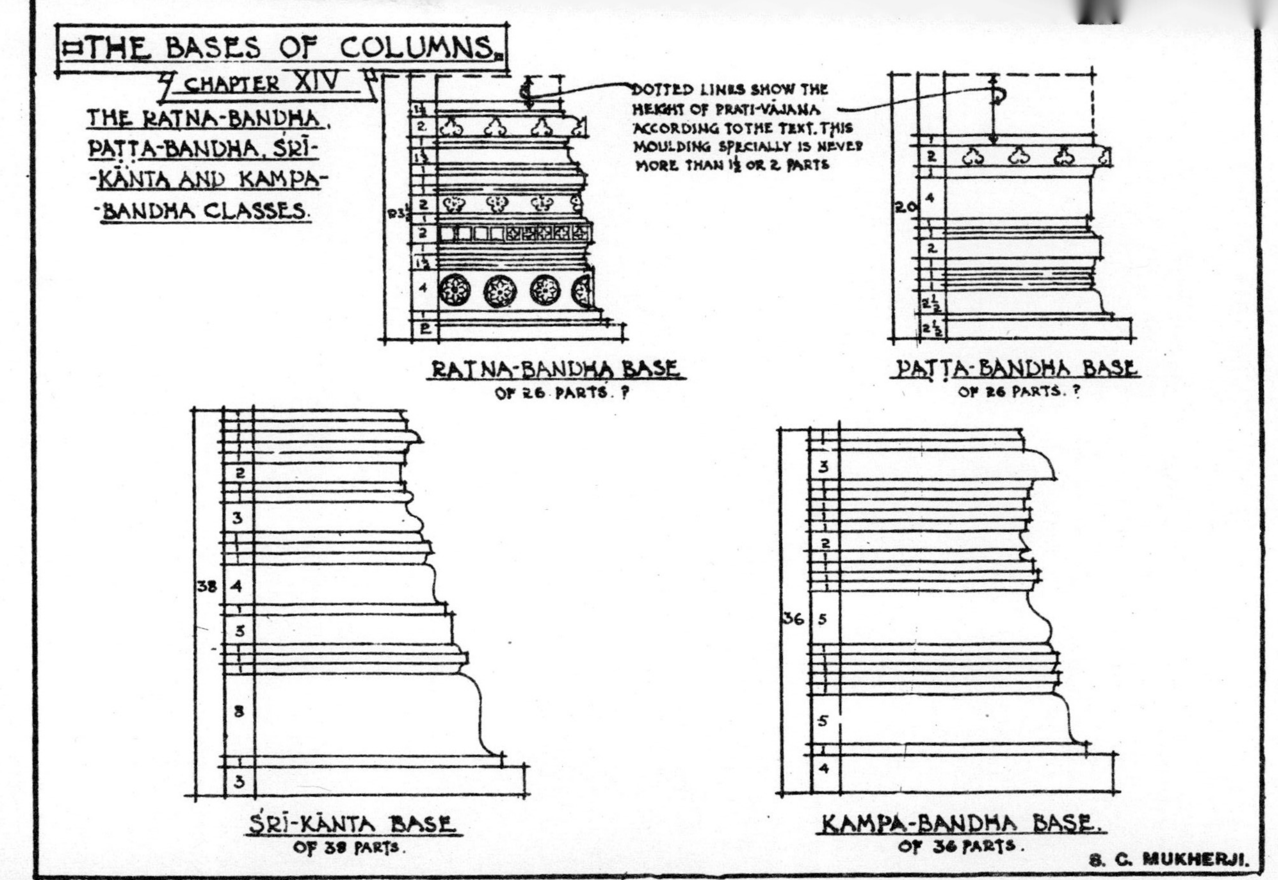
THE BASES OF COLUMNS.
CHAPTER XIV
THE RATNA-BANDHA, PATTA-BANDHA, ŚRĪ-KĀNTA AND KAMPA-BANDHA CLASSES.
DOTTED LINES SHOW THE HEIGHT OF PRATI-VĀJANA ACCORDING TO THE TEXT. THIS MOULDING SPECIALLY IS NEVER MORE THAN 1½ OR 2 PARTS
RATNA-BANDHA BASE
OF 26 PARTS. ?
PATTA-BANDHA BASE
OF 26 PARTS. ?
ŚRĪ-KĀNTA BASE
OF 38 PARTS.
KAMPA-BANDHA BASE.
OF 36 PARTS.
S. C. MUKHERJI.

THE BASES OF COLUMNS

CHAPTER XIV

KUKSHI-BANDHA CLASS

NOTE:- IN THE TWO TYPES FIRST AND THIRD, THE TOTALS OF THE NUMBER OF PARTS FOR DIFFERENT MOULDINGS VARY FROM THOSE GIVEN IN THE TEXT

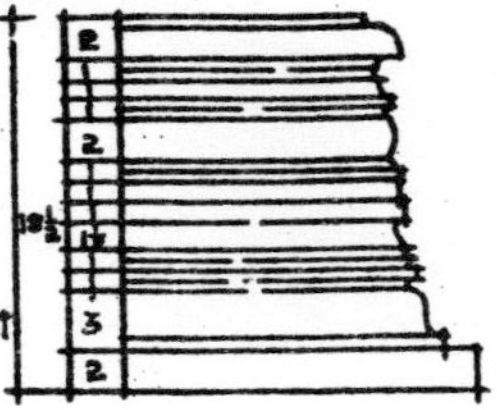

2 2 $1\frac{1}{2}$ 3 2 $18\frac{1}{2}$

FIRST TYPE
OF 18 PARTS ?

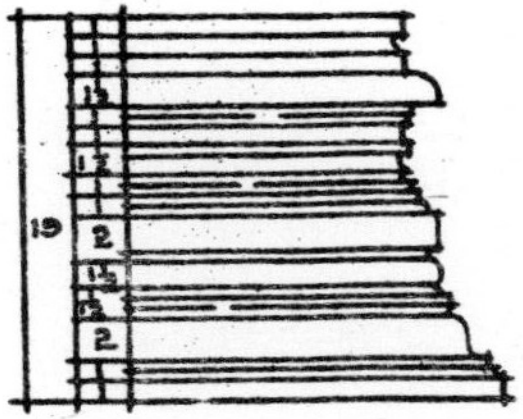

$1\frac{1}{2}$ $1\frac{1}{2}$ 2 $1\frac{1}{2}$ $1\frac{1}{2}$ 2 19

SECOND TYPE
OF 19 PARTS

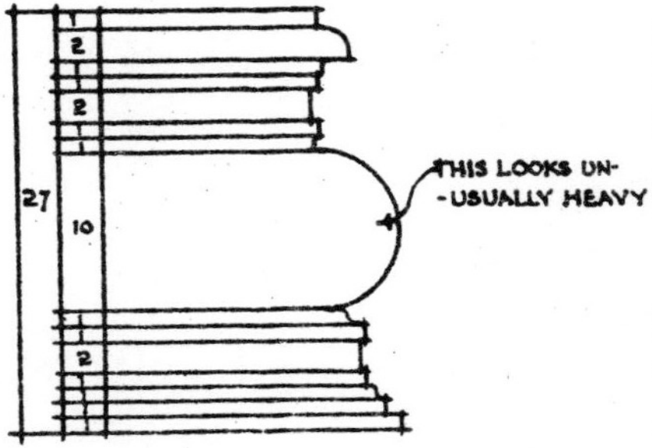

2 2 10 2 27

THIS LOOKS UN-USUALLY HEAVY

THIRD TYPE
OF 26 PARTS ?

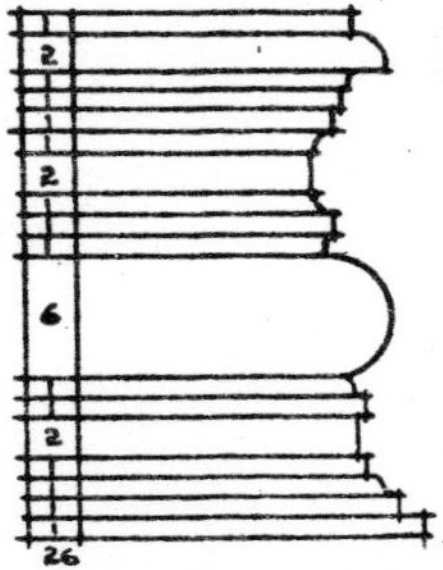

2 2 6 2 26

SUGGESTED ALTERNATIVE OF THIRD TYPE

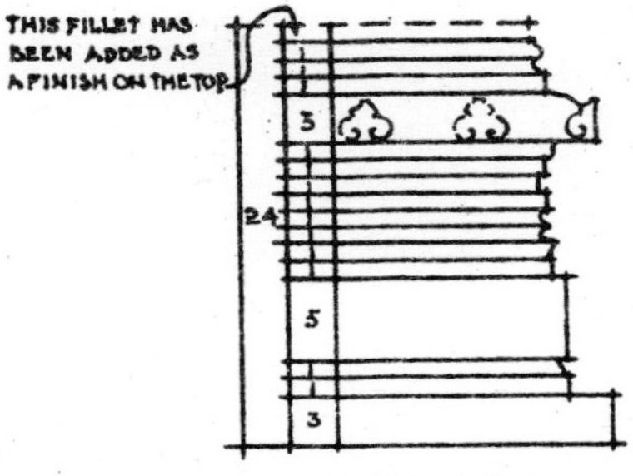

THIS FILLET HAS BEEN ADDED AS A FINISH ON THE TOP

3 5 3 24

FOURTH TYPE
OF 24 PARTS.

S. C. MUKHERJI.

SHEET No. XLIV

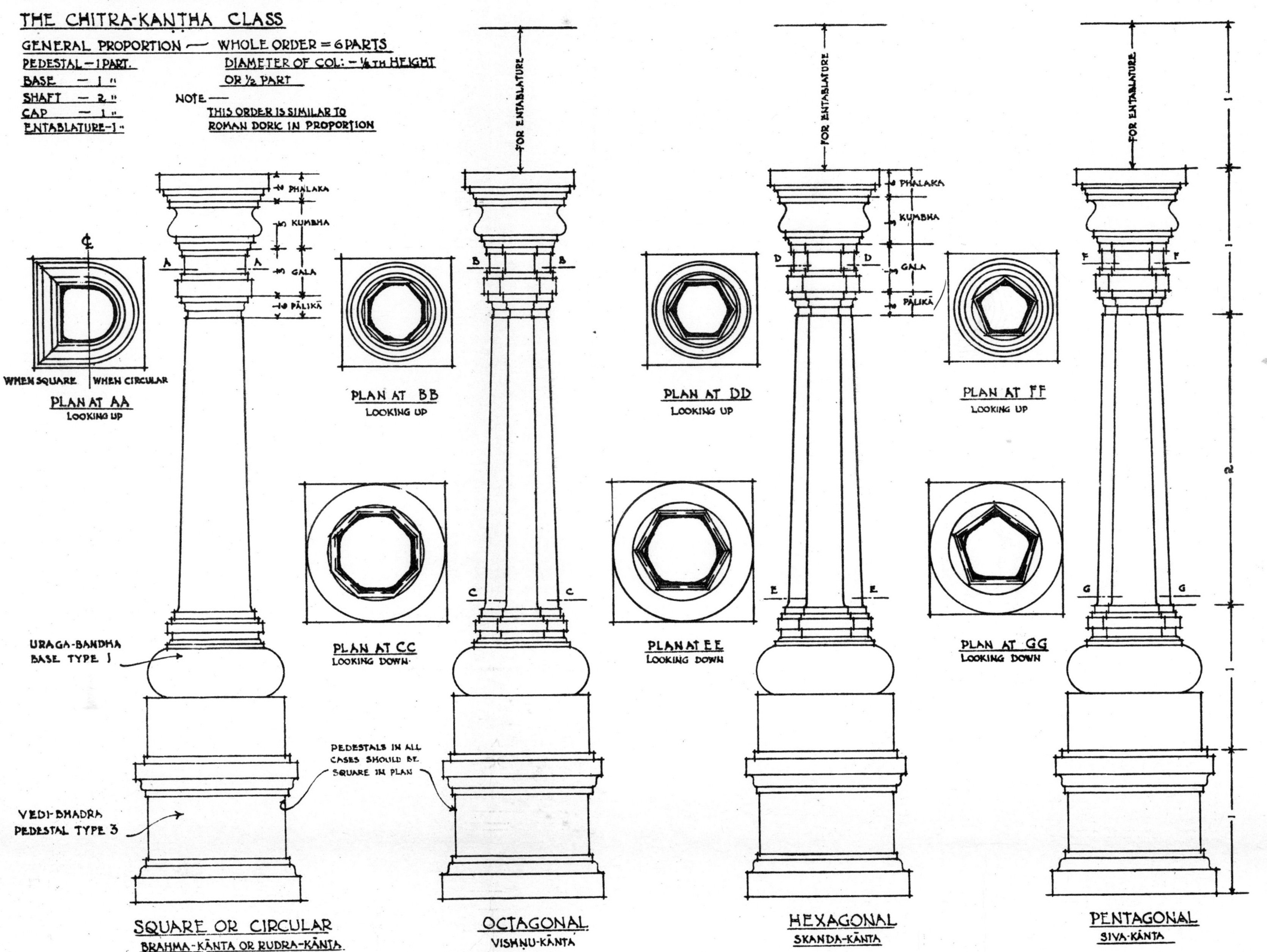

S. C. MUKHERJI.

SHEET NO. XLV

THE COLUMNS — CHAPTER XV

THE PADMA-KĀNTA AND CHITRA-SKAMBHA CLASSES

GENERAL PROPORTION— WHOLE ORDER = 6 PARTS

PEDESTAL — 1 PART
BASE — 1 "
SHAFT — 2 "
CAP — 1 "
ENTABLATURE — 1 "

DIAMETER OF PADMA-KĀNTA = 1/9 TH HEIGHT OF COL:
DIAMETER OF CHITRA-SKAMBHA = 1/10TH HEIGHT OF COL:
THEY ARE RESPECTIVELY SIMILAR TO IONIC AND CORINTHIAN IN PROPORTION.

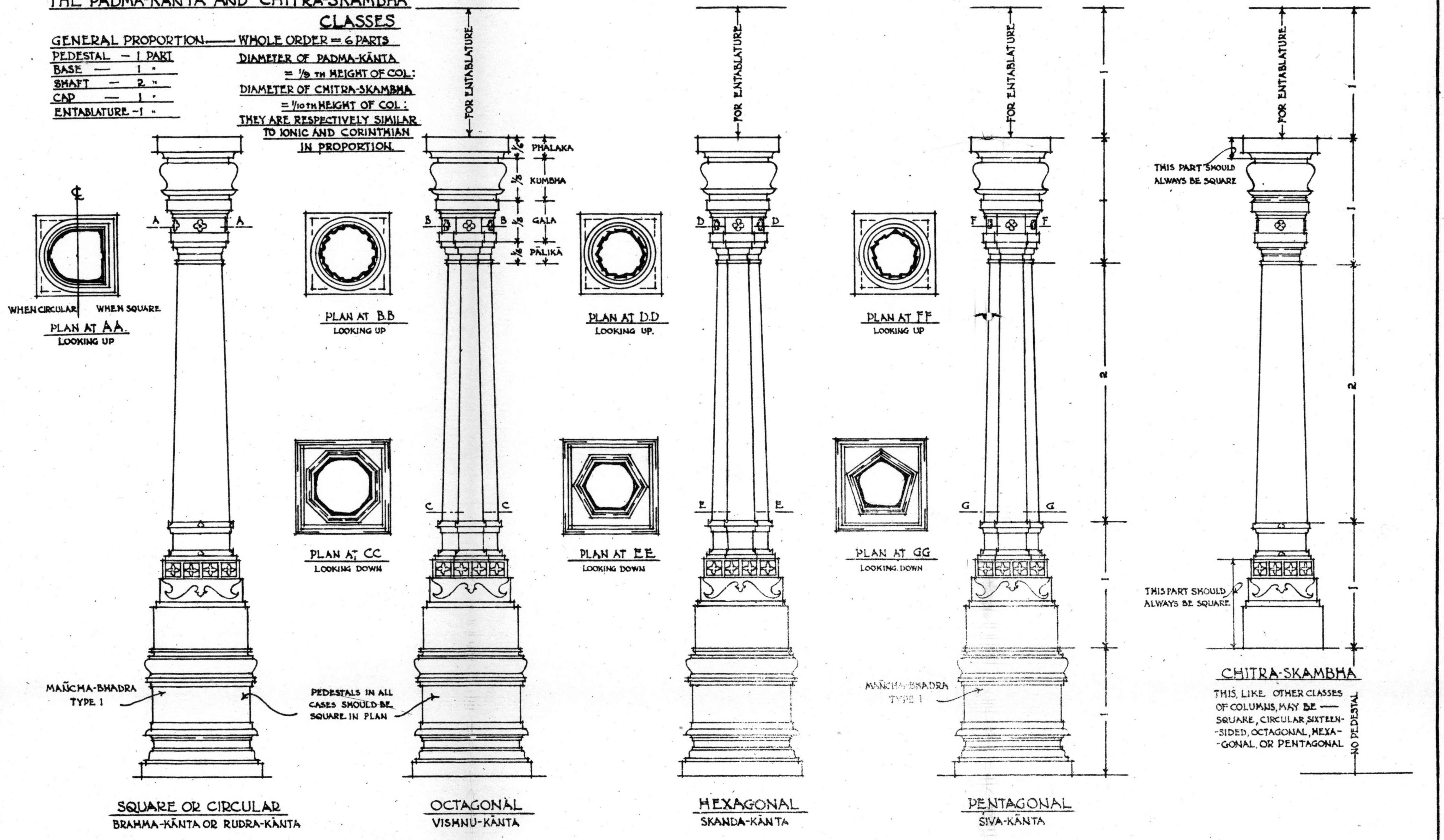

FOR ENTABLATURE

PHALAKA
KUMBHA
GALA
PĀLIKĀ

WHEN CIRCULAR — WHEN SQUARE
PLAN AT AA. LOOKING UP

PLAN AT B.B LOOKING UP

PLAN AT D.D LOOKING UP.

PLAN AT FF LOOKING UP

PLAN AT CC LOOKING DOWN

PLAN AT EE LOOKING DOWN

PLAN AT GG LOOKING DOWN

THIS PART SHOULD ALWAYS BE SQUARE

MAÑCHA-BHADRA TYPE 1

PEDESTALS IN ALL CASES SHOULD BE SQUARE IN PLAN

MAÑCHA-BHADRA TYPE 1

NO PEDESTAL

SQUARE OR CIRCULAR
BRAHMA-KĀNTA OR RUDRA-KĀNTA

OCTAGONAL
VISHNU-KĀNTA

HEXAGONAL
SKANDA-KĀNTA

PENTAGONAL
SIVA-KĀNTA

CHITRA-SKAMBHA

THIS, LIKE OTHER CLASSES OF COLUMNS, MAY BE — SQUARE, CIRCULAR, SIXTEEN-SIDED, OCTAGONAL, HEXAGONAL, OR PENTAGONAL

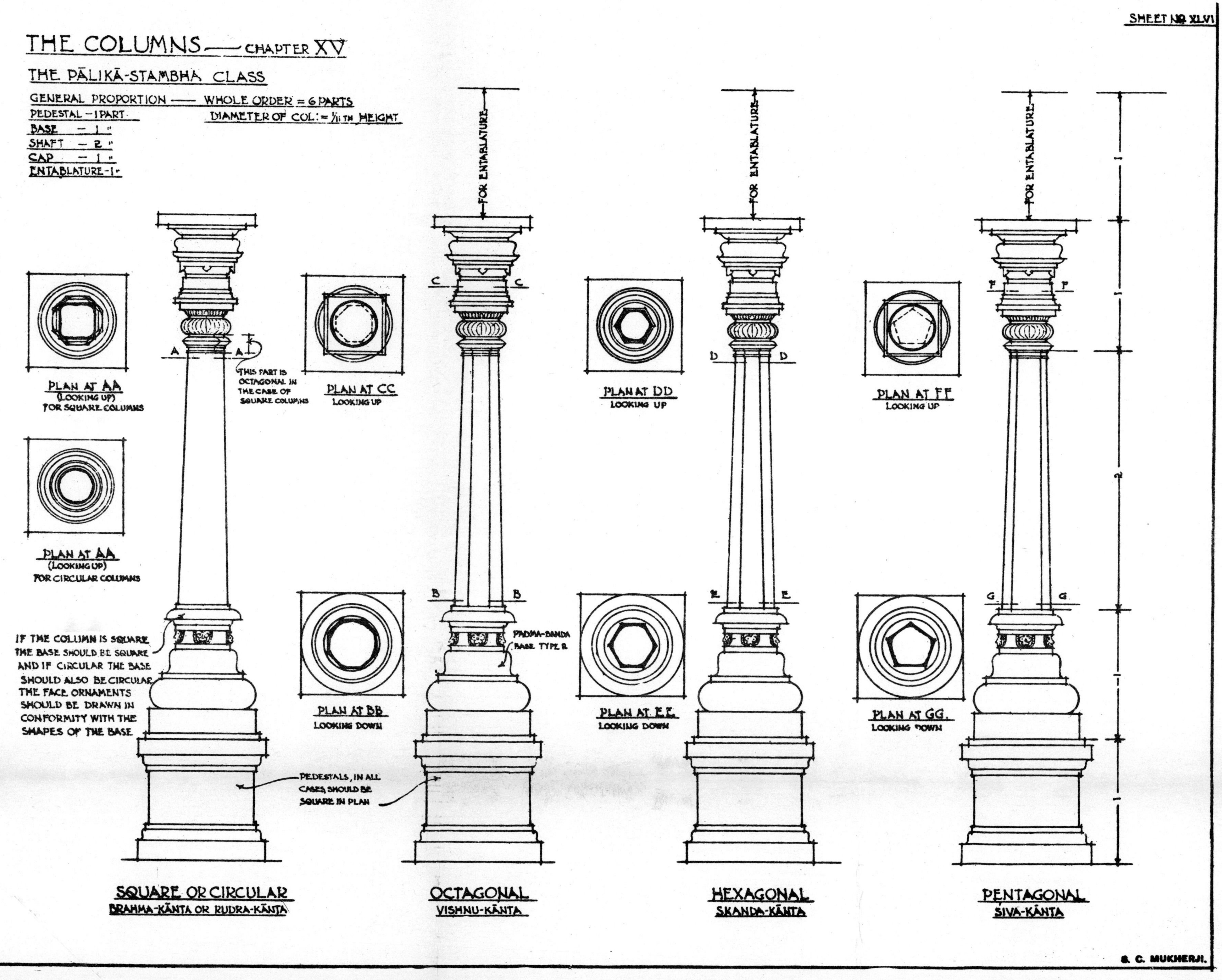

THE COLUMNS — CHAPTER XV

THE PĀLIKĀ-STAMBHA CLASS

GENERAL PROPORTION — WHOLE ORDER = 6 PARTS
DIAMETER OF COL: = 1/11TH HEIGHT

PEDESTAL – 1 PART
BASE – 1 "
SHAFT – 2 "
CAP – 1 "
ENTABLATURE – 1 "

FOR ENTABLATURE

PLAN AT AA (LOOKING UP) FOR SQUARE COLUMNS

PLAN AT AA (LOOKING UP) FOR CIRCULAR COLUMNS

THIS PART IS OCTAGONAL IN THE CASE OF SQUARE COLUMNS

IF THE COLUMN IS SQUARE THE BASE SHOULD BE SQUARE AND IF CIRCULAR THE BASE SHOULD ALSO BE CIRCULAR. THE FACE ORNAMENTS SHOULD BE DRAWN IN CONFORMITY WITH THE SHAPES OF THE BASE

PLAN AT CC LOOKING UP

PLAN AT BB LOOKING DOWN

PADMA-BANDA BASE TYPE B

PEDESTALS, IN ALL CASES, SHOULD BE SQUARE IN PLAN

PLAN AT DD LOOKING UP

PLAN AT EE LOOKING DOWN

PLAN AT FF LOOKING UP

PLAN AT GG LOOKING DOWN

1 1 2 1 1

SQUARE OR CIRCULAR
BRAHMA-KĀNTA OR RUDRA-KĀNTA

OCTAGONAL
VISHNU-KĀNTA

HEXAGONAL
SKANDA-KĀNTA

PENTAGONAL
ŚIVA-KĀNTA

S. C. MUKHERJI.

THE COLUMNS

CHAPTER XV

THE KUMBHA-STAMBHA AND KOSHTHA-STAMBHA CLASSES

GENERAL PROPORTION

PEDESTAL	1 PART
BASE	1 "
SHAFT	2 "
CAP	1 "
ENTABLATURE	1 "

WHOLE ORDER = 6 PARTS

DIAMETER OF BOTH THE CLASSES = 1/12TH HEIGHT OF COL:

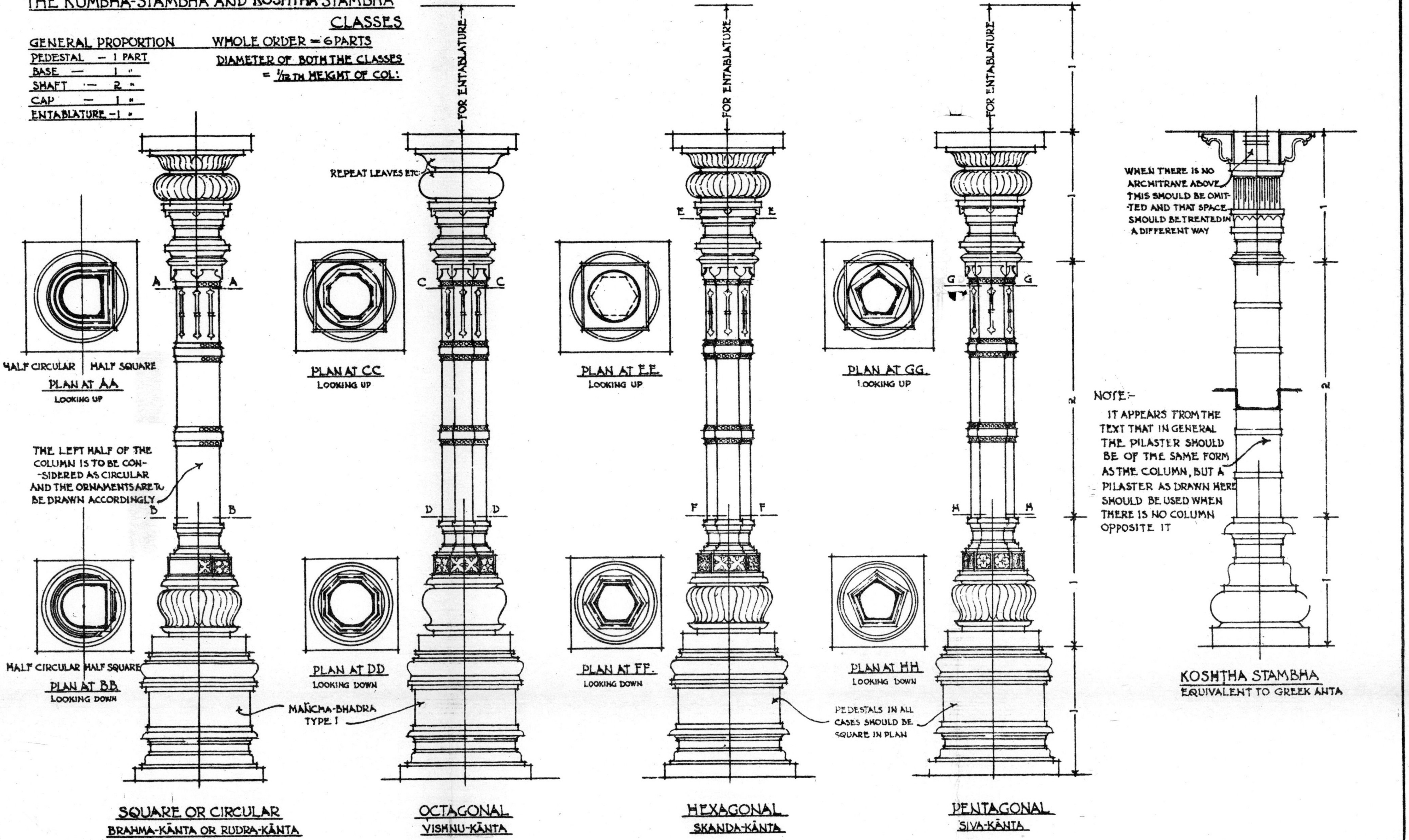

SQUARE OR CIRCULAR
BRAHMA-KĀNTA OR RUDRA-KĀNTA

OCTAGONAL
VISHNU-KĀNTA

HEXAGONAL
SKANDA-KĀNTA

PENTAGONAL
SIVA-KĀNTA

KOSHTHA STAMBHA
EQUIVALENT TO GREEK ANTA

S. C. MUKHERJI.

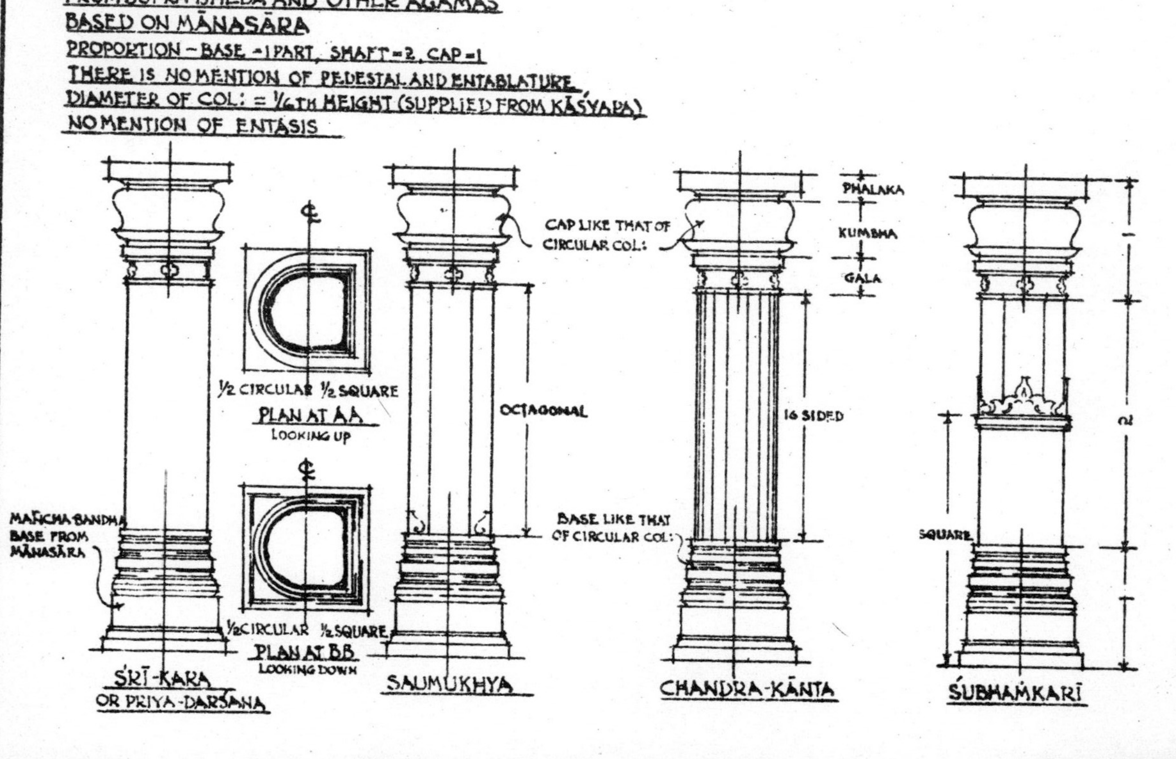
THE COLUMNS —— CHAPTER XV
THE SET OF FIVE ORDERS
FROM SUPRA-BHEDA AND OTHER ĀGAMAS
BASED ON MĀNASĀRA
PROPORTION – BASE – 1 PART, SHAFT = 2, CAP = 1
THERE IS NO MENTION OF PEDESTAL AND ENTABLATURE
DIAMETER OF COL: = 1/6TH HEIGHT (SUPPLIED FROM KĀŚYAPA)
NO MENTION OF ENTASIS
MAÑCHA-BANDHA BASE FROM MĀNASĀRA
ŚRĪ-KARA
OR PRIYA-DARŚANA
½ CIRCULAR ½ SQUARE
PLAN AT AA
LOOKING UP
½ CIRCULAR ½ SQUARE
PLAN AT BB
LOOKING DOWN
OCTAGONAL
SAUMUKHYA
CAP LIKE THAT OF CIRCULAR COL:
BASE LIKE THAT OF CIRCULAR COL:
16 SIDED
PHALAKA
KUMBHA
GALA
CHANDRA-KĀNTA
SQUARE
1
2
ŚUBHAMKARĪ
S. C. MUKHERJI.

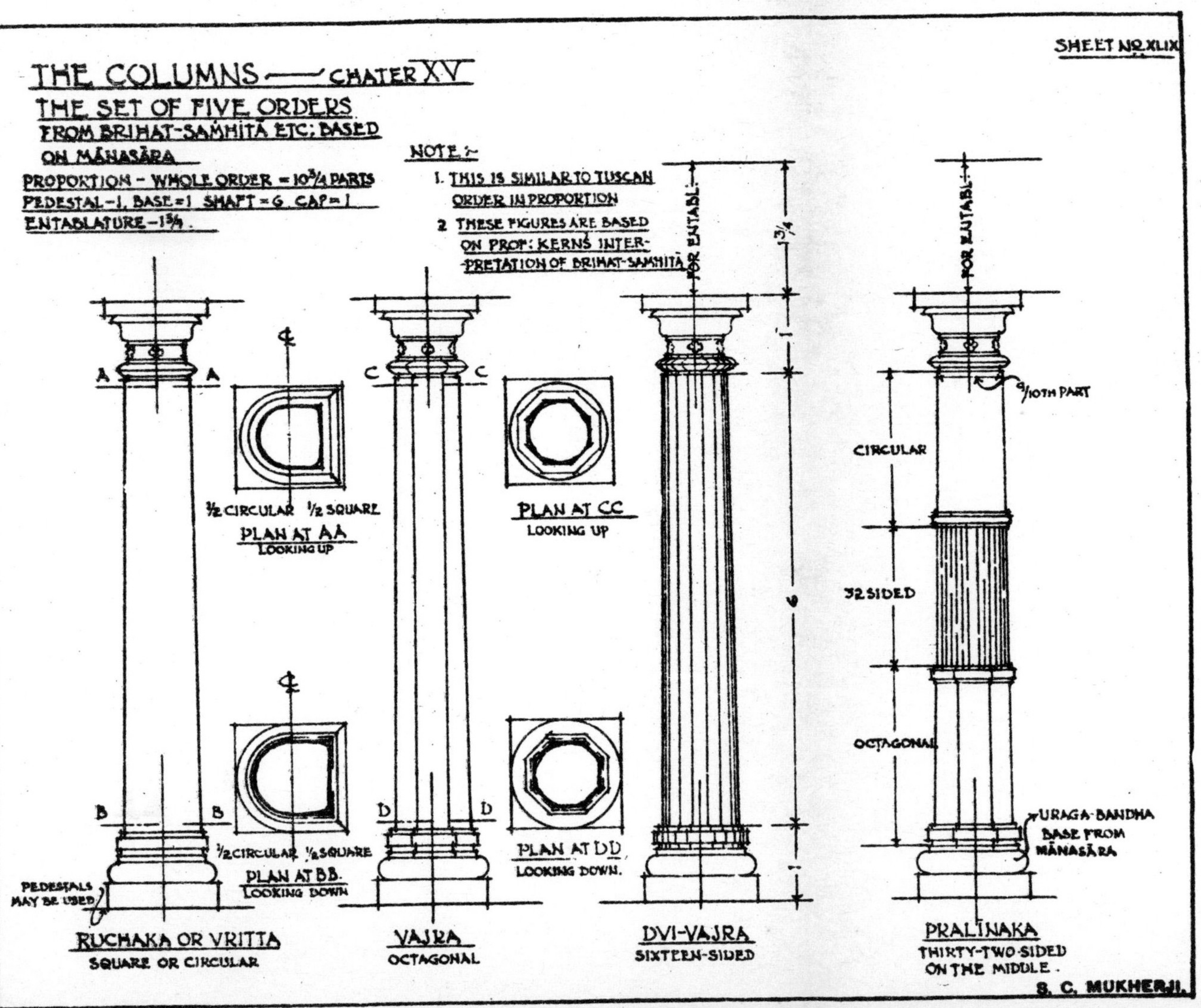
SHEET NO. XLIX
THE COLUMNS — CHATER XV
THE SET OF FIVE ORDERS
FROM BRIHAT-SAMHITĀ ETC; BASED
ON MĀNASĀRA
PROPORTION - WHOLE ORDER = 10¾ PARTS
PEDESTAL-1, BASE=1 SHAFT=6 CAP=1
ENTABLATURE-1¾.
NOTE :-
1. THIS IS SIMILAR TO TUSCAN
ORDER IN PROPORTION
2. THESE FIGURES ARE BASED
ON PROF: KERNS INTER-
-PRETATION OF BRIHAT-SAMHITĀ
FOR ENTABL.
1¾
1
6
1
½ CIRCULAR ½ SQUARE
PLAN AT AA
LOOKING UP
PLAN AT CC
LOOKING UP
½ CIRCULAR ½ SQUARE
PLAN AT BB.
LOOKING DOWN
PLAN AT DD
LOOKING DOWN.
9/10TH PART
CIRCULAR
32 SIDED
OCTAGONAL
URAGA-BANDHA
BASE FROM
MĀNASĀRA
PEDESTALS
MAY BE USED
RUCHAKA OR VRITTA
SQUARE OR CIRCULAR
VAJRA
OCTAGONAL
DVI-VAJRA
SIXTEEN-SIDED
PRALĪNAKA
THIRTY-TWO SIDED
ON THE MIDDLE.
S. C. MUKHERJI.

SHEET NO. 1

THE ENTABLATURES AND ROOFS — CHAPTER XVI

NOTE:–

1. THE TOTAL OF THE NUMBER OF PARTS FOR EACH TYPE VARIES FROM WHAT IS GIVEN IN THE TEXT
2. EXCEPTING THE TYPES SECOND AND THIRD, IMAGES AND LEOGRAPHS DO NOT SUIT OTHERS

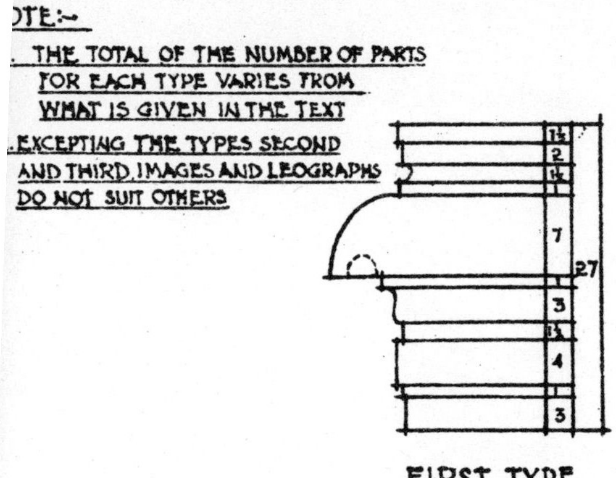

FIRST TYPE

SECOND TYPE

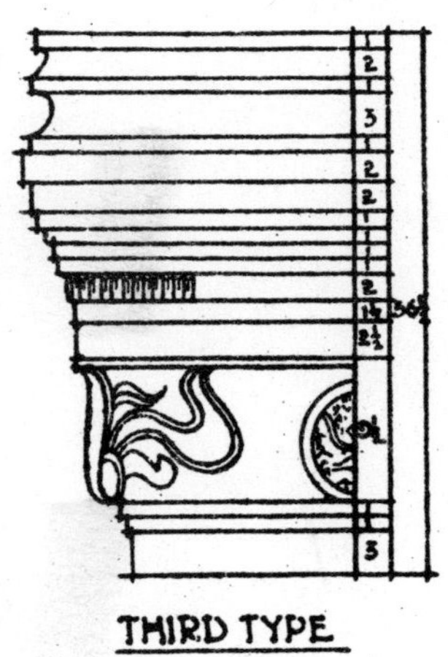

THIRD TYPE

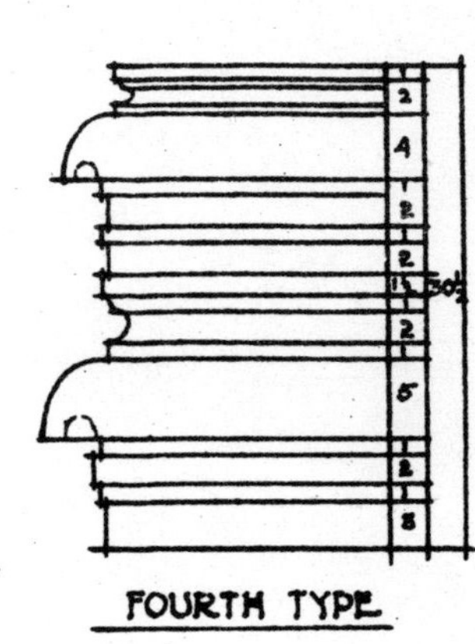

FOURTH TYPE

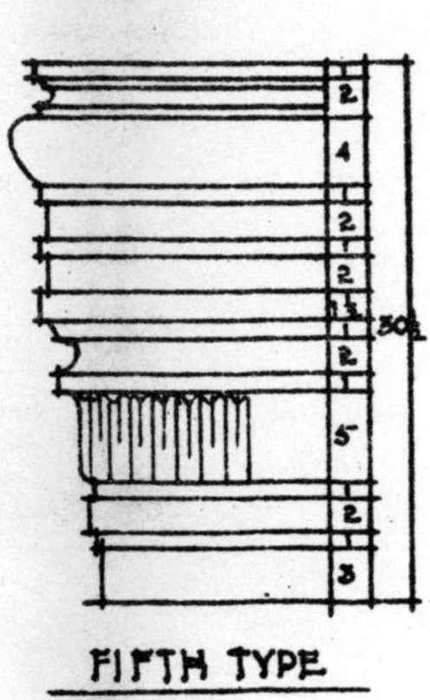

FIFTH TYPE

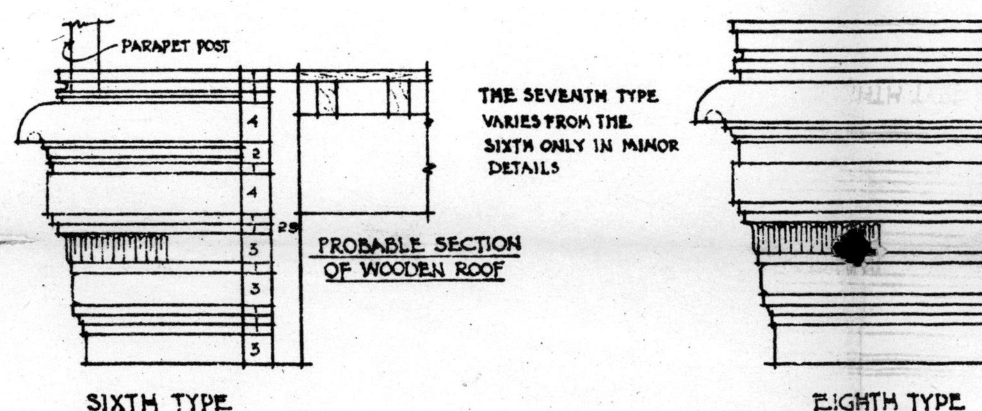

SIXTH TYPE

EIGHTH TYPE

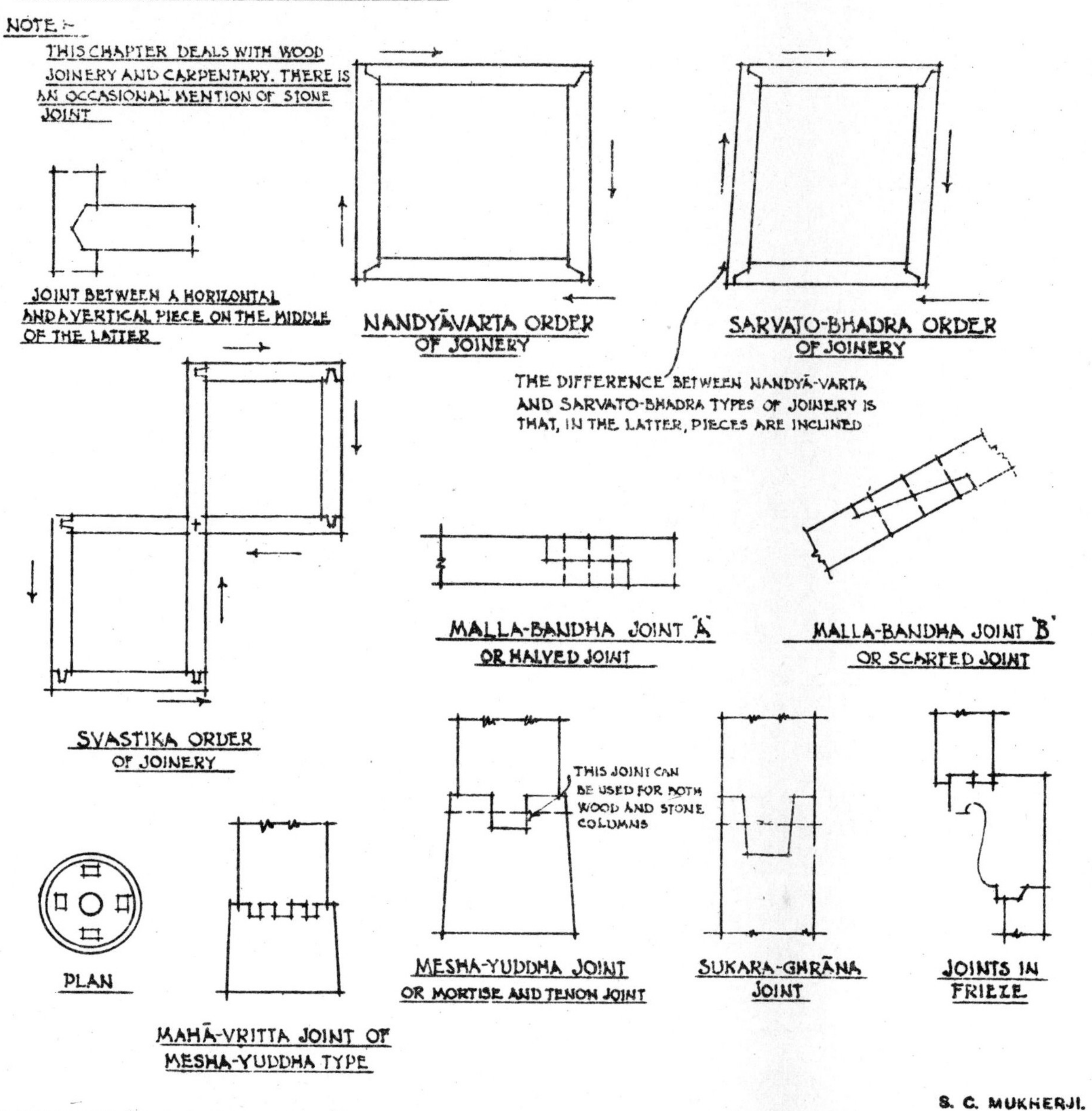
SHEET No. LI
THE JOINERY — CHAPTER XVII
NOTE :-
THIS CHAPTER DEALS WITH WOOD JOINERY AND CARPENTARY. THERE IS AN OCCASIONAL MENTION OF STONE JOINT
JOINT BETWEEN A HORIZONTAL AND A VERTICAL PIECE ON THE MIDDLE OF THE LATTER
NANDYĀVARTA ORDER OF JOINERY
SARVATO-BHADRA ORDER OF JOINERY
THE DIFFERENCE BETWEEN NANDYĀ-VARTA AND SARVATO-BHADRA TYPES OF JOINERY IS THAT, IN THE LATTER, PIECES ARE INCLINED
MALLA-BANDHA JOINT 'A' OR HALVED JOINT
MALLA-BANDHA JOINT 'B' OR SCARFED JOINT
SVASTIKA ORDER OF JOINERY
THIS JOINT CAN BE USED FOR BOTH WOOD AND STONE COLUMNS
PLAN
MESHA-YUDDHA JOINT OR MORTISE AND TENON JOINT
SUKARA-GHRĀNA JOINT
JOINTS IN FRIEZE
MAHĀ-VRITTA JOINT OF MESHA-YUDDHA TYPE
S. C. MUKHERJI.

THE ONE-STOREYED BUILDINGS — CHAPTER XIX

THE ELEVATION TOWARDS THE BREADTH

NOTE:—

I. ALL THESE TYPES MAY BE UTILISED BOTH AS TEMPLES AND DWELLING HOUSES WITH SLIGHT DIFFERENCE IN DETAILS TO BE INDICATED IN THE SECTION.

THE REMAINING FOUR TYPES ARE TO BE DRAWN SIMILARLY WITH DIFFERENT PROPORTIONS

FIRST TYPE
OF SMALL PROPORTION

HEIGHT = 1¼ BREADTH
= 8 PARTS.

SCALE OF 1 0 4 PARTS

S. C. MUKHERJI.

SHEET NO LIII

THE ONE-STOREYED BUILDINGS — CHAPTER XIX

THE TYPICAL PLAN

NOTE:—

ALL THESE TYPES MAY BE UTILISED BOTH AS TEMPLES AND DWELLING HOUSES WITH SLIGHT DIFFERENCE IN DETAILS

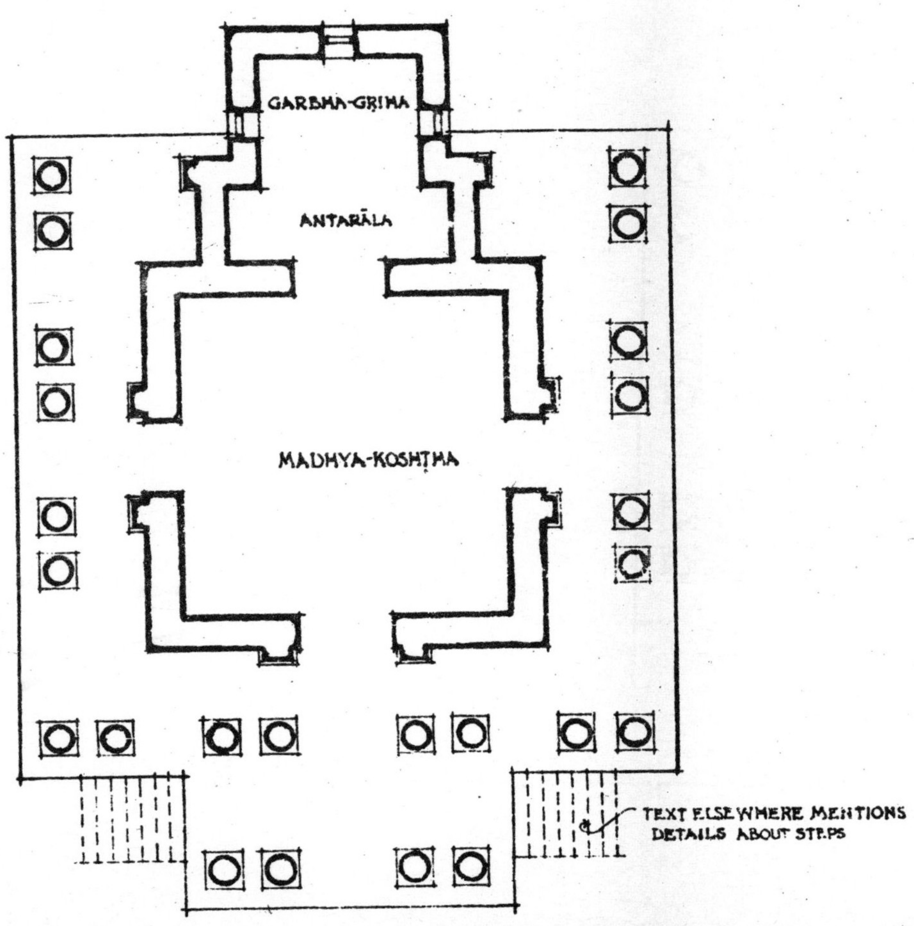

SUGGESTED PLAN

BASED ON FIRST TYPE

GARBHA-GRIHA = 1/3RD BREADTH IN THIS CASE

SCALE OF 1 0 5 PARTS

S. C. MUKHERJI.

THE ONE-STOREYED BUILDINGS — CHAPTER XIX

THE ELEVATION TOWARDS THE BREADTH

NOTE :-

ALL THESE TYPES MAY BE UTILISED BOTH AS TEMPLES AND DOMESTIC BUILDINGS WITH SLIGHT DIFFERENCE IN DETAILS TOBE INDICATED IN THE SECTION

THE REMAINING FOUR TYPES ARE TOBE DRAWN SIMILARLY WITH DIFFERENT PROPORTIONS.

THE SECOND TYPE
OF SMALL PROPORTION

HEIGHT = 1¼ BREADTH
= 10 PARTS

SCALE OF 1 0 5 PARTS

S. C. MUKHERJI.

THE ONE-STOREYED BUILDINGS — CHAPTER XIX

THE ELEVATION TOWARDS THE BREADTH

NOTE :-

ALL THESE TYPES MAY BE UTILISED BOTH AS TEMPLES AND DOMESTIC BUILDINGS WITH SLIGHT DIFFERENCE IN DETAILS TO BE INDICATED IN THE SECTION

THE REMAINING FOUR TYPES ARE TO BE DRAWN SIMILARLY WITH DIFFERENT PROPORTIONS.

THE THIRD TYPE
OF INTERMEDIATE PROPORTION.

HEIGHT = 1½ BREADTH
= 12 PARTS.

SCALE OF . 1 0 4 8 PARTS

S. C. MUKHERJI.

SHEET NO. LVI

HE ONE-STOREYED BUILDINGS — CHAPTER XIX

HE ELEVATION TOWARDS THE BREADTH

IOTE :—

ALL THESE TYPES MAY BE UTILISED
BOTH AS TEMPLES AND DOMESTIC BUILDINGS.
WITH SLIGHT DIFFERENCE IN DETAILS TO BE
INDICATED IN THE SECTION.

THE REMAINING FOUR TYPES ARE TO BE DRAWN
SIMILARLY WITH DIFFERENT PROPORTIONS

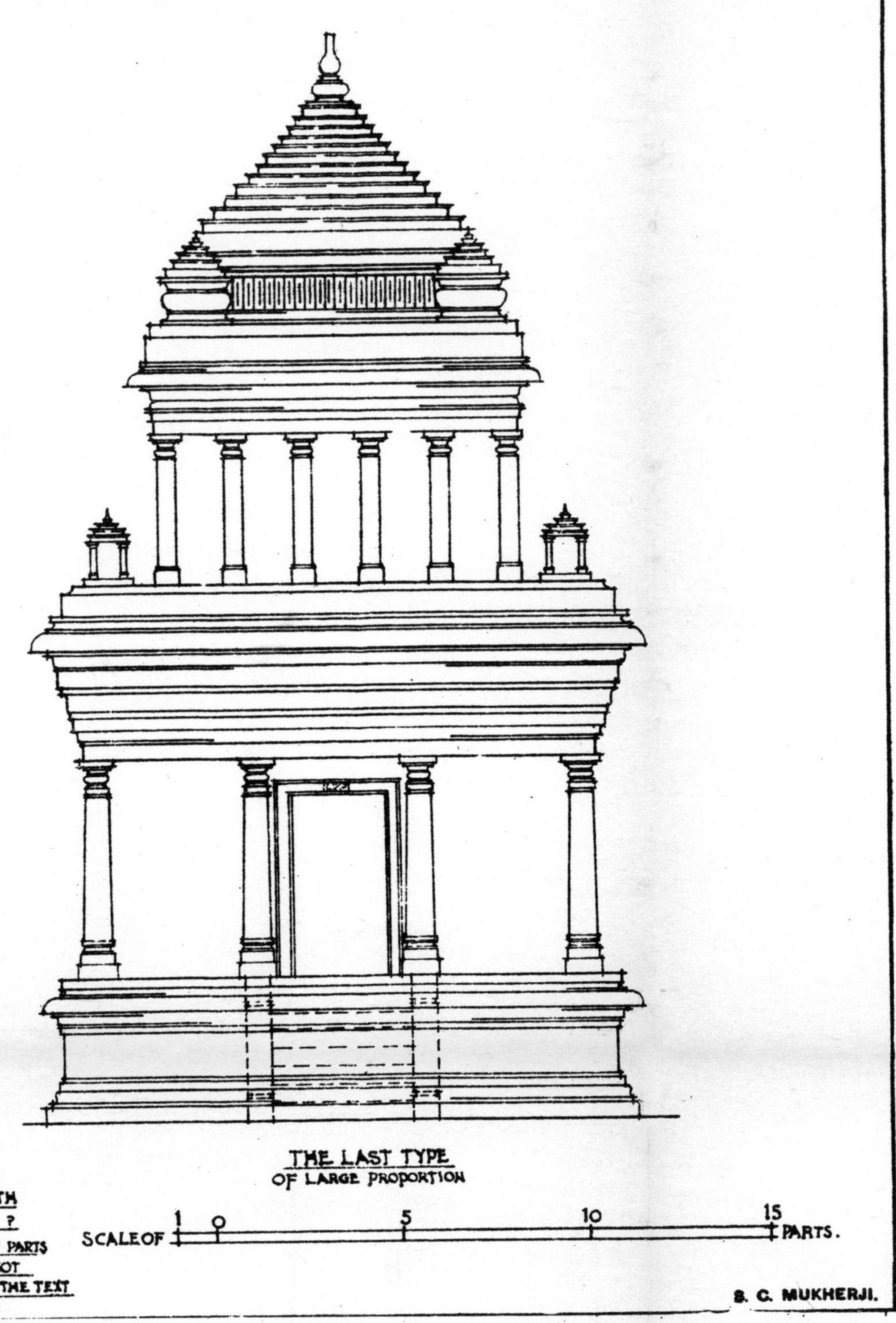

THE LAST TYPE
OF LARGE PROPORTION

IGHT = 2 BREADTH
= 32 PARTS ?
NUMBER OF PARTS
ED AND NOT
NED IN THE TEXT

S. C. MUKHERJI.

THE TO
SHOULD B
32 AS MEN

SHEET No. LVII

THE ONE-STOREYED BUILDINGS — CHAPTER XIX.

THE TYPICAL SECTION.

NOTE :-

IF THIS IS TOBE USED AS A TEMPLE THE FRIEZE AND PARAPET SHOULD ALSO BE DECORATED WITH IMAGES OF GODS.

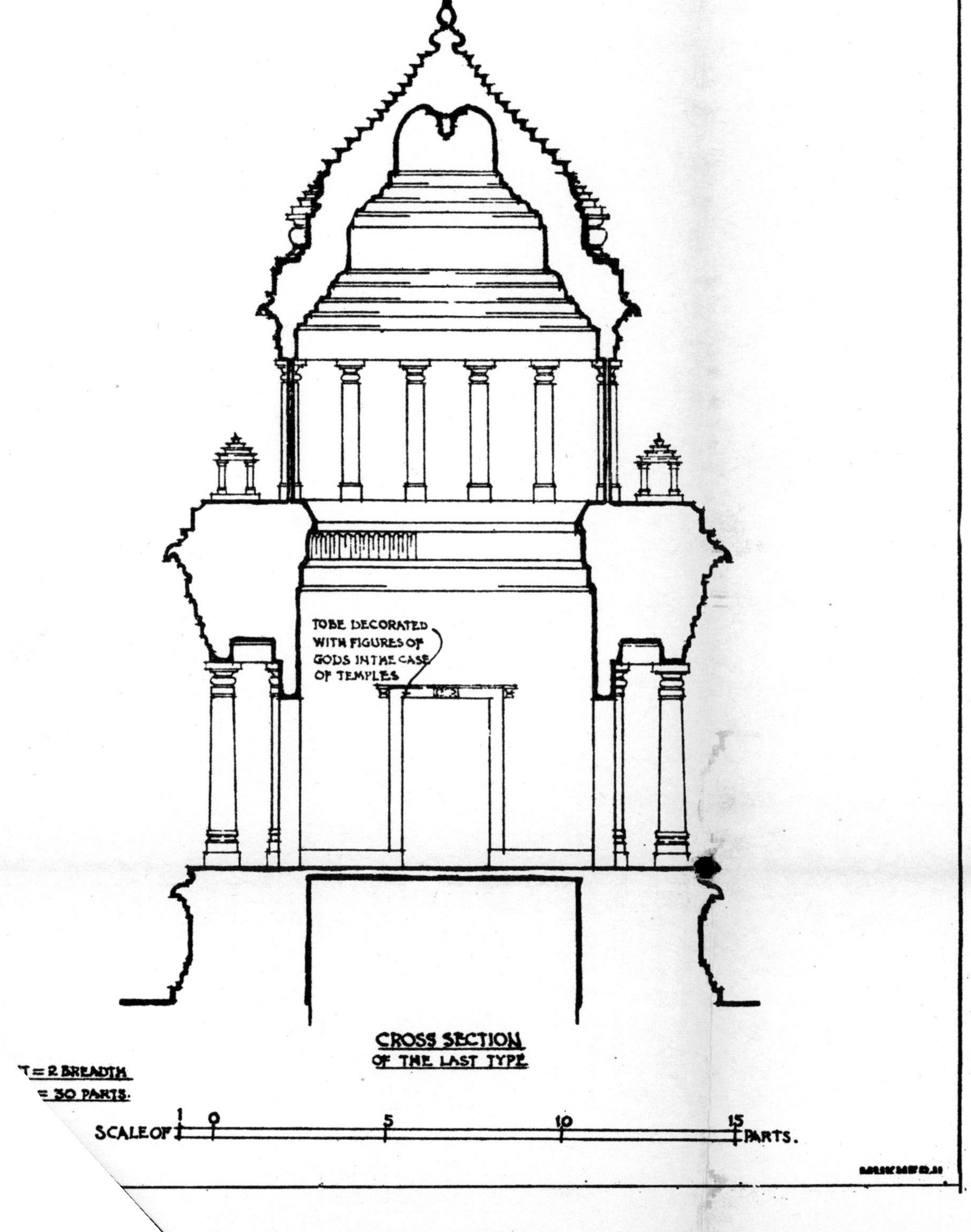

SHEET NO. LVIII

THE TWO-STOREYED BUILDINGS — CHAPTER XX

THE ELEVATION TOWARDS THE BREADTH

NOTE :-

ALL THESE TYPES MAY BE UTILISED BOTH AS TEMPLES AND DOMESTIC BUILDINGS WITH SLIGHT DIFFERENCE IN DETAIL TOBE INDICATED IN THE SECTION.

THE REMAINING FIVE TYPES ARE TOBE DRAWN SIMILARLY, WITH DIFFERENT PROPORTIONS

HEIGHT = 1½ BREADTH
= 16 PARTS.

B. C. MUKHERJI.

SHEET No LIX

THE TWO-STOREYED BUILDINGS — CHAPTER XX

THE ELEVATION TOWARDS THE BREADTH

NOTE:-

ALL THESE TYPES MAY BE UTILISED BOTH AS TEMPLES AND DOMESTIC BUILDINGS WITH SLIGHT DIFFERENCE IN DETAIL TO BE INDICATED IN THE SECTION.

THE REMAINING FIVE TYPES ARE TO BE DRAWN SIMILARLY WITH DIFFERENT PROPORTIONS

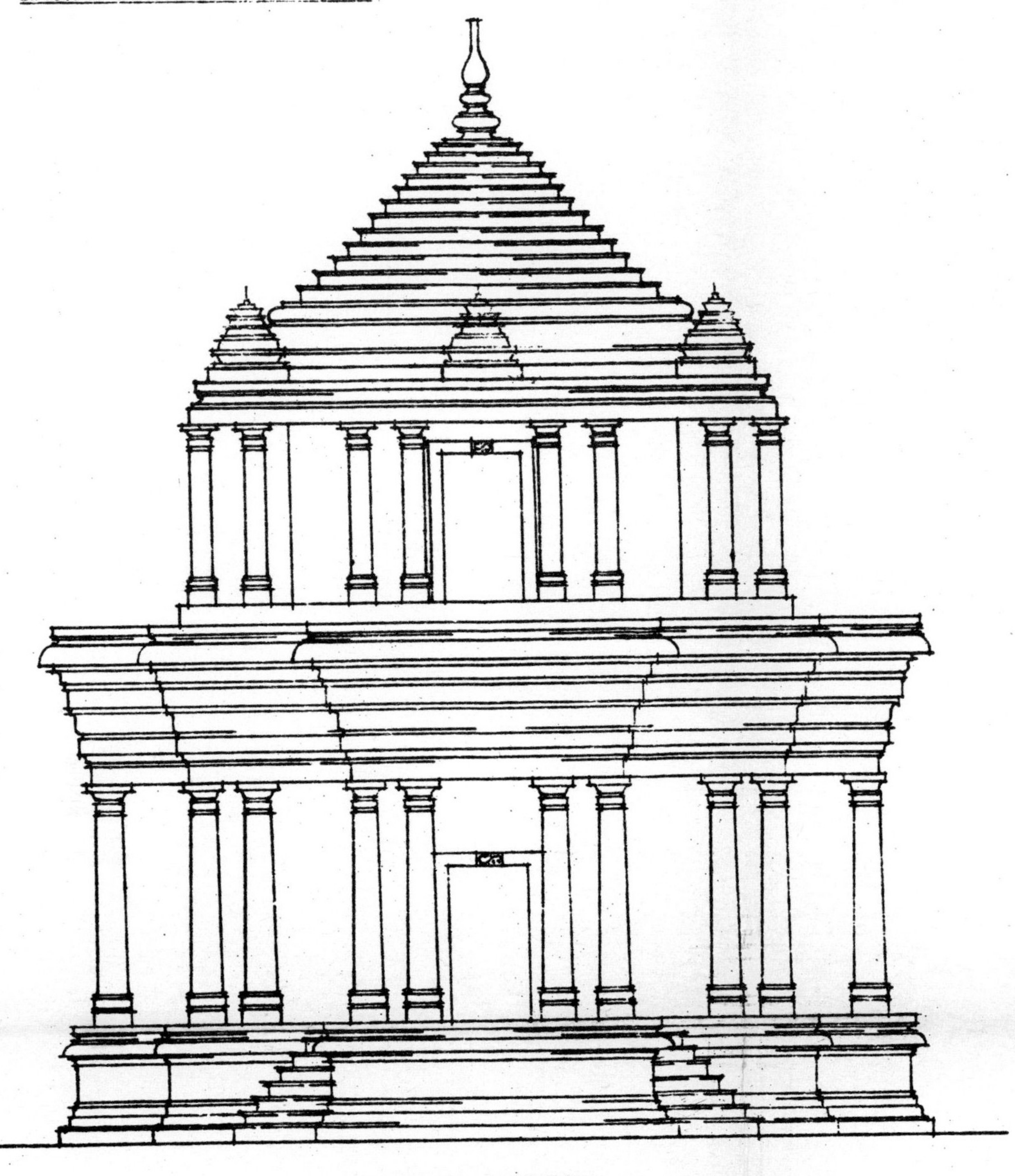

INTERMEDIATE TYPE

HEIGHT = 1¾ TH BREADTH
= 28 PARTS.

SCALE OF 0 1 5 10 15 PARTS

S. C. MUKHERJI.

THE TWO-STOREYED BUILDINGS — CHAPTER XX

THE TYPICAL PLAN

NOTE :-

ALL THESE TYPES MAY BE UTILISED
BOTH AS TEMPLES AND DOMESTIC BUILDINGS
WITH SLIGHT DIFFERENCE IN DETAILS

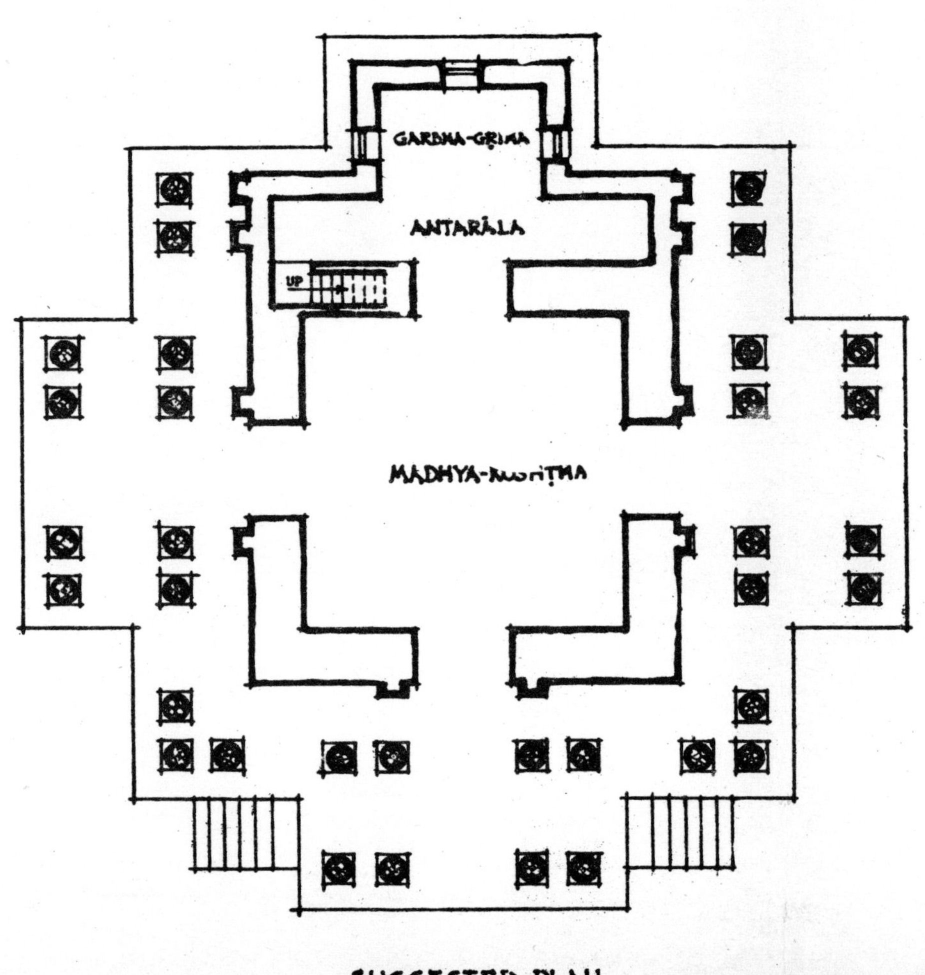

SUGGESTED PLAN
BASED ON INTERMEDIATE TYPE

SCALE OF 1 0 5 10 15 PARTS.

S. C. MUKHERJI.

SHEET NO. LXI

THE TWO-STOREYED BUILDINGS — CHAPTER XX

THE ELEVATION TOWARDS THE BREADTH

NOTE:-

ALL THESE TYPES MAY BE UTILISED BOTH AS TEMPLES AND DOMESTIC BUILDINGS WITH SLIGHT DIFFERENCE IN DETAIL TO BE INDICATED IN THE SECTION

THE REMAINING FIVE TYPES MAY BE DRAWN SIMILARLY WITH DIFFERENT PROPORTIONS.

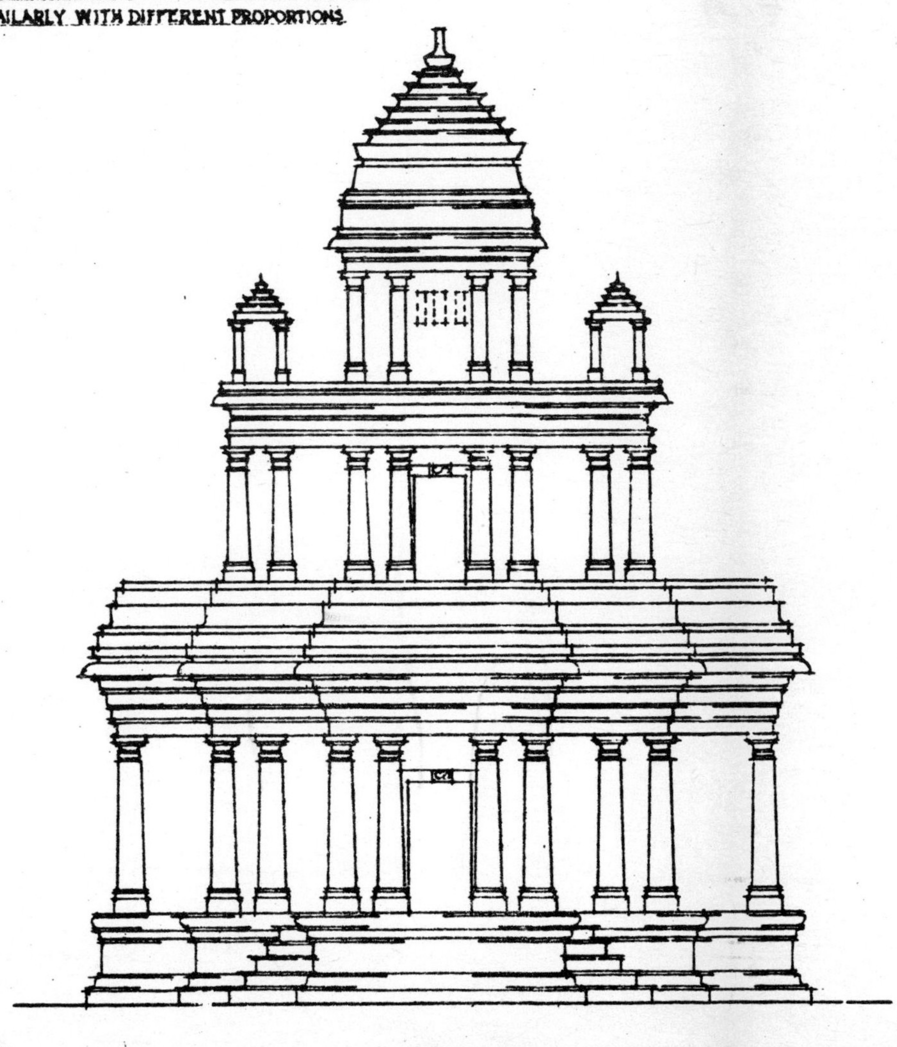

LARGE TYPE

HEIGHT = 2 BREADTH = 11 PARTS

SCALE OF 0 1 2 3 4 5 6 PARTS

S. C. MUKHERJI.

THE TWO-STOREYED BUILDINGS — CHAPTER XX

THE TYPICAL SECTION

NOTE:-

IF THIS IS TO BE USED AS A TEMPLE THE FRIEZE AND PARAPET SHOULD ALSO BE DECORATED WITH IMAGES OF GODS

CROSS SECTION
BASED ON LARGE TYPE.

HEIGHT = 2 BREADTH
= 11 PARTS.

SCALE OF 0 1 2 3 4 5 6 PARTS

S. C. MUKHERJI.

SHEET NO LXIII

THE THREE-STOREYED BUILDINGS — CHAPTER XXI

THE ELEVATION TOWARDS THE BREADTH

NOTE:-

ALL THESE TYPES MAY BE UTILISED BOTH AS TEMPLES AND DOMESTIC BUILDINGS WITH SLIGHT DIFFERENCE IN DETAIL TO BE INDICATED IN THE SECTION

THE OTHER FIVE TYPES SHOULD BE DRAWN WITH PROPORTIONS AS FOLLOW - SRĪKANTA = 6 PARTS AS HEIGHT. KESARA = 13 — — KAMALĀÑGA AND BRAHMA-KĀNTA = 24 — — MERU-KĀNTA = 30 PARTS — — —

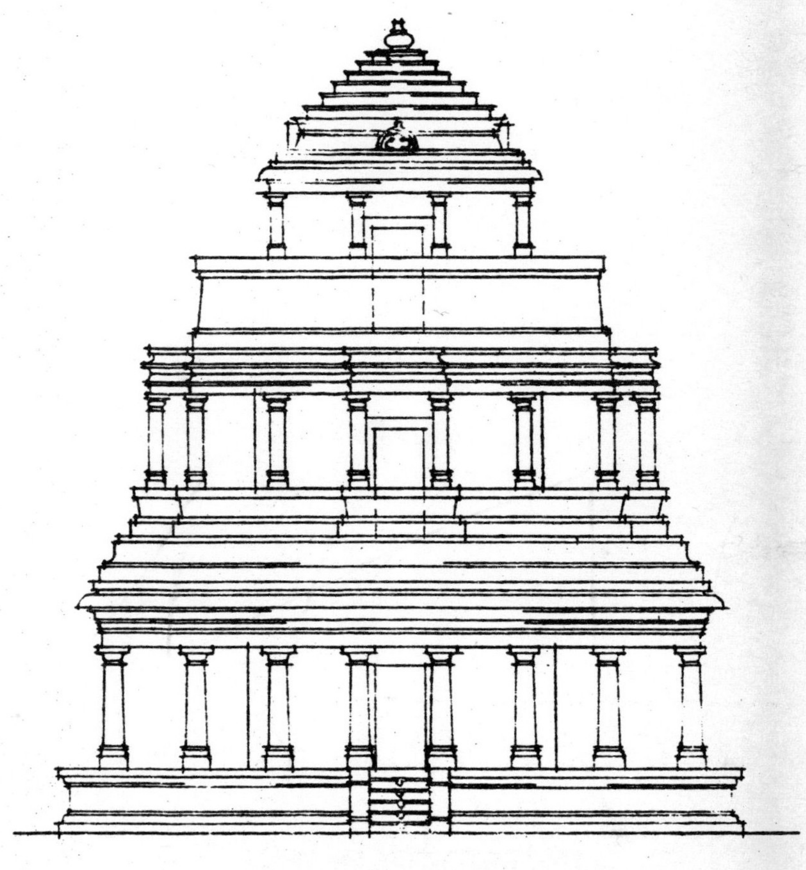

SUKHĀLAYA OR SMALL TYPE

HEIGHT = 1¼TH BREADTH = 13 PARTS.

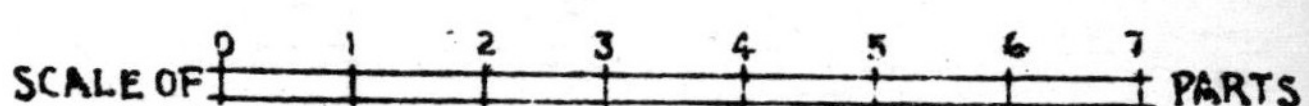

S. C. MUKHERJI.

THE THREE-STOREYED BUILDINGS — CHAPTER XXI

THE ELEVATION TOWARDS THE BREADTH

NOTE :-

ALL THESE TYPES MAY BE UTILISED BOTH AS TEMPLES AND DOMESTIC BUILDINGS WITH SLIGHT DIFFERENCE IN DETAIL TO BE INDICATED IN THE SECTION.

THE OTHER FIVE TYPES SHOULD BE DRAWN WITH PROPORTIONS AS FOLLOW — ŚRĪ-KĀNTA = 6 PARTS AS HEIGHT, KESARA = 13 —— KAMALĀNGA AND BRAHMA-KĀNTA = 24 —— MERU-KĀNTA = 30 PARTS ——

KAILĀSA OR INTERMEDIATE TYPE

HEIGHT = 1½ BREADTH
= 31 PARTS.

17½ PARTS OF MERU-KĀNTA + 12 PARTS OF KAILĀSA + 1½ PARTS FOR FINIAL MAKE UP 31 PARTS.

S. C. MUKHERJI.

THE THREE-STOREYED BUILDINGS — CHAPTER XXI

THE ELEVATION TOWARDS THE BREADTH

NOTE :-

ALL THESE TYPES MAY BE UTILISED BOTH AS TEMPLES AND DOMESTIC BUILDINGS WITH SLIGHT DIFFERENCE IN DETAIL TO BE INDICATED IN THE SECTION

THE OTHER FIVE TYPES SHOULD BE DRAWN WITH PROPORTIONS AS FOLLOW :- ŚRĪ-KĀNTA = 6 PARTS AS HEIGHT, KESARA = 13 KAMALĀNGA AND BRAHMA-KĀNTA = 24 MERU-KĀNTA = 30 PARTS

ĀSANA OR LARGE TYPE

HEIGHT = 1 3/4 TH BREADTH = 49 PARTS

THE TOTAL NUMBER OF PARTS SHOULD BE 47½ AND NOT 49 AS MENTIONED IN THE TEXT.

B. C. MUKHERJI

SHEET No LXVI

THE THREE-STOREYED BUILDINGS — CHAPTER XXI

THE TYPICAL SECTION

NOTE:-

IF THIS IS TO BE USED AS A TEMPLE
THE FRIEZE AND PARAPET SHOULD ALSO
BE DECORATED WITH IMAGES OF GODS.

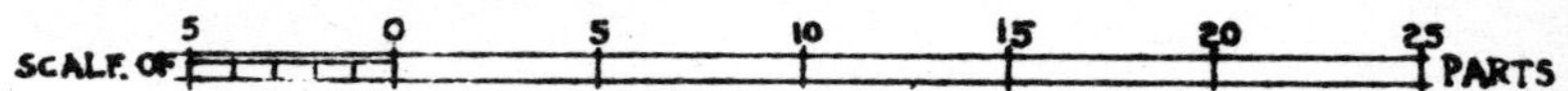

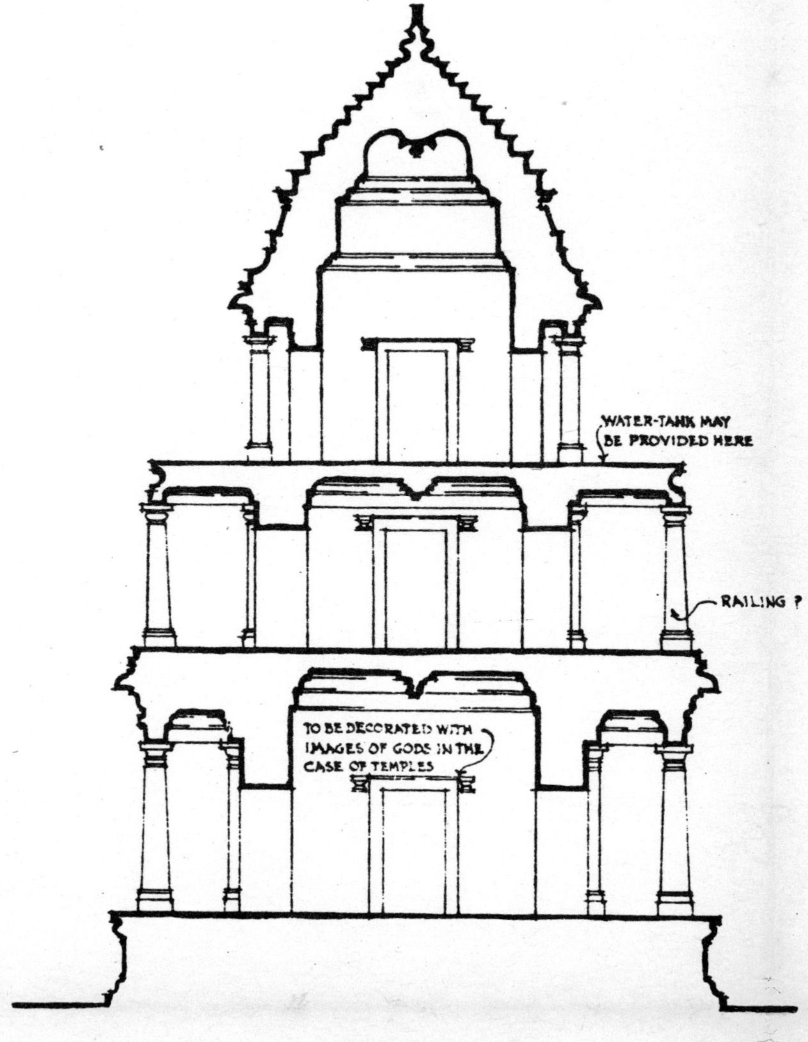

CROSS SECTION

BASED ON ĀSANA OR LARGE TYPE

HEIGHT = 1¾TH BREADTH

S. C. MUKHERJI.

THE THREE-STOREYED BUILDINGS — CHAPTER XXI

THE TYPICAL PLAN

NOTE:—

ALL THESE TYPES MAY BE UTILISED
BOTH AS TEMPLES AND DOMESTIC BUILDINGS.
WITH SLIGHT DIFFERENCE IN DETAILS.

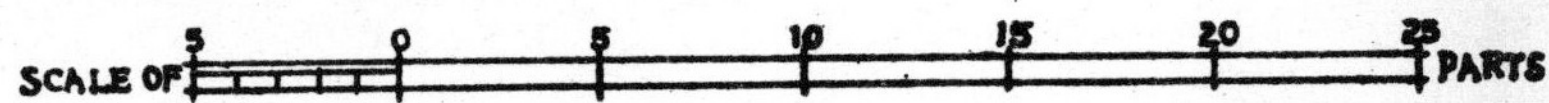

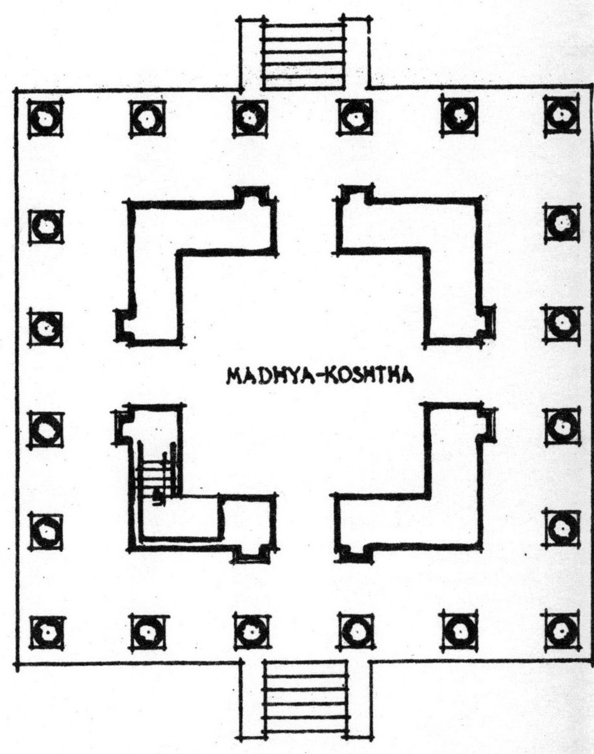

SUGGESTED PLAN (GROUND FLOOR)
BASED ON LARGE TYPE

S. C. MUKHERJI.

SHEET No. LXVIII

THE FOUR-STOREYED BUILDINGS — CHAPTER XXII

THE ELEVATION TOWARDS THE BREADTH

SCALE OF 1 0 5 10 15 PARTS

NOTE:-

ALL THESE TYPES MAY BE UTILISED BOTH AS TEMPLES AND DOMESTIC BUILDINGS WITH SLIGHT MODIFICATION IN DETAIL TO BE INDICATED IN THE SECTION

THE OTHER FIVE TYPES SHOULD BE DRAWN WITH PROPORTIONS AS FOLLOW - SADĀ-ŚIVA = 41 PARTS AS HEIGHT, ĪSVARA-KĀNTA = 32 — MAÑCHA-KĀNTA AND VEDI-KĀNTA = 15 — INDRA-KĀNTA = 26 PARTS —

VISHNU-KĀNTA OR SMALL TYPE

HEIGHT = 1¼ BREADTH
= 18 PARTS.

THE TOTAL NUMBER OF PARTS SHOULD BE 18¼ AND NOT 18 AS GIVEN IN THE TEXT.

S. C. MUKHERJI.

THE FOUR-STOREYED BUILDINGS — CHAPTER XXII

THE ELEVATION TOWARDS THE BREADTH

SCALE OF 1 0 5 10 15 PARTS

NOTE:—

ALL THESE TYPES MAY BE UTILISED BOTH AS TEMPLES AND DOMESTIC BUILDINGS WITH SLIGHT MODIFICATION IN DETAIL TO BE INDICATED IN THE SECTION.

THE OTHER FIVE TYPES SHOULD BE DRAWN WITH PROPORTIONS AS FOLLOW — SADĀ-ŚIVA = 41 PARTS AS HEIGHT, ĪŚVARA-KĀNTA = 32 — MAÑCHA-KĀNTA AND VEDI-KĀNTA = 15 — INDRA-KĀNTA = 26 PARTS.

RUDRA-KĀNTA OR INTERMEDIATE TYPE.

HEIGHT = 1½ BREADTH
= 32 PARTS.

THE TOTAL NUMBER OF PARTS SHOULD BE 32¼ AND NOT 32 AS GIVEN IN THE TEXT.

S. C. MUKHERJI.

THE FOUR-STOREYED BUILDINGS — CHAPTER XXII

THE TYPICAL SECTION

SCALE OF 1 0 5 10 15 PARTS

NOTE:—

IF THIS IS TO BE USED AS A TEMPLE THE FRIEZE AND PARAPET SHOULD ALSO BE DECORATED WITH IMAGES OF GODS.

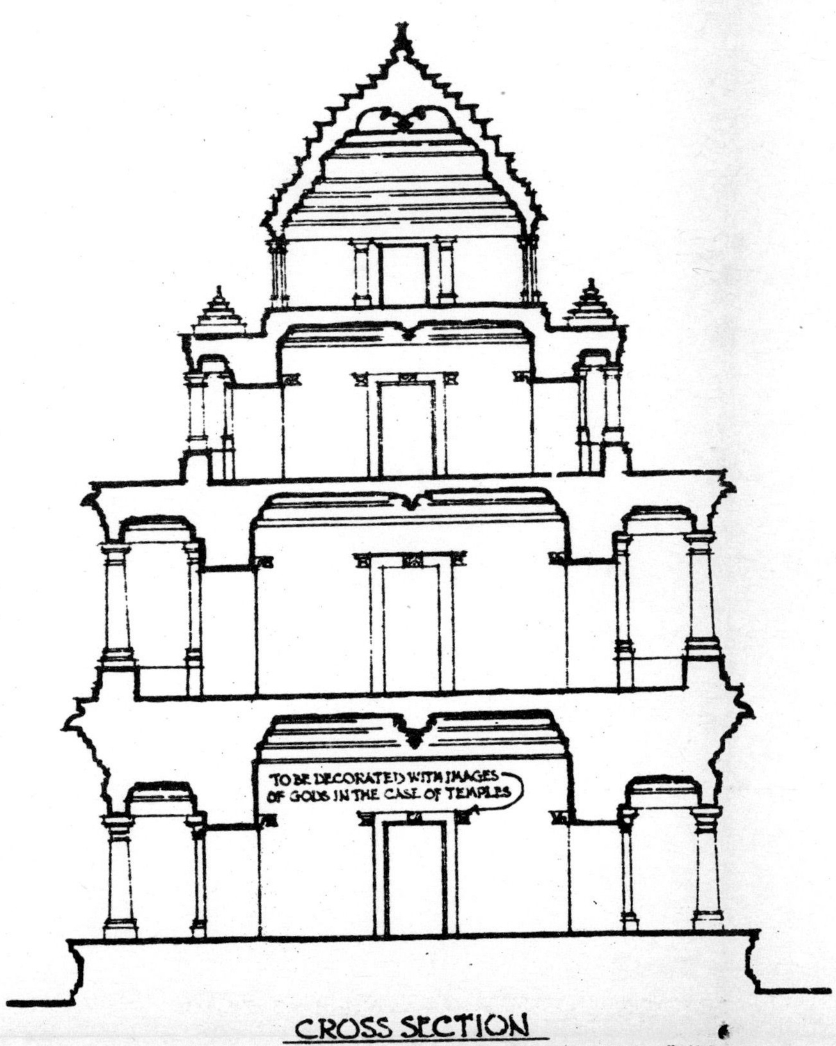

CROSS SECTION

BASED ON RUDRA-KĀNTA OR INTERMEDIATE TYPE

HEIGHT = $1\frac{1}{2}$ BREADTH

S. C. MUKHERJI.

THE FOUR-STOREYED BUILDINGS — CHAPTER XXII

THE TYPICAL PLAN.

SCALE OF 1 0 5 10 15 PARTS

NOTE:-

ALL THESE TYPES MAY BE UTILISED
BOTH AS TEMPLES AND DOMESTIC BUILDINGS
WITH SLIGHT DIFFERENCE IN DETAILS

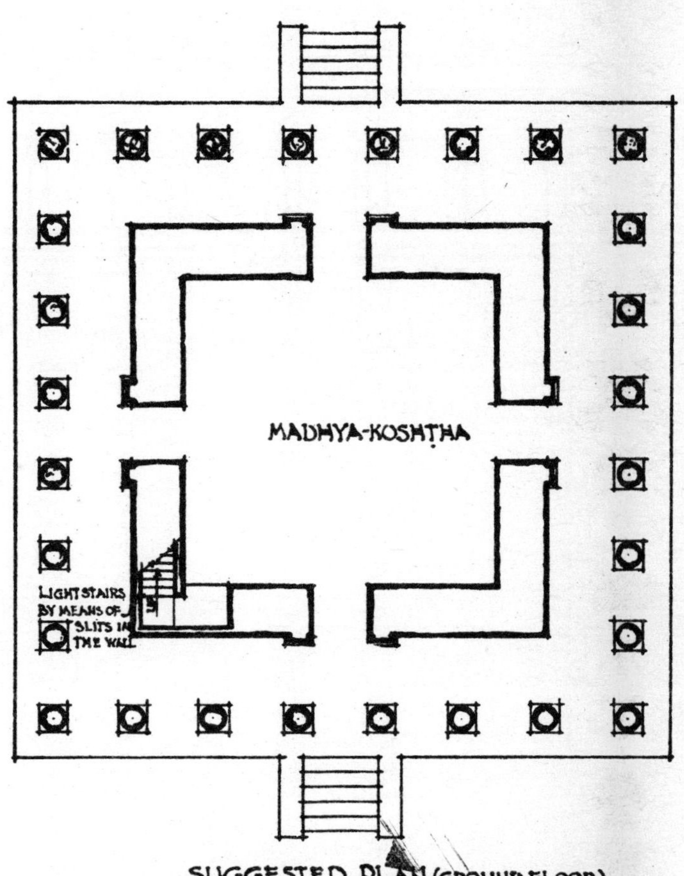

SUGGESTED PLAN (GROUND FLOOR)
BASED ON RUDRA-KĀNTA OR INTER-MEDIATE TYPE

S. C. MUKHERJI.

SHEET No. LXXIII

THE FIVE-STOREYED BUILDINGS — CHAPTER XXIII

THE ELEVATION TOWARDS THE BREADTH

SCALE OF 0 5 10 15 PARTS

NOTE :-

ALL THE TYPES MAY BE UTILISED BOTH AS TEMPLES AND DOMESTIC BUILDINGS WITH SLIGHT MODIFICATION IN DETAIL TO BE INDICATED IN THE SECTION.

THE OTHER SEVEN TYPES SHOULD BE DRAWN WITH THE SAME NUMBER OF PARTS AS HEIGHT, BUT THEY DIFFER FROM EACH OTHER ONLY IN MINOR DETAILS

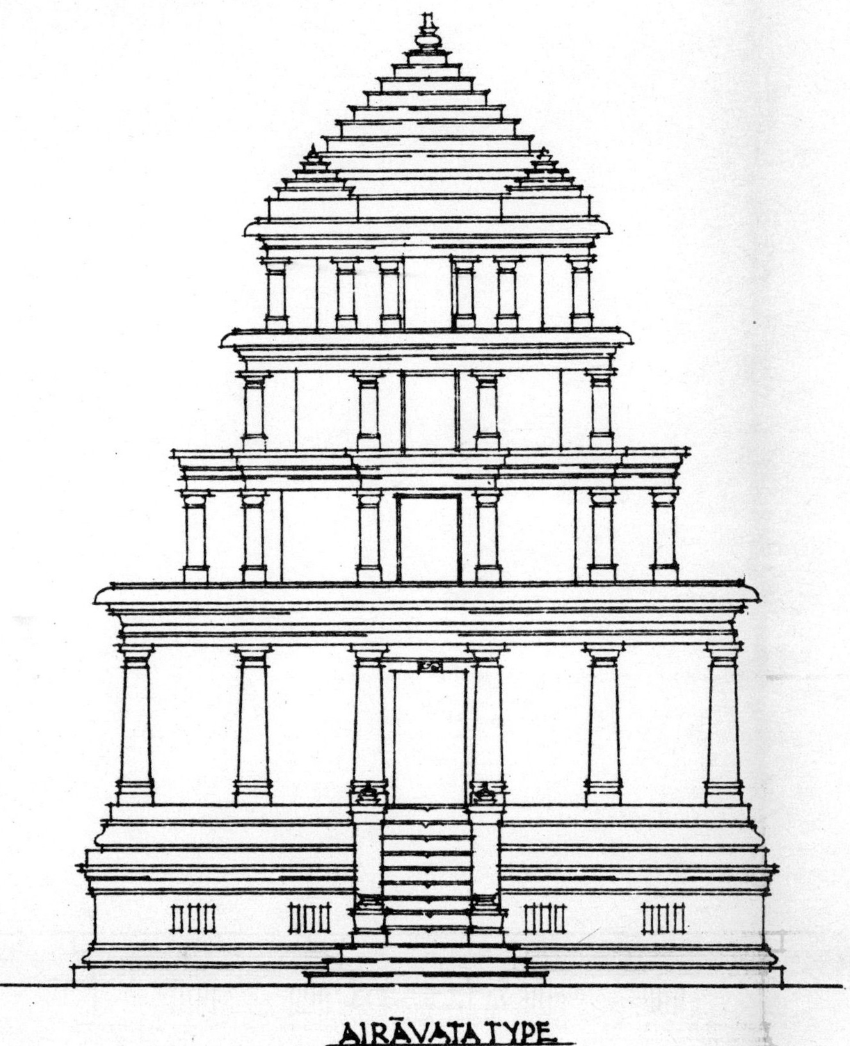

AIRĀVATA TYPE

HEIGHT = 1½ BREADTH
= 24 PARTS.

THE TEXT GIVES AN ACCOUNT OF 20 PARTS ONLY.

S. C. MUKHERJI.

SHEET NO LXXIV

THE FIVE-STOREYED BUILDINGS — CHAPTER XXIII

THE TYPICAL SECTION

SCALE OF 0 5 10 15 PARTS

NOTE:–
IF THIS IS TO BE USED AS A TEMPLE
THE FRIEZE AND PARAPET SHOULD ALSO
BE DECORATED WITH IMAGES OF GODS.

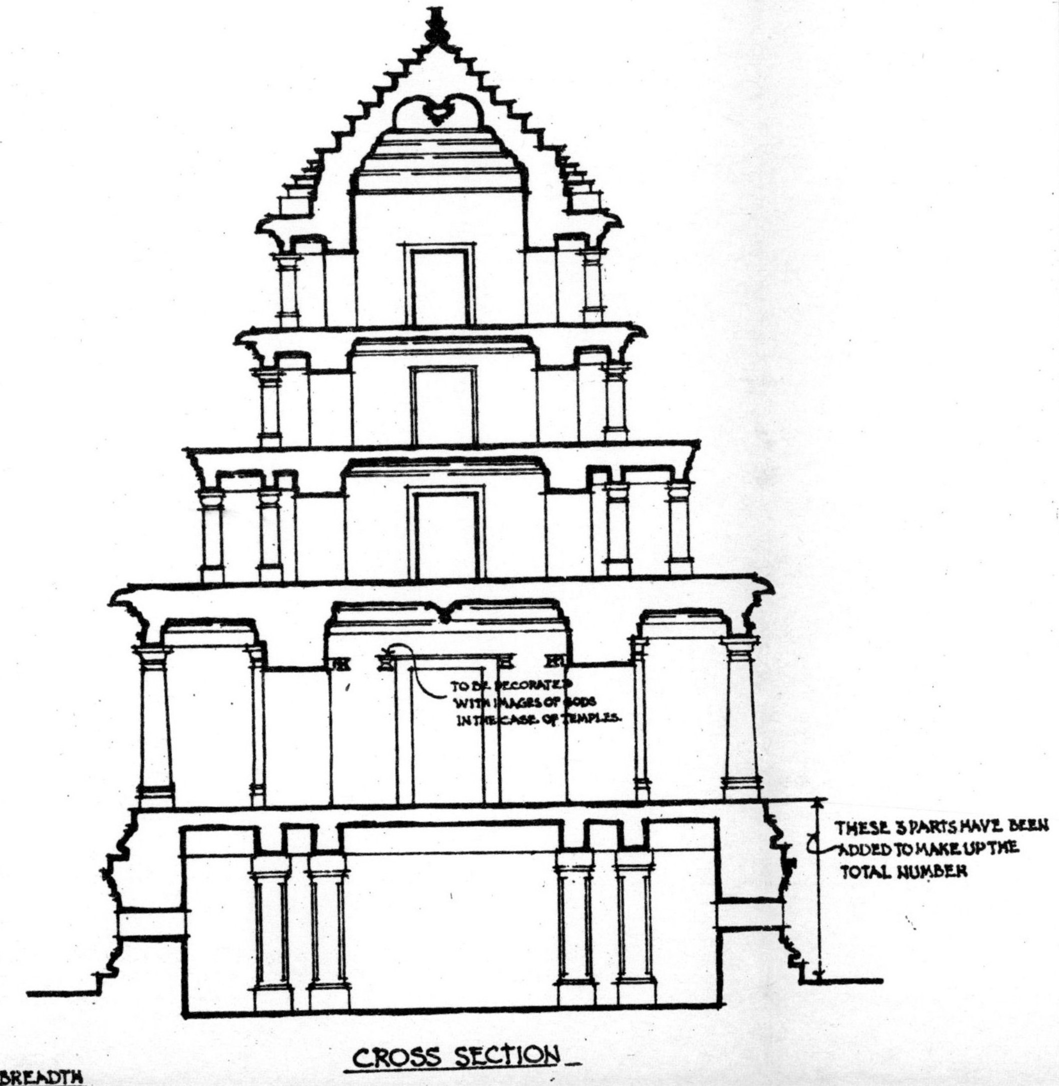

CROSS SECTION

HEIGHT = 1½ BREADTH
= 24 PARTS.

THE TEXT GIVES AN ACCOUNT OF 20 PARTS
WITH FOUR SETS OF COLUMNS. OF THE REMAINING
FOUR PARTS, 1 FOR FINIAL AND 3 FOR BASEMENT HAVE
BEEN USED

S. C. MUKHERJI.

SHEET No. LXXV

THE FIVE-STOREYED BUILDINGS.—CHAPTER XXIII

THE TYPICAL PLAN.

SCALE OF 1 0 5 10 15 PARTS

NOTE:—

ALL THESE TYPES MAY BE UTILISED BOTH AS TEMPLES AND DOMESTIC BUILDINGS WITH SLIGHT DIFFERENCE IN DETAIL.

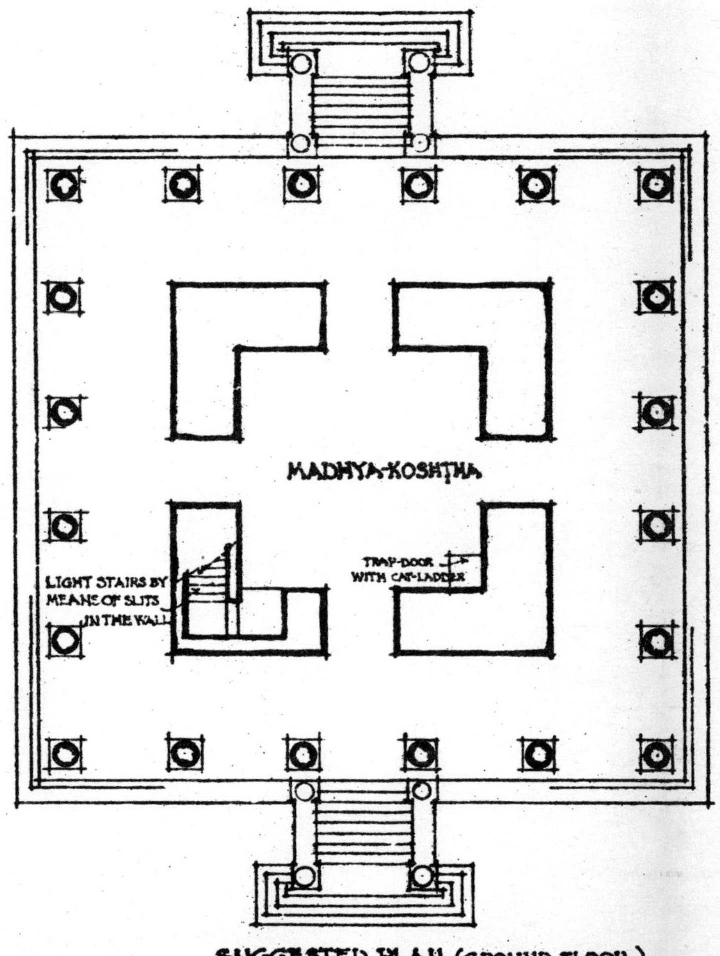

SUGGESTED PLAN (GROUND FLOOR)

S. C. MUKHERJI.

THE SIX-STOREYED BUILDINGS — CHAPTER XXIV

THE ELEVATION TOWARDS THE BREADTH

SCALE OF 1 0 5 10 15 20 25 PARTS

NOTE:–

ALL THESE TYPES MAY BE UTILISED BOTH AS TEMPLES AND DOMESTIC BUILDINGS WITH SLIGHT MODIFICATION IN DETAIL TO BE INDICATED IN THE SECTION.

THE OTHER TWELVE TYPES SHOULD BE DRAWN WITH THE SAME NUMBER OF PARTS AS HEIGHT, BUT THEY DIFFER FROM EACH OTHER ONLY IN MINOR DETAILS

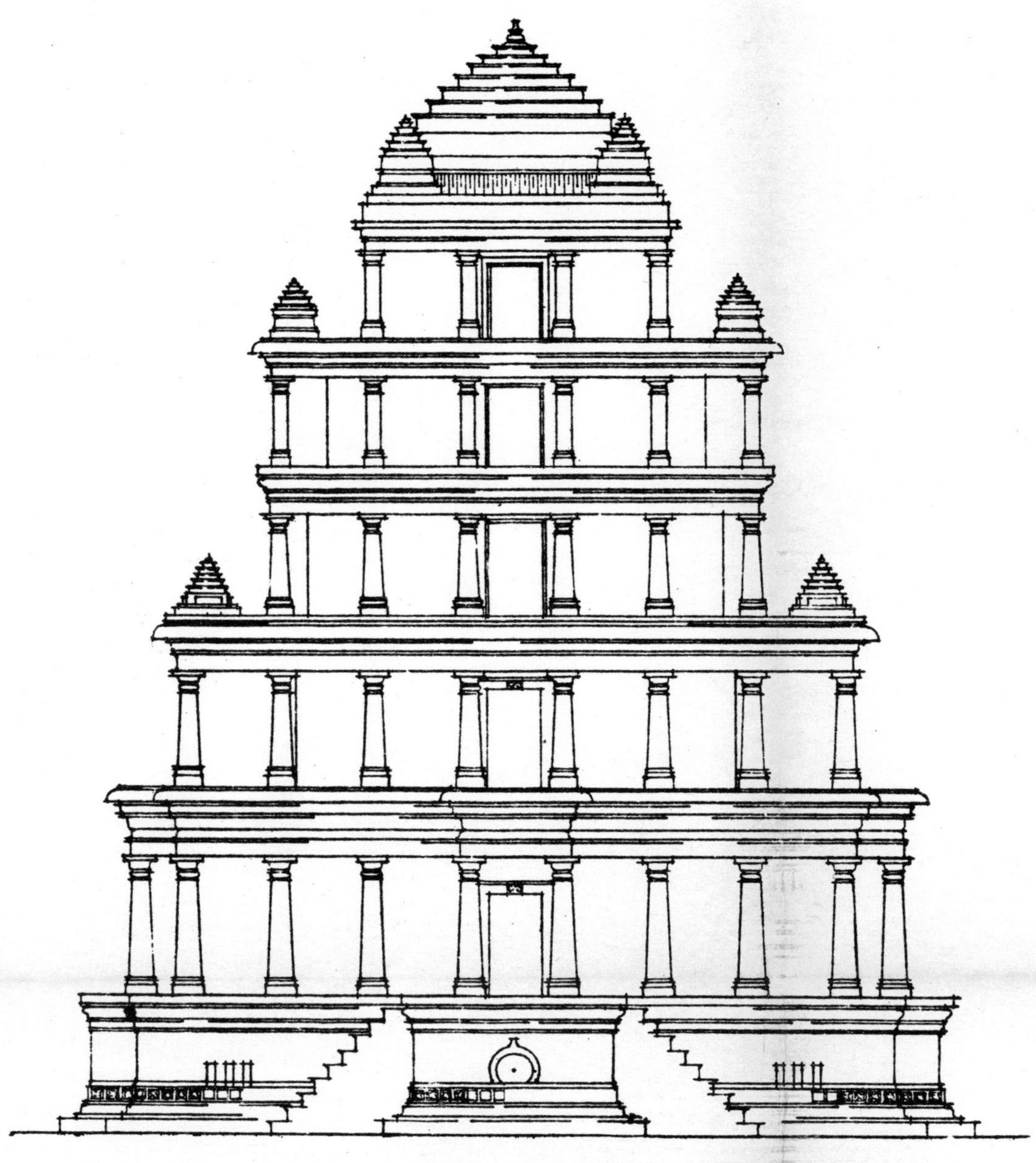

PADMA-KĀNTA TYPE

HEIGHT = $1\frac{1}{2}$ BREADTH
= 57 PARTS.

THE TEXT GIVES AN ACCOUNT 54 PARTS ONLY.

S. C. MUKHERJI.

SHEET NO LXXVII

THE SIX-STOREYD BUILDINGS — CHAPTER XXIV

THE TYPICAL SECTION

SCALE OF 1 0 5 10 15 20 25 PARTS

NOTE :-

IF THIS IS TO BE USED AS A TEMPLE THE FRIEZE AND PARAPET SHOULD ALSO BE DECORATED WITH IMAGES OF GODS

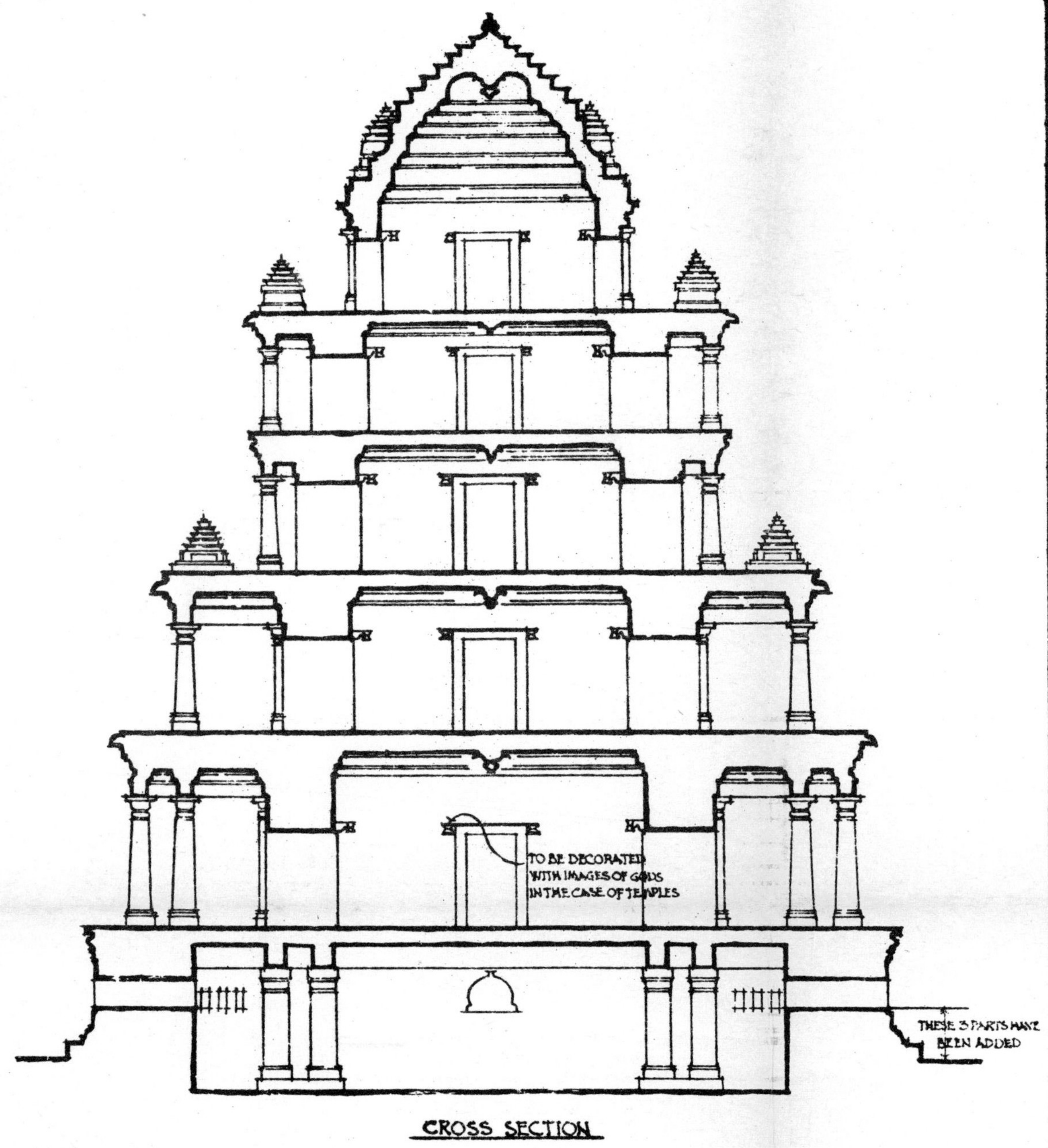

CROSS SECTION

HEIGHT = $1\frac{1}{2}$ BREADTH
= 57 PARTS.

THE TEXT GIVES AN ACCOUNT OF 54 PARTS ONLY WITH FIVE SETS OF COLUMNS. OF THE REMAINING 4 PARTS, 1 FOR FOR FINIAL AND 3 FOR EXTRA PLINTH HAVE BEEN USED

S. C. MUKHERJI.

SHEET No. LXXVIII

THE SIX-STOREYED BUILDINGS — CHAPTER XXIV

THE TYPICAL PLAN

SCALE OF 0 5 10 15 20 25 PARTS

NOTE:—

ALL THESE TYPES MAY BE UTILISED BOTH AS TEMPLES AND DOMESTIC BUILDINGS WITH SLIGHT DIFFERENCE IN DETAIL.

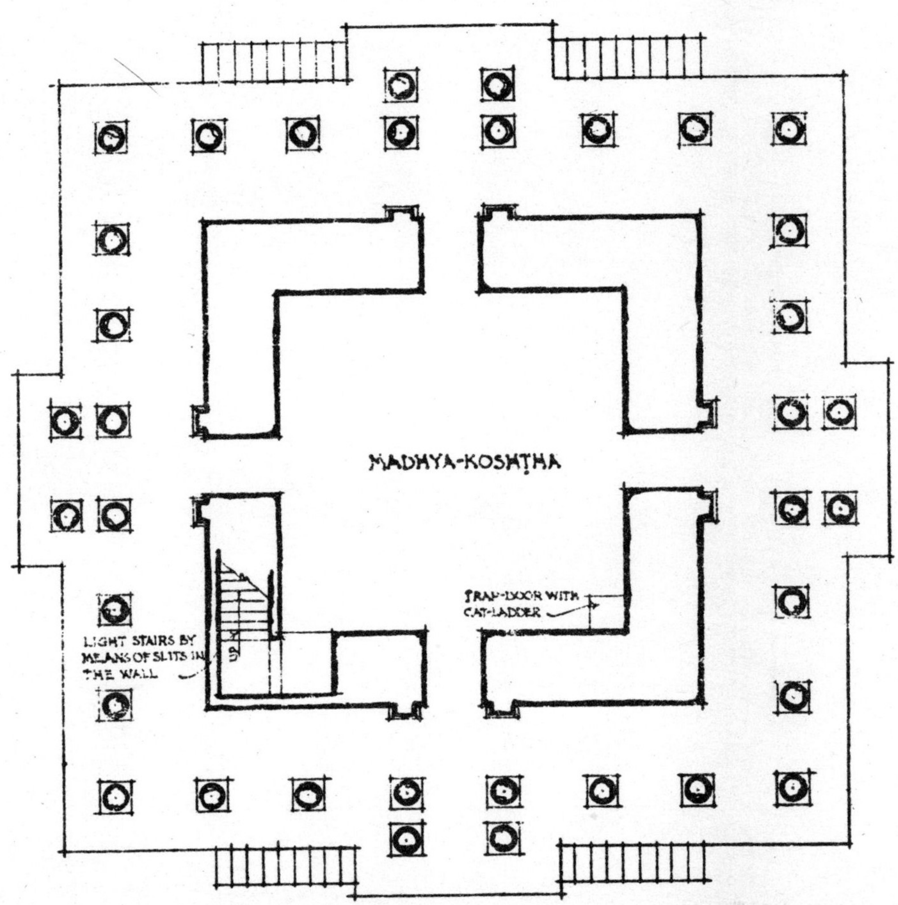

SUGGESTED PLAN. (GROUND FLOOR)

S. C. MUKHERJI.

THE SEVEN-STOREYED BUILDINGS — CHAPTER XXV
THE ELEVATION TOWARDS THE BREADTH

NOTE :-

ALL THESE TYPES MAY BE UTILISED BOTH AS TEMPLES AND DOMESTIC BUILDINGS WITH SLIGHT MODIFICATION IN DETAIL TO BE INDICATED IN THE SECTION

THE OTHER SEVEN TYPES SHOULD BE DRAWN WITH THE SAME NUMBER OF PARTS AS HEIGHT BUT THEY DIFFER FROM EACH OTHER ONLY IN MINOR DETAILS

PUṆḌARĪKA TYPE

HEIGHT = 1½ BREADTH
= 33 PARTS.

THE TOTAL NUMBER OF PARTS SHOULD BE 37½ AND NOT 33 AS MENTIONED IN THE TEXT.

SCALE OF 1 0 5 10 15 20 PARTS

S. C. MUKHERJI.

SHEET NO. LXXX

THE SEVEN-STOREYED BUILDINGS — CHAPTER XXV

THE TYPICAL SECTION

SCALE OF 0 5 10 15 20 PARTS

NOTE:-

IF THIS IS TO BE USED AS A TEMPLE THE FRIEZE AND PARAPET SHOULD ALSO BE DECORATED WITH IMAGES OF GODS

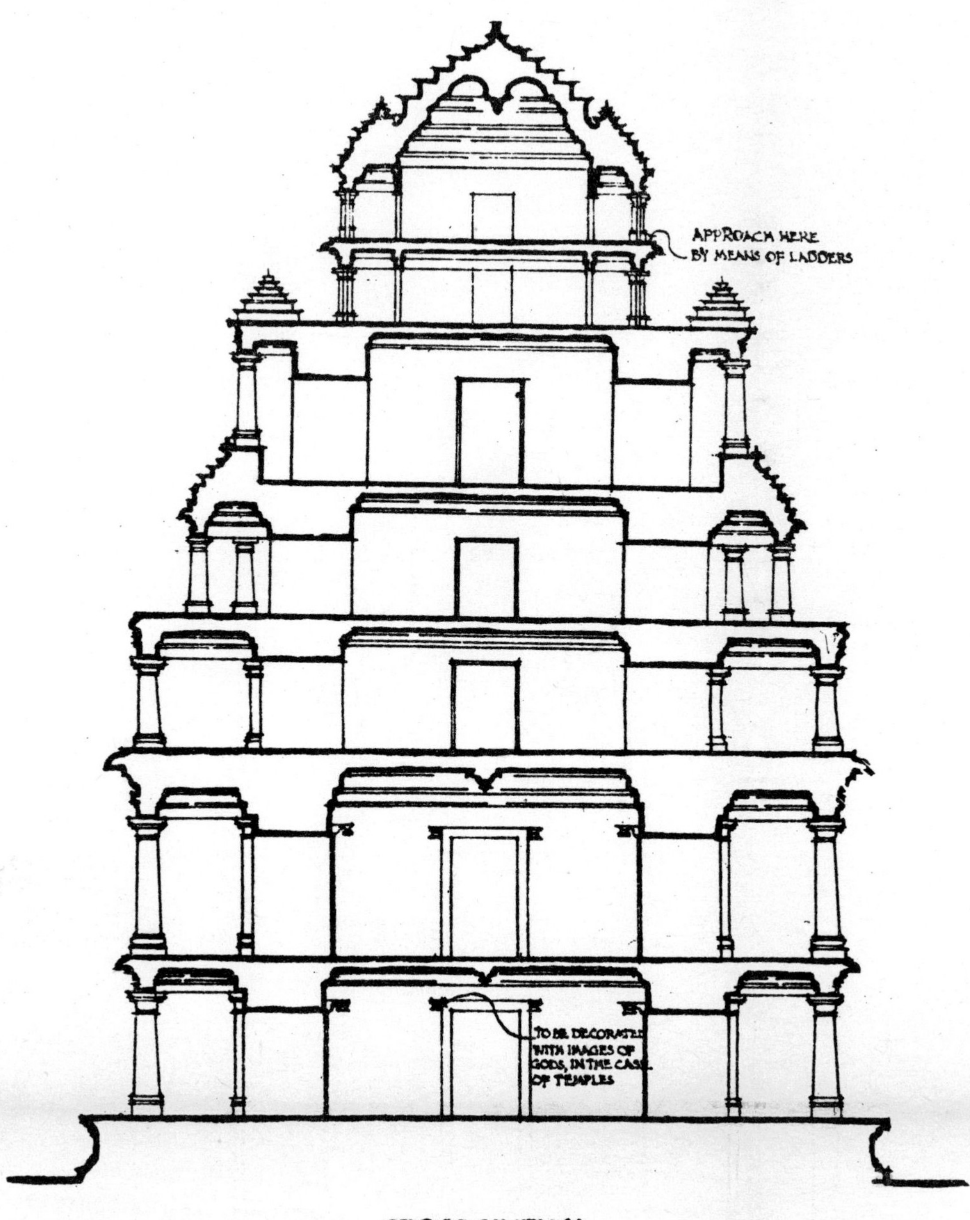

CROSS SECTION.

HEIGHT = 1½ BREADTH
= 33 PARTS ;

THE TOTAL NUMBER OF PARTS SHOULD BE 37½ AND NOT 33 AS MENTIONED IN THE TEXT.

S. C. MUKHERJI.

THE SEVEN-STOREYED BUILDINGS — CHAPTER XXV

THE TYPICAL PLAN

NOTE:-

ALL THESE TYPES MAY BE UTILISED BOTH AS TEMPLES AND DOMESTIC BUILDINGS WITH SLIGHT DIFFERENCE IN DETAIL.

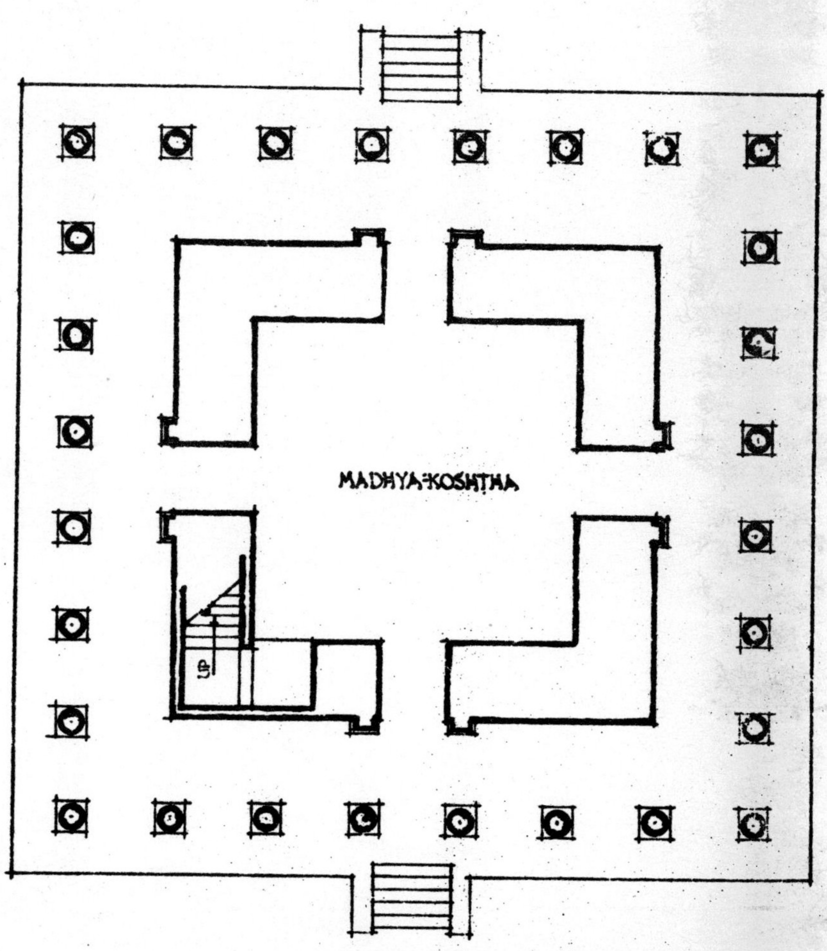

SUGGESTED PLAN (GROUND FLOOR)

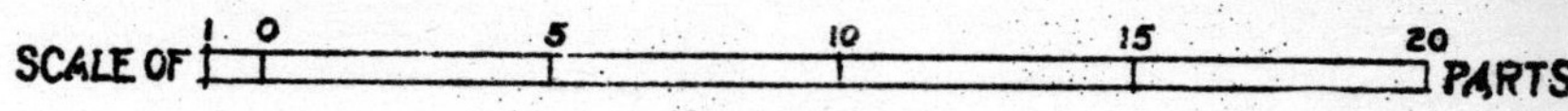

S. C. MUKHERJI.

THE EIGHT-STOREYED BUILDINGS — CHAPTER XXVI

THE ELEVATION TOWARDS THE BREADTH

NOTE :—

ALL THESE TYPES MAY BE UTILISED BOTH AS TEMPLES AND DOMESTIC BUILDINGS WITH SLIGHT MODIFICATION IN DETAIL TO BE INDICATED IN THE SECTION

THE OTHER TYPE NOT DRAWN SHOULD HAVE 48 PARTS AS HEIGHT. IT DIFFERS FROM THIS ONE IN MINOR DETAILS

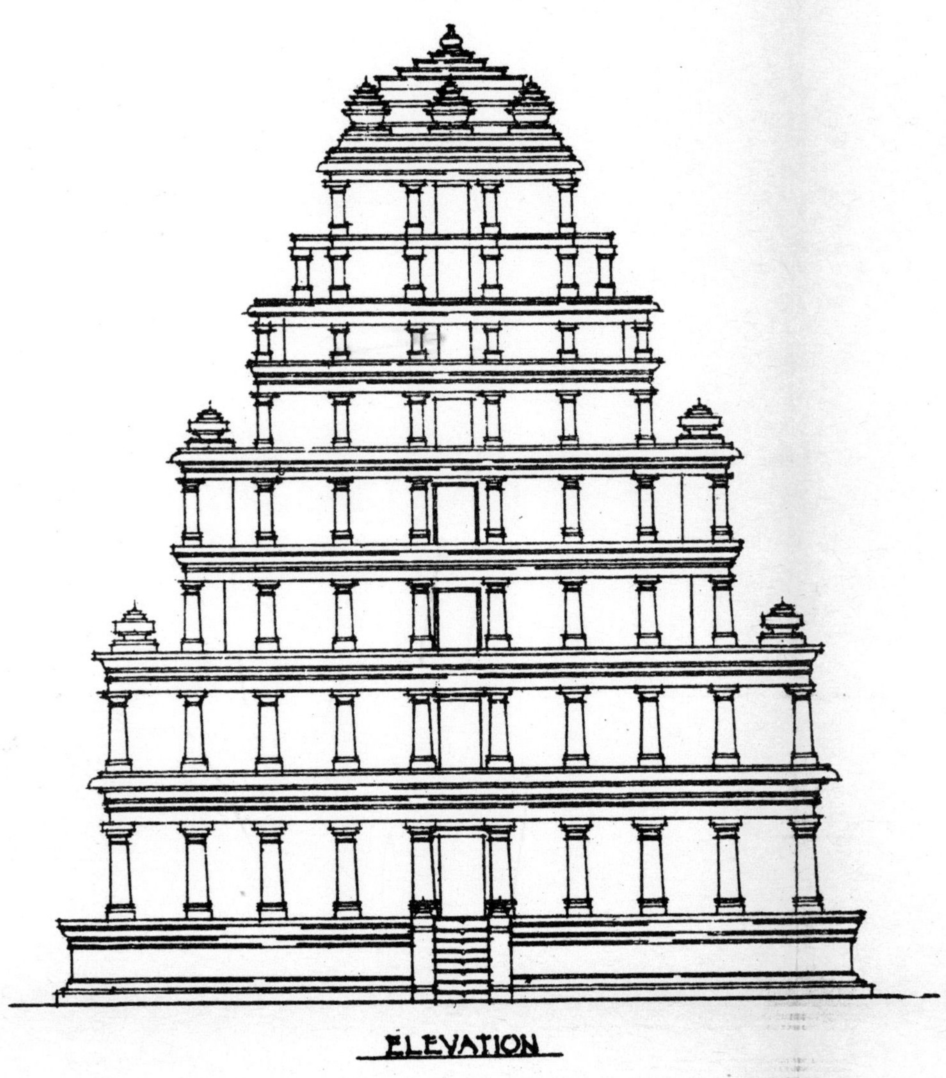

ELEVATION

HEIGHT = 1¼ BREADTH
= 41 PARTS

SCALE OF 1 0 5 10 15 20 PARTS

THE HEIGHT OF THE PLINTH HAS BEEN TAKEN TO BE 3½ IN-STEAD OF 8 TO MAKE THE TOTAL NUMBER OF PARTS 41.

S. C. MUKHERJI

SHEET No. LXXXIII

THE EIGHT-STOREYED BUILDINGS — CHAPTER XXVI.

THE TYPICAL SECTION

NOTE:—

IF THIS IS TO BE USED AS A TEMPLE THE FRIEZE AND PARAPET SHOULD ALSO BE DECORATED WITH IMAGES OF GODS

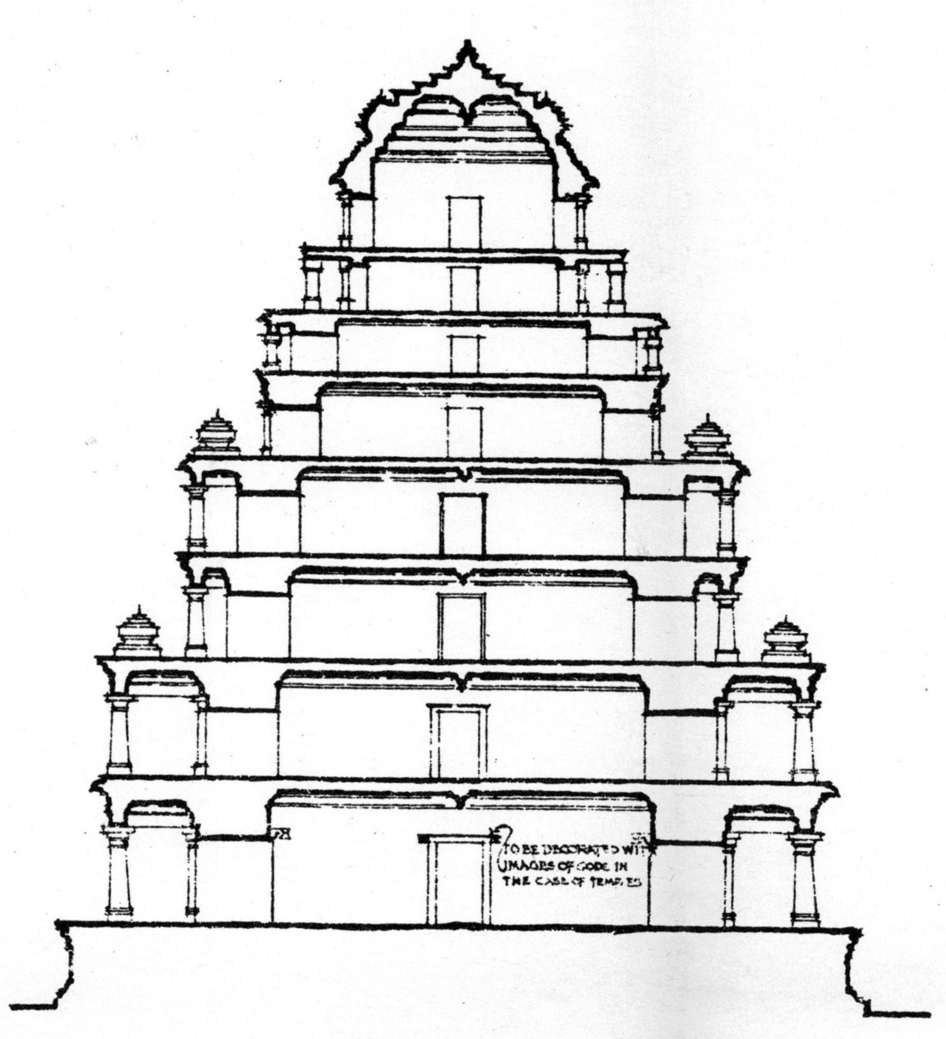

CROSS SECTION.

HEIGHT = 1¼ BREADTH
= 41 PARTS

SCALE OF 0 5 10 15 20 PARTS

THE HEIGHT OF THE PLINTH HAS BEEN TAKEN TO BE 3½ INSTEAD OF 8 TO MAKE THE TOTAL NUMBER OF PARTS 41

S. C. MUKHERJI

THE NINE-STOREYED BUILDINGS — CHAPTER XXVII

THE ELEVATION TOWARDS THE BREADTH

NOTE:-

ALL THESE TYPES MAY BE UTILISED BOTH AS TEMPLES AND DOMESTIC BUILDINGS WITH SLIGHT MODIFICATION IN DETAIL TO BE INDICATED IN THE SECTION

SCALE OF 0 5 10 15 20 25 PARTS

ELEVATION.

HEIGHT = 1½ BREADTH
= 51 PARTS

THE HEIGHT (51 PARTS) HAS BEEN OBTAINED BY ADDING 10 WITH 41 PARTS (THE HEIGHT OF THE EIGHT-STOREYED BUILDING)

S. C. MUKHERJI.

SHEET No. LXXXVI

THE NINE-STOREYED BUILDINGS — CHAPTER XXVII.

THE TYPICAL SECTION.

NOTE :—

IF THIS IS TO BE USED AS A TEMPLE THE FRIEZE AND PARAPET SHOULD ALSO BE DECORATED WITH IMAGES OF GODS

TO BE DECORATED WITH IMAGES OF GODS IN THE CASE OF TEMPLES

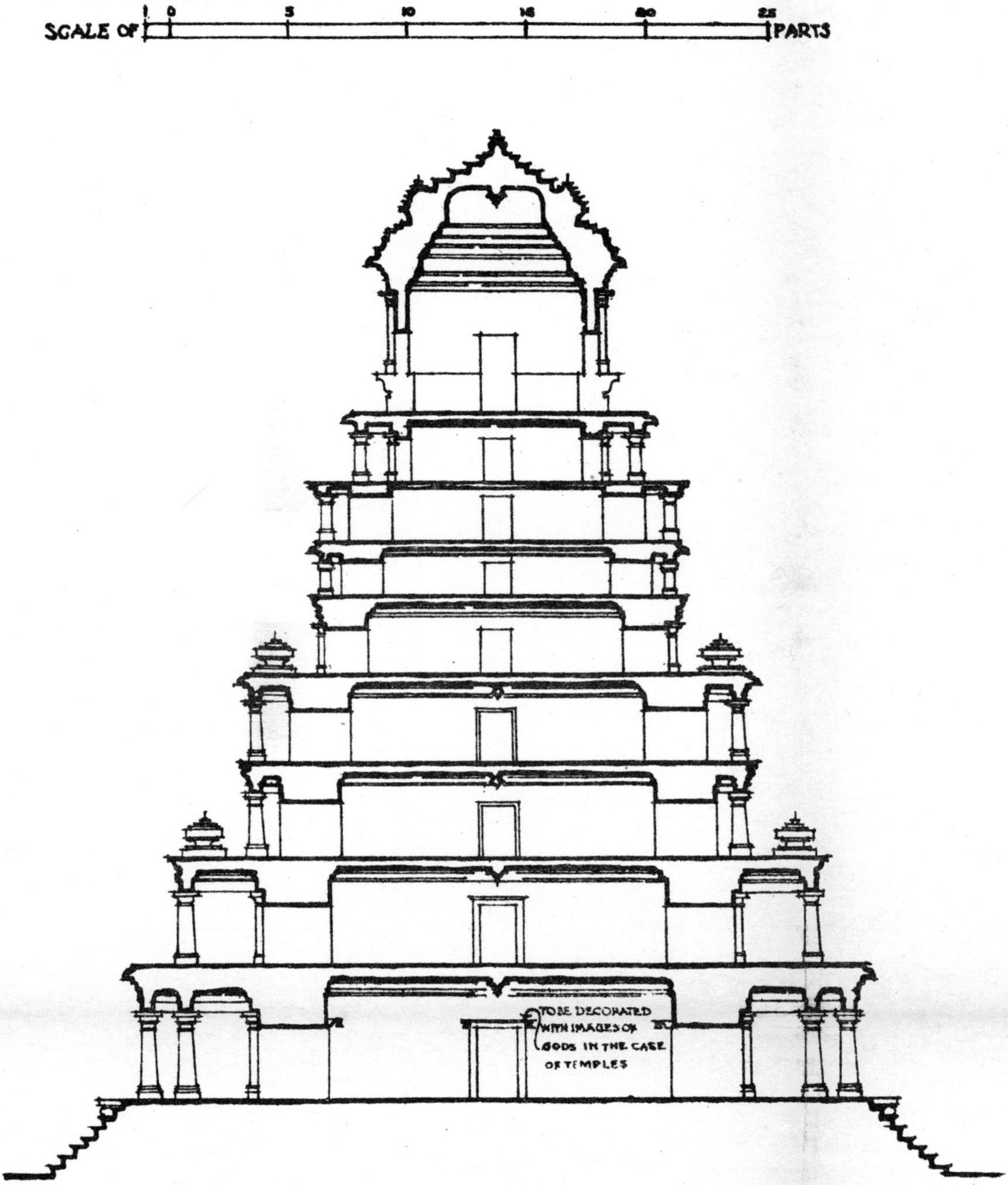

CROSS SECTION.

HEIGHT = 1½ BREADTH
= 51 PARTS

THE HEIGHT (51 PARTS) HAS BEEN OBTAINED BY ADDING 10 WITH 41 PARTS (THE HEIGHT OF THE EIGHT-STOREYED BUILDING)

S. C. MUKHERJI.

SHEET No LXXXVII

THE NINE-STOREYED BUILDINGS — CHAPTER XXVII

SUGGESTIONS FOR PLANS IN GENERAL

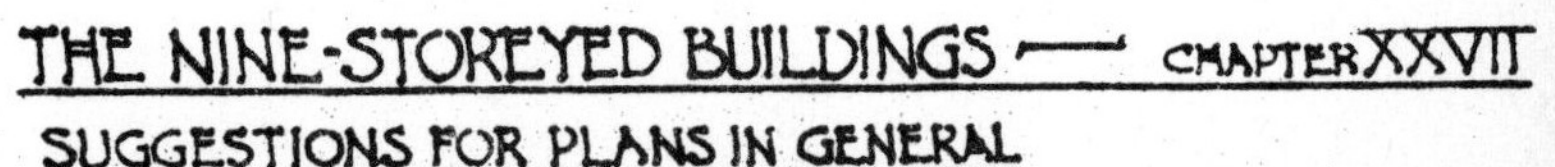

NOTE :—

FIG.1- SAURA-KĀNTA-SMALL TYPE, FIG:2 VIŚVA-KĀNTA-LARGE TYPE
FIG.3 VIVRITA-INTERMEDIATE TYPE.

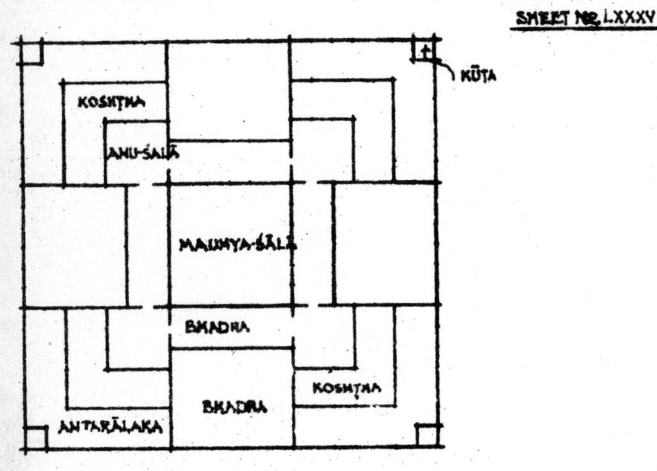

PLAN WITH 20 PARTS
FIG. 1

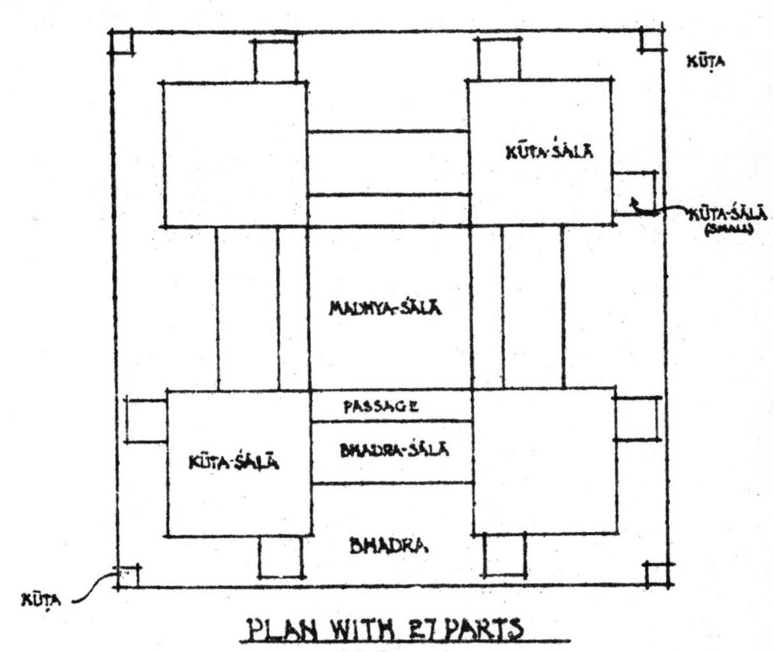

PLAN WITH 27 PARTS
FIG: 2

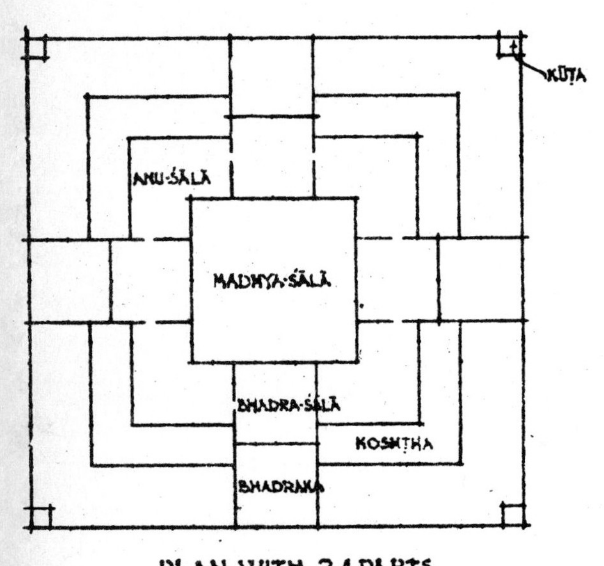

PLAN WITH 24 PARTS
FIG: 3

S. C. MUKHERJI.

THE TEN-STOREYED BUILDINGS — CHAPTER XXVIII

THE ELEVATION TOWARDS THE BREADTH

NOTE :-

ALL THESE TYPES MAY BE UTILISED BOTH AS TEMPLES AND DOMESTIC BUILDINGS WITH SLIGHT MODIFICATION IN DETAIL TO BE INDICATED IN THE SECTION.

ELEVATION

HEIGHT = 1½ BREADTH
= 63 PARTS

SCALE OF 1 0 5 10 15 20 PARTS

S. C. MUKHERJI.

THE TEN-STOREYED BUILDINGS — CHAPTER XXVIII
THE TYPICAL SECTION

NOTE:—

IF THIS .. TO BE USED AS A TEMPLE THE FRIEZE AND PARAPET SHOULD ALSO BE DECORATED WITH IMAGES OF GODS

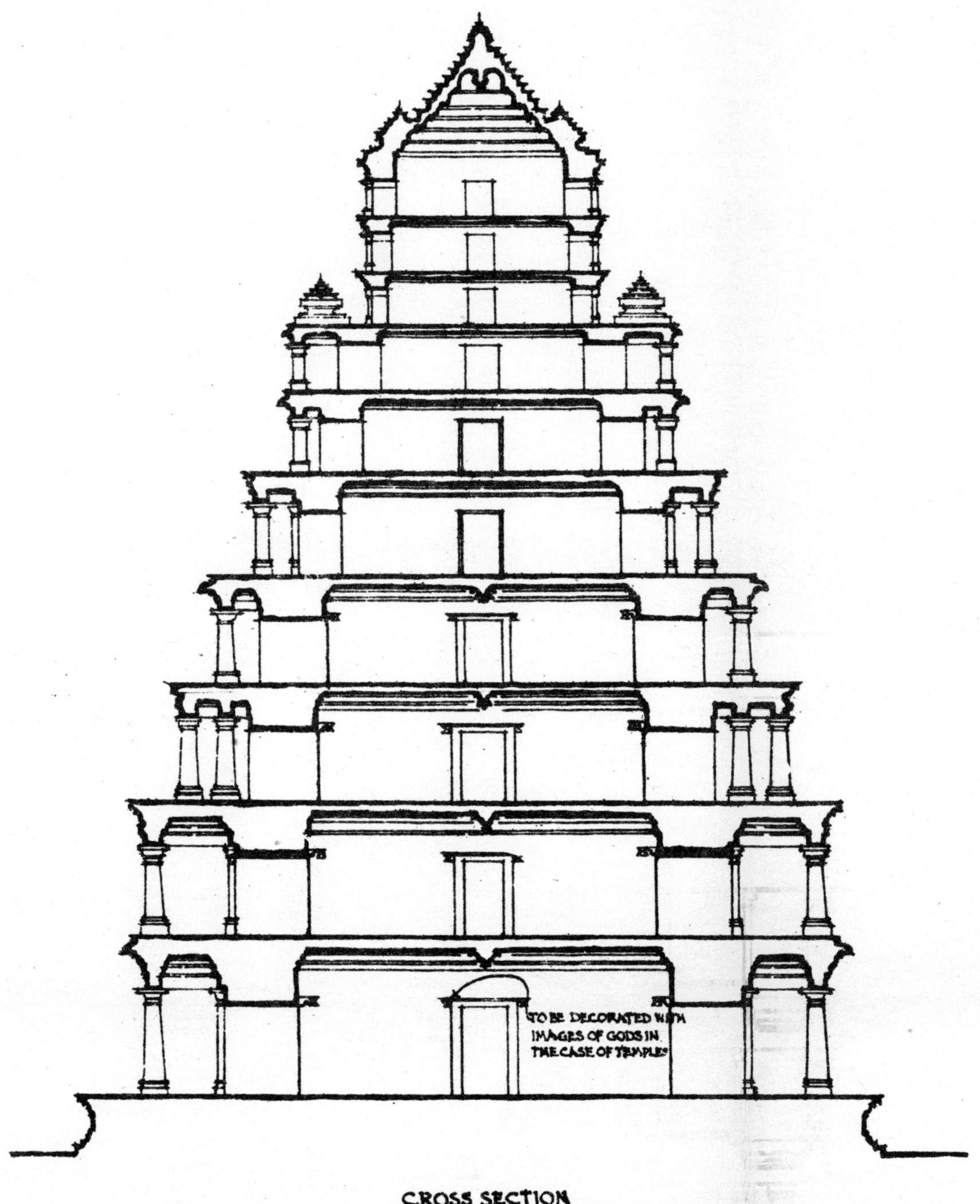

CROSS SECTION

HEIGHT = 1½ BREADTH
= 63 PARTS

SCALE OF 1 0 5 10 15 20 25 PARTS

S. C. MUKHERJI.

SHEET No. XC

THE TEN-STOREYED BUILDINGS — CHAPTER XXVIII

SUGGESTIONS FOR PLANS IN GENERAL

NOTE:—

THE OTHER TYPES NOT DRAWN VARY ONLY IN MINOR DETAILS

THE IDEA OF KŪTA-ŚĀLĀ HAS BEEN TAKEN FROM THE PLANS OF NINE-STOREYED BUILDINGS (CHAP: XXVII)

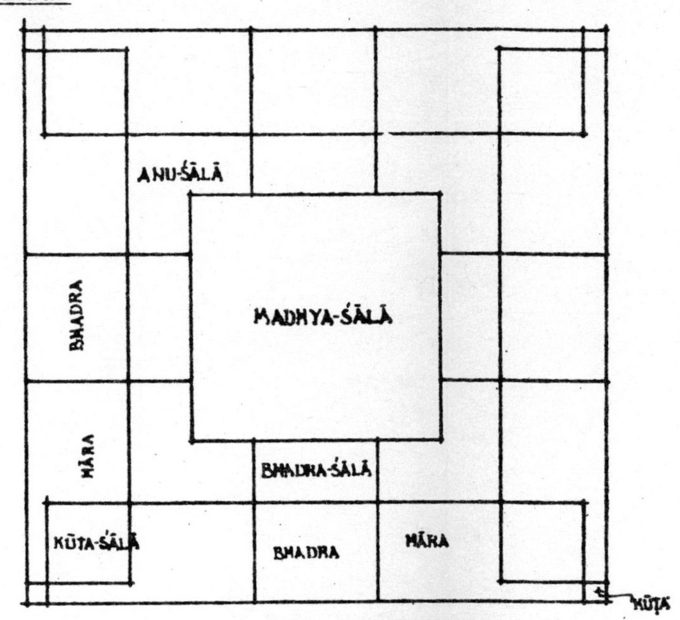

BHAVANA-KĀNTA TYPE OF 28 PARTS ONLY

SCALE OF 0 5 10 15 20 25 PARTS

S. C. MUKHERJI.

THE ELEVEN-STOREYED BUILDINGS — CHAPTER XXIX.

THE ELEVATION TOWARDS THE BREADTH

NOTE:-

ALL THESE TYPES MAY BE UTILISED BOTH AS TEMPLES AND DOMESTIC BUILDINGS WITH SLIGHT MODIFICATION IN DETAIL TO BE INDICATED IN THE SECTION.

ELEVATION.

HEIGHT = 1½ BREADTH
= 74 PARTS

SCALE OF 0 5 10 15 20 25 30 PARTS

S. C. MUKHERJI.

THE ELEVEN-STOREYED BUILDINGS — CHAPTER XXIX

THE TYPICAL SECTION.

NOTE:—

IF THIS IS TO BE USED AS A TEMPLE THE FRIEZE AND PARAPET SHOULD ALSO BE DECORATED WITH IMAGES OF GODS

ROOMS SHOWN IN THE GENERAL PLAN SHOULD BE PROVIDED WITHIN THIS SPACE
TO BE DECORATED WITH IMAGES OF GODS IN THE CASE OF TEMPLES

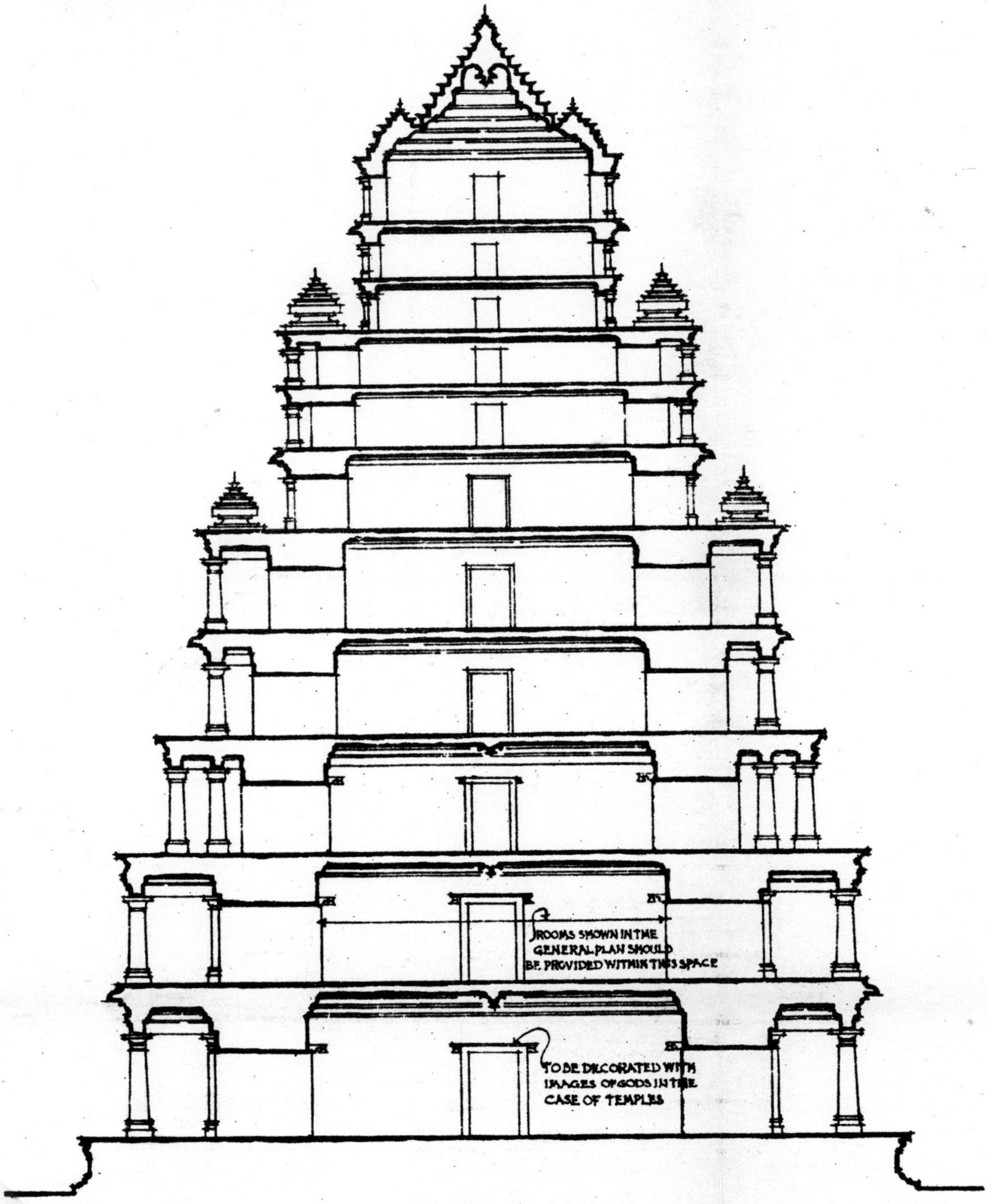

CROSS SECTION

HEIGHT = 1½ BREADTH
= 74 PARTS

SCALE OF 0 5 10 15 20 25 30 PARTS

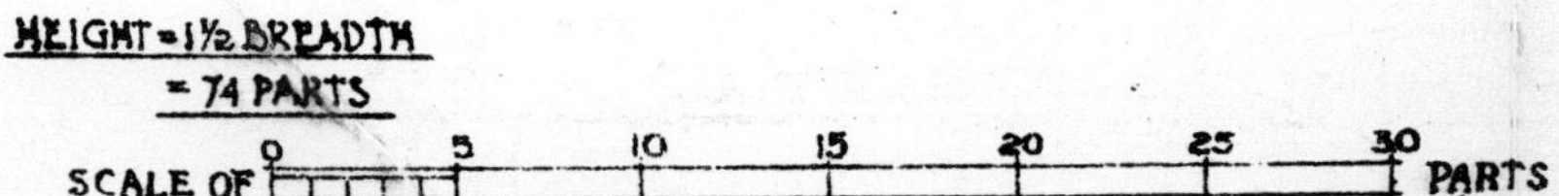

S. C. MUKHERJI.

THE ELEVEN-STOREYED BUILDINGS — CHAPTER XXIX

SUGGESTIONS FOR PLANS IN GENERAL

NOTE:—

FIG. 1 - ŚAMBHU-KĀNTA, SMALL TYPE.
FIG. 2 - VAJRA-KĀNTA, INTERMEDIATE TYPE.
FIG. 3 - CHAKRA-KĀNTA, LARGE TYPE.
OTHER TYPES NOT DRAWN VARY ONLY IN MINOR DETAILS.

SCALE OF 0 5 10 15 20 25 PARTS

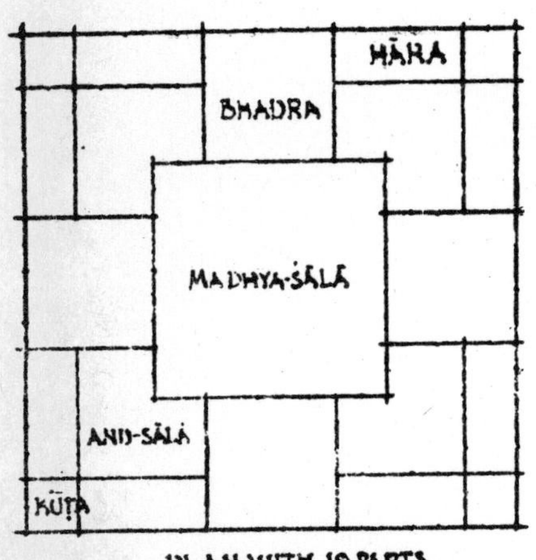

PLAN WITH 19 PARTS
FIG. 1

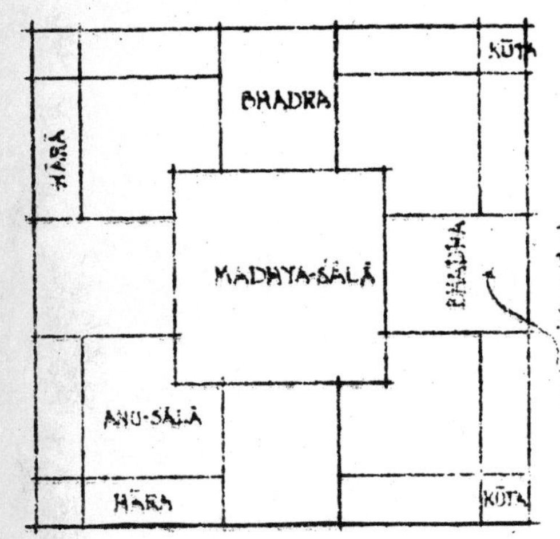

THE TEXT PRESCRIBES TWO BHADRAS AND A BHADRA-ŚĀLĀ WHICH CAN NOT POSSIBLY BE PROVIDED IN THIS FIGURE WITHOUT DIMINISHING THE SIZES OF OTHER ROOMS

PLAN WITH 21 PARTS.
FIG. 2

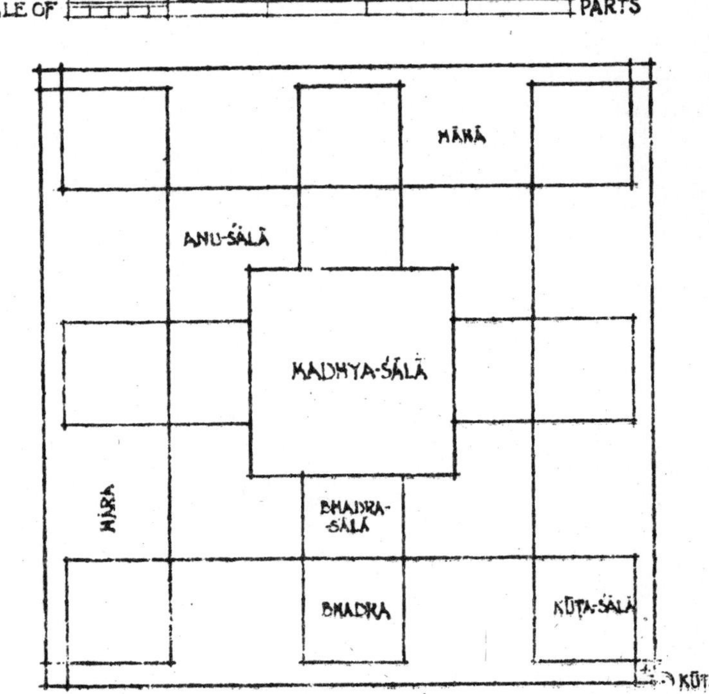

PLAN WITH 30 PARTS
FIG. 3

S. C. MUKHERJI

SHEET NO XCIV

THE TWELVE-STOREYED BUILDINGS — CHAPTER XXX

THE ELEVATION TOWARDS THE BREADTH

NOTE :-

ALL THESE TYPES MAY BE UTILISED BOTH AS TEMPLES AND DOMESTIC BUILDINGS WITH SLIGHT DIFFERENCE IN DETAIL TO BE INDICATED IN THE SECTION

G. C. MUKHERJI.

SHEET NO XCV

THE TWELVE-STOREYED BUILDINGS.— CHAPTER XXX

THE TYPICAL SECTION

NOTE:-

IF THIS IS TO BE USED AS A TEMPLE, THE FRIEZE AND PARAPET SHOULD ALSO BE DECORATED WITH IMAGES OF GODS

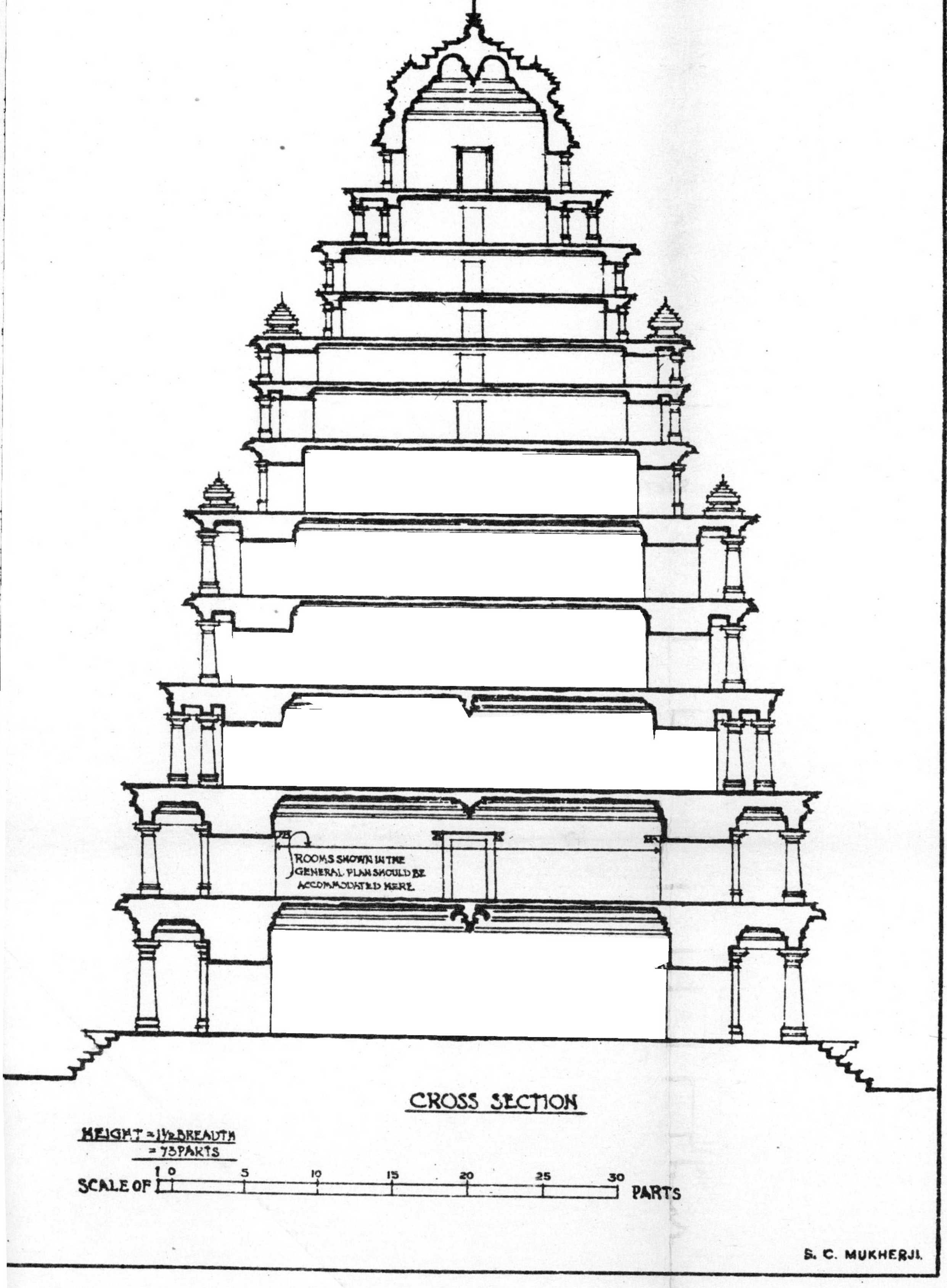

THE TWELVE-STOREYED BUILDINGS — CHAPTER XXX

SUGGESTIONS FOR PLANS IN GENERAL

NOTE:-

FIG.1. SMALL SIZE ~ 28 PARTS

FIG 2. INTERMEDIATE SIZE ~ 34 PARTS

SCALE 0 4 8 12 16 20 24 OF PARTS

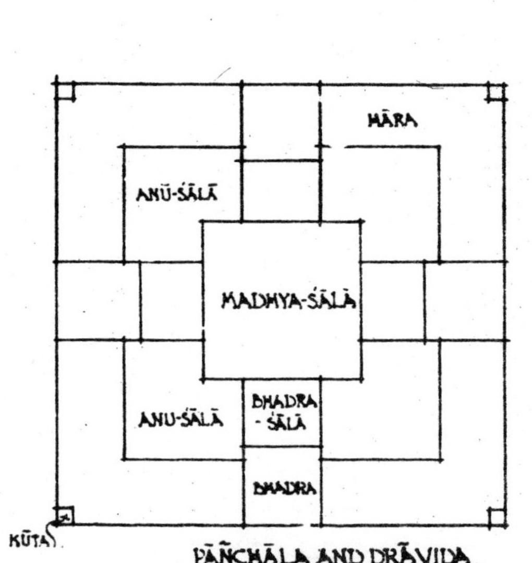

PĀÑCHĀLA AND DRĀVIḌA

FIG I.

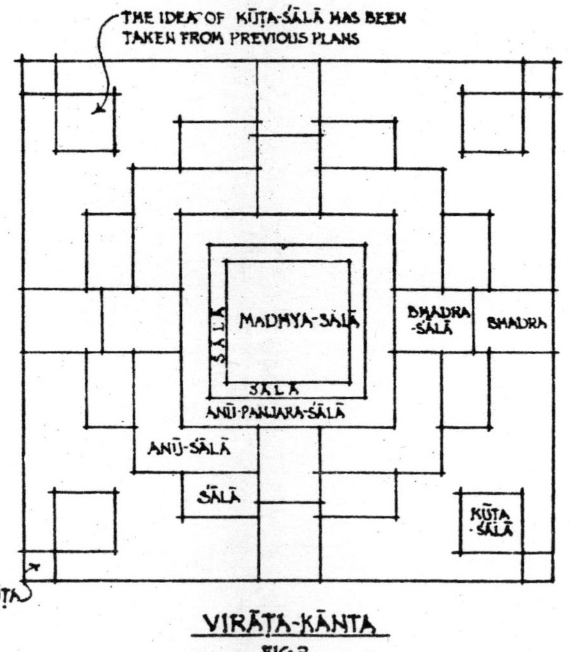

VIRĀṬA-KĀNTA

FIG.2

S. C. MUKHERJI.

SHEET NO. XCVII

THE TWELVE-STOREYED BUILDINGS — CHAPTER XXX

SUGGESTIONS FOR PLANS IN GENERAL

NOTE:-

FIG 1. INTERMEDIATE SIZE, 33 PARTS

FIG 2. INTERMEDIATE SIZE, 34 PARTS

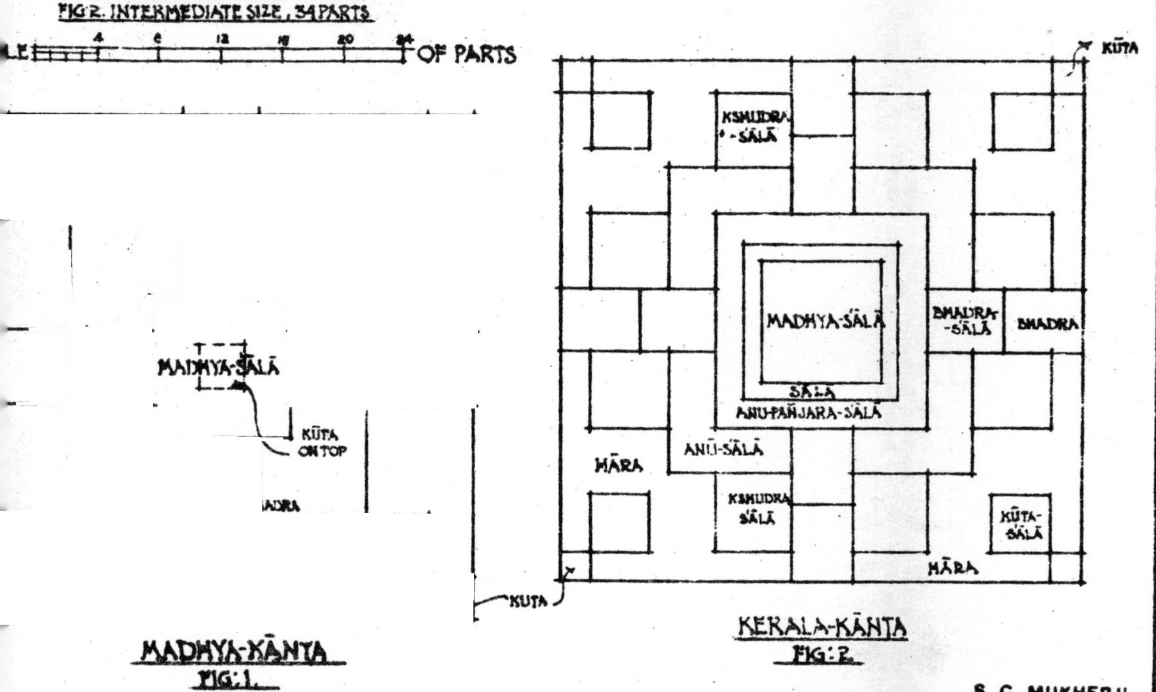

MADHYA-KĀNTA
FIG: 1.

KERALA-KĀNTA
FIG: 2.

S. C. MUKHERJI.

SHEET No XCVIII

THE TWELVE-STOREYED BUILDINGS — CHAPTER XXX

SUGGESTIONS FOR PLANS IN GENERAL

NOTE:-

FIG: 1 INTERMEDIATE SIZE, 33 PARTS

FIG. 2 INTERMEDIATE SIZE, 34 PARTS

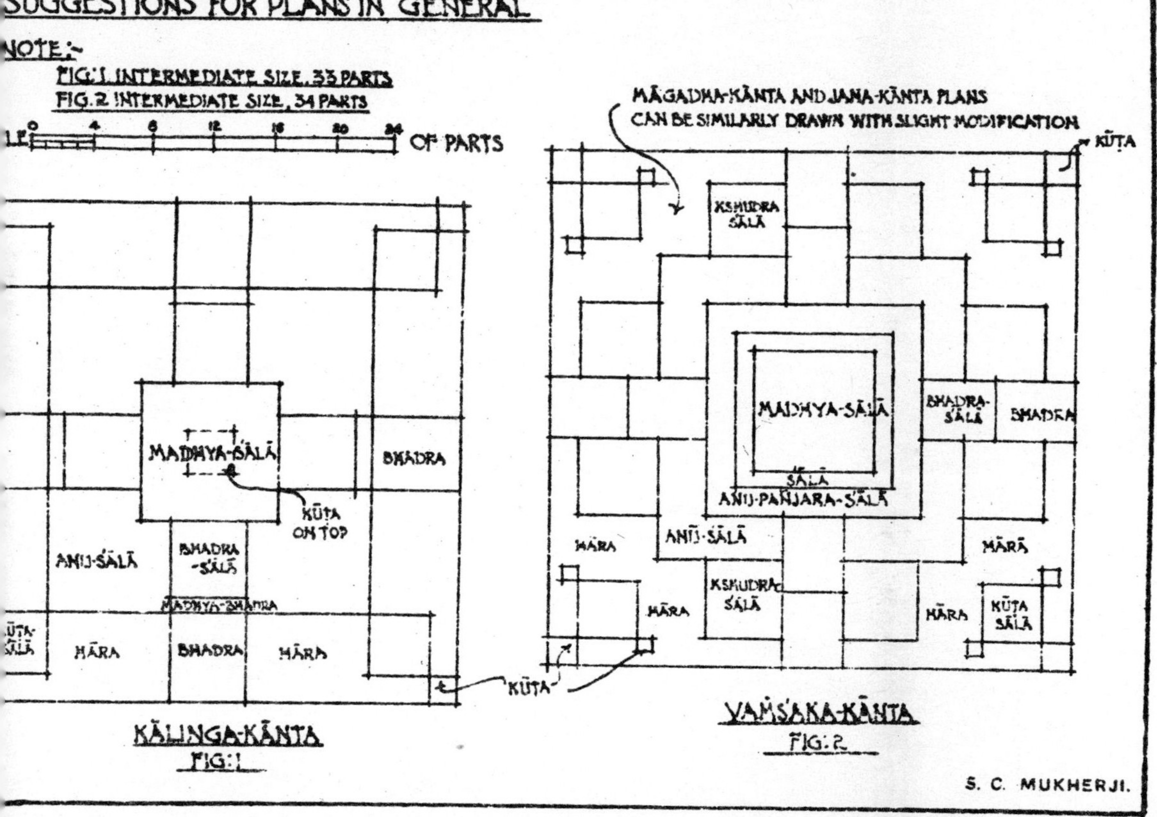

KĀLINGA-KĀNTA

FIG: 1

VAṀŚAKA-KĀNTA

FIG: 2

S. C. MUKHERJI.

SHEET NO. XCIX

TWELVE-STOREYED BUILDINGS — CHAPTER XXX

STEPS AND STAIR-CASES

SCALE ½ INCH = 1 FOOT

NOTE:-

THERE ARE OTHER TYPES OF STAIRS.
SUCH AS THOSE FOR TANKS AND MOUNTAINS.
THEY ARE TO BE DESIGNED SIMILARLY.

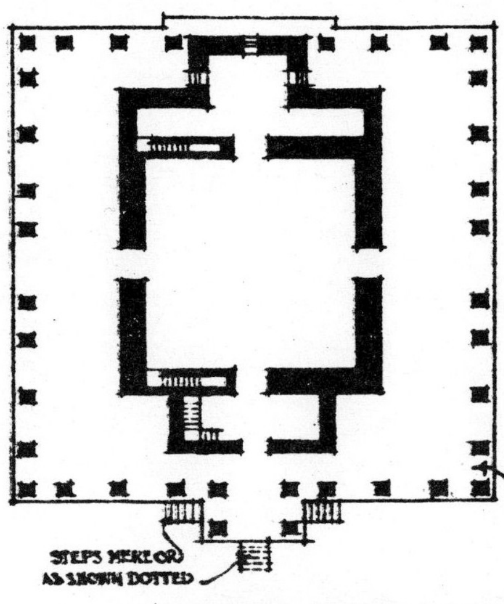

PLAN SHOWING VARIOUS POSITIONS
OF STEPS AND STAIR-CASES
FIXED STAIR-CASE

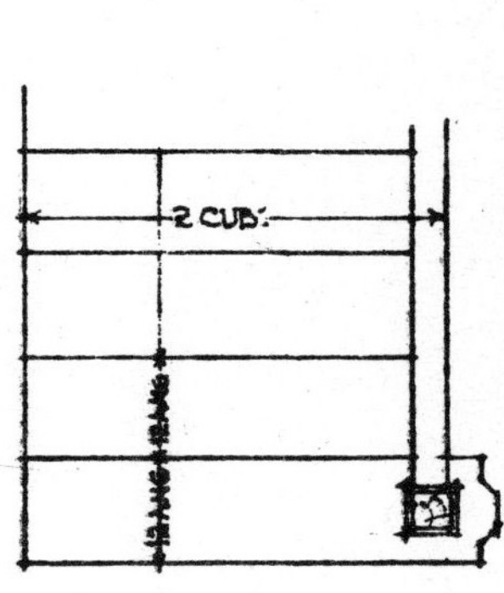

PLAN

REPEAT

SIDE ELEVATION

FIXED STAIR-CASE

NOTE:-
THE GENERAL PLANS ARE
NOT TO SCALE

UP

UP

PLAN SHOWING POSSIBLE POSITIONS
OF MOVABLE STAIR-CASES

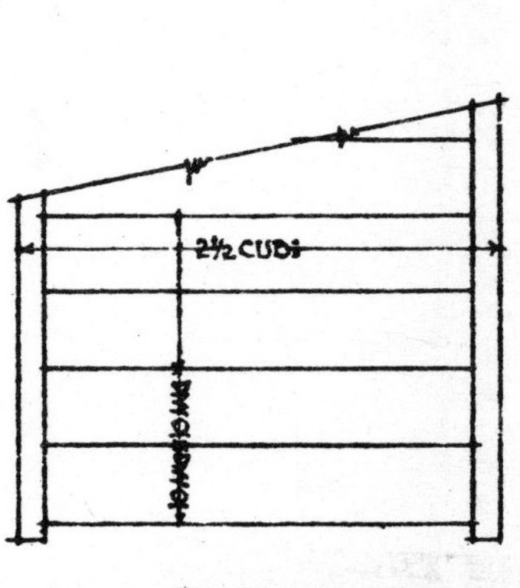

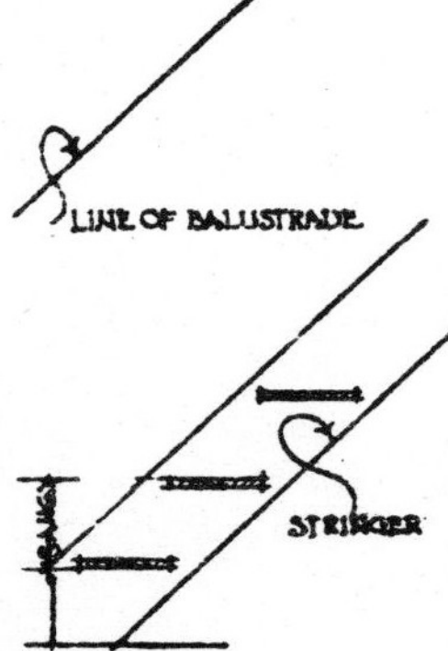

PLAN

SECTION

MOVABLE STAIR-CASE

S. C. MUKHERJI.

SHEET No. C

THE COURTS — CHAPTER XXXI

NOTE:–

THE COURTS FOR ĀBHĀSA AND VIKALPA MAY LIKE-WISE BE DRAWN WITH THE ABSOLUTE MEASUREMENT GIVEN IN THE TEXT

THE HEIGHT OF A COURT WALL SHOULD EXTEND UP TO THE NECK OF THE MAIN EDIFICE OR OTHERWISE, IF SPECIFIED

THE NUMBER OF COURTS MAY EVEN BE SEVEN IN VERY LARGE BUILDINGS SUCH AS PALACES (CHAP XL.) BUT THE TEXT DOES NOT GIVE ANY DESCRIPTION HERE

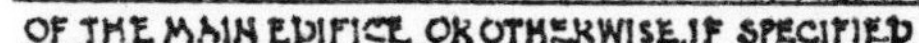

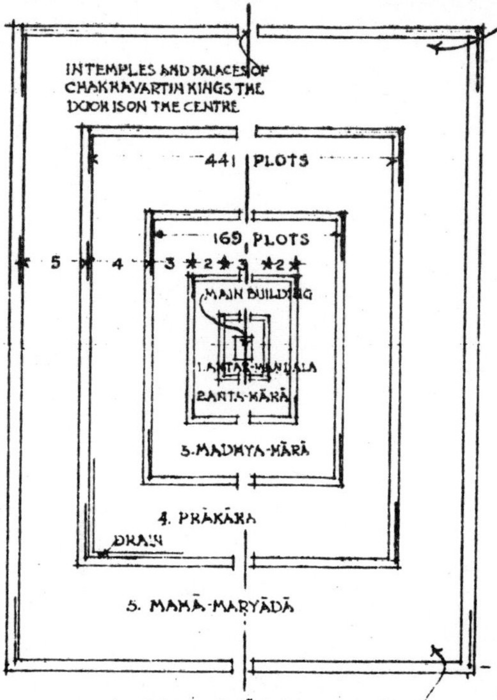

COURTS FOR JĀTI BUILDINGS

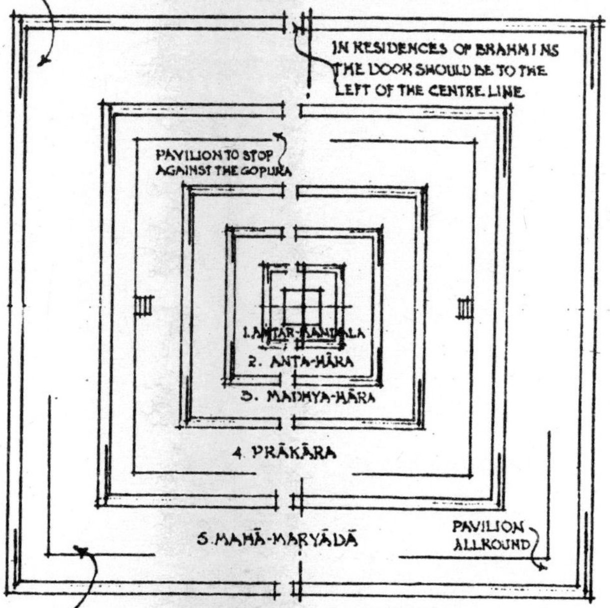

COURTS FOR CHHANDA BUILDINGS

THE COURTS FOR JĀTI HAS BEEN DRAWN WITH RECTANGULAR UNITS AND THOSE FOR CHHANDA WITH SQUARE UNITS

S. C. MUKHERJI.

SHEET NO. C1

A TEMPLE OF VISHNU WITH HIS ATTENDANT DEITIES — CHAPTER XXXII

NOT TO SCALE

NOTE :—
ŚIVA AND OTHER TEMPLES MAY LIKE-WISE BE ARRANGED
WITH SLIGHT CHANGES IN DETAIL

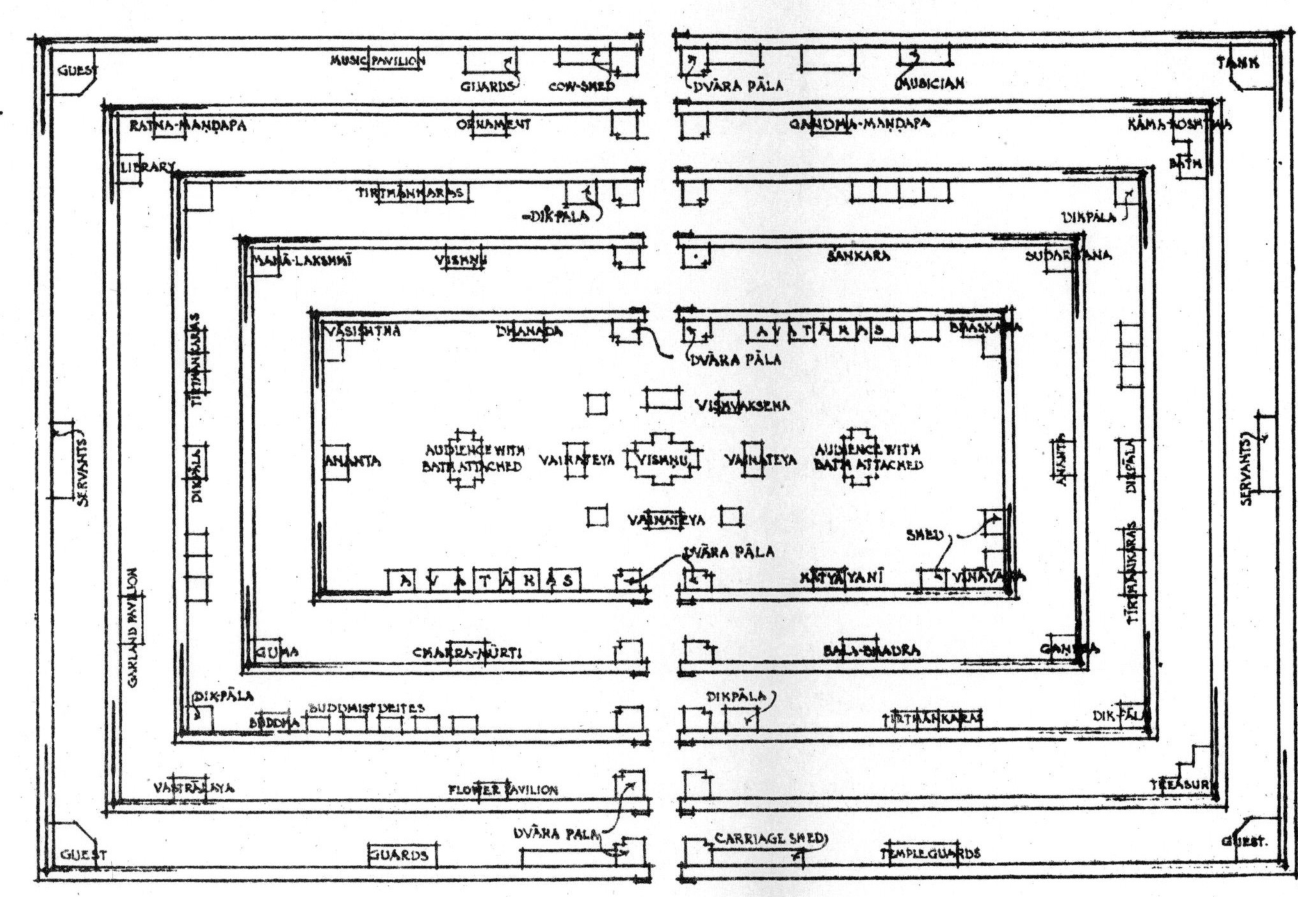

S. C. MUKHERJI.

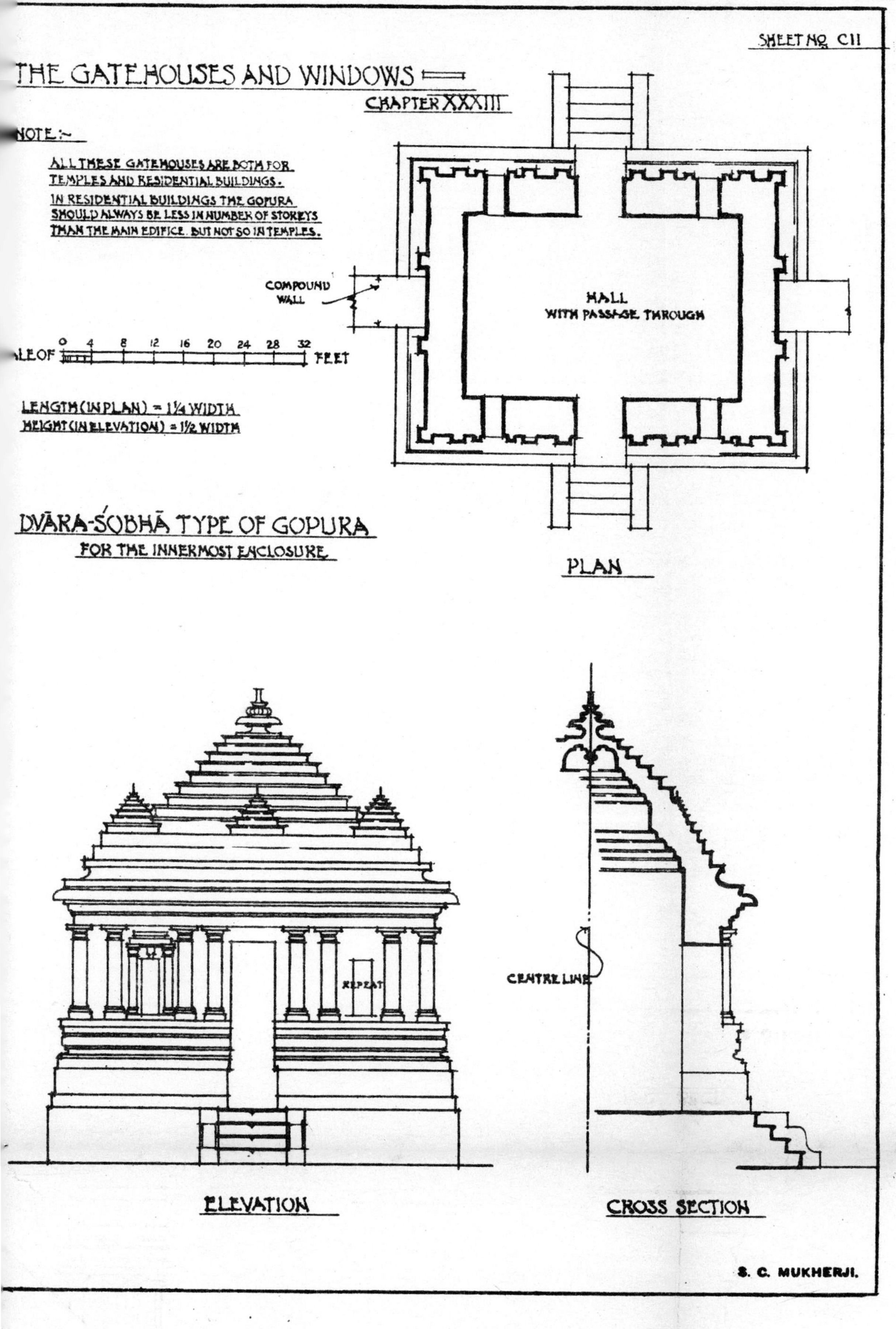

SHEET NO. C11
THE GATEHOUSES AND WINDOWS
CHAPTER XXXIII
NOTE :-
ALL THESE GATEHOUSES ARE BOTH FOR TEMPLES AND RESIDENTIAL BUILDINGS.
IN RESIDENTIAL BUILDINGS THE GOPURA SHOULD ALWAYS BE LESS IN NUMBER OF STOREYS THAN THE MAIN EDIFICE. BUT NOT SO IN TEMPLES.
COMPOUND WALL
HALL
WITH PASSAGE THROUGH
0 4 8 12 16 20 24 28 32
ALE OF
FEET
LENGTH (IN PLAN) = 1¼ WIDTH
HEIGHT (IN ELEVATION) = 1½ WIDTH
DVĀRA-ŚOBHĀ TYPE OF GOPURA
FOR THE INNERMOST ENCLOSURE
PLAN
REPEAT
CENTRE LINE
ELEVATION
CROSS SECTION
S. C. MUKHERJI.

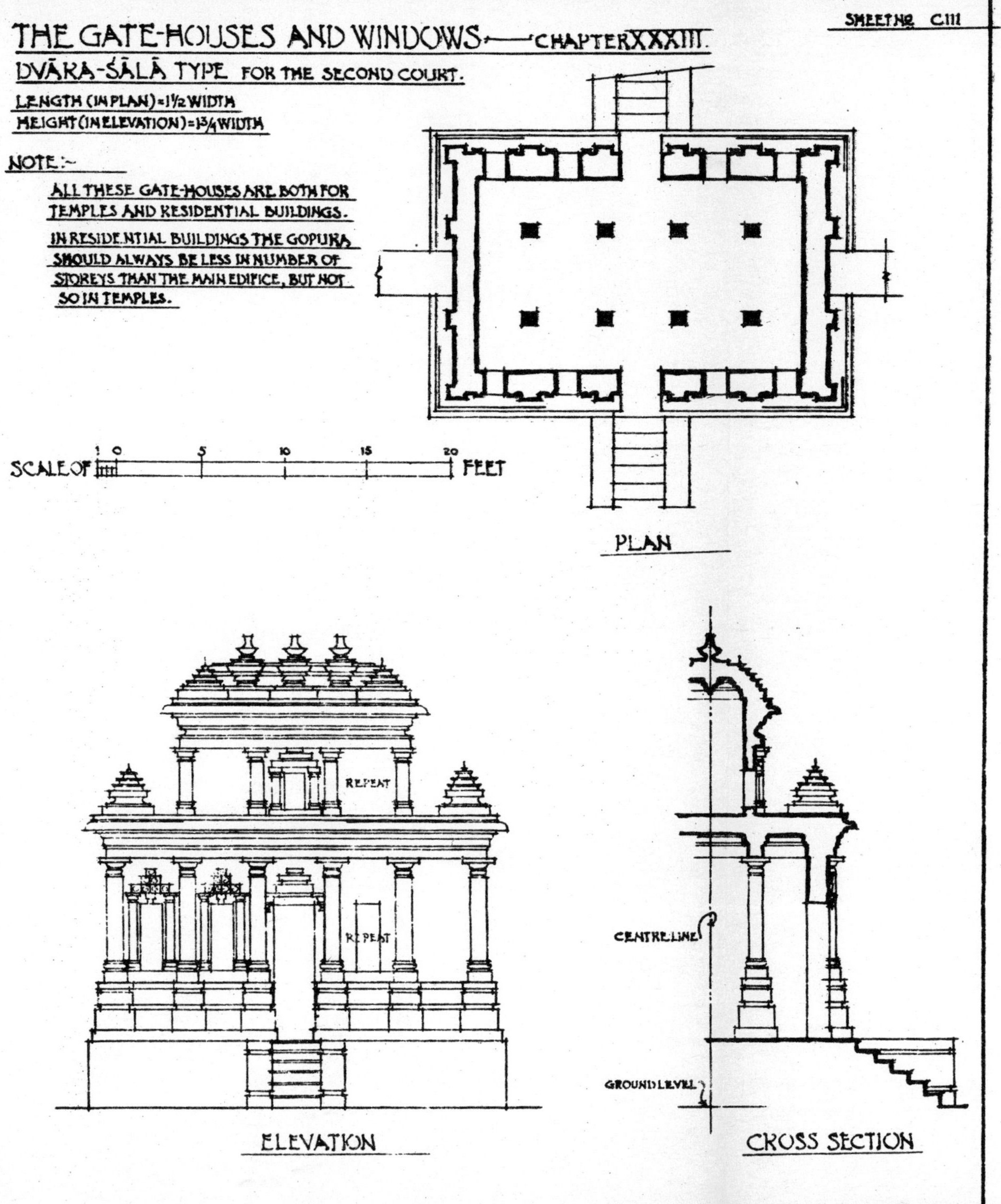
SHEET NO. C111
THE GATE-HOUSES AND WINDOWS — CHAPTER XXXIII.
DVĀRA-ŚĀLĀ TYPE FOR THE SECOND COURT.
LENGTH (IN PLAN) = 1½ WIDTH
HEIGHT (IN ELEVATION) = 1¾ WIDTH
NOTE:-
ALL THESE GATE-HOUSES ARE BOTH FOR TEMPLES AND RESIDENTIAL BUILDINGS.
IN RESIDENTIAL BUILDINGS THE GOPURA SHOULD ALWAYS BE LESS IN NUMBER OF STOREYS THAN THE MAIN EDIFICE, BUT NOT SO IN TEMPLES.
SCALE OF 1 0 5 10 15 20 FEET
PLAN
REPEAT
REPEAT
CENTRE LINE
GROUND LEVEL
ELEVATION
CROSS SECTION
S. C. MUKHERJI.

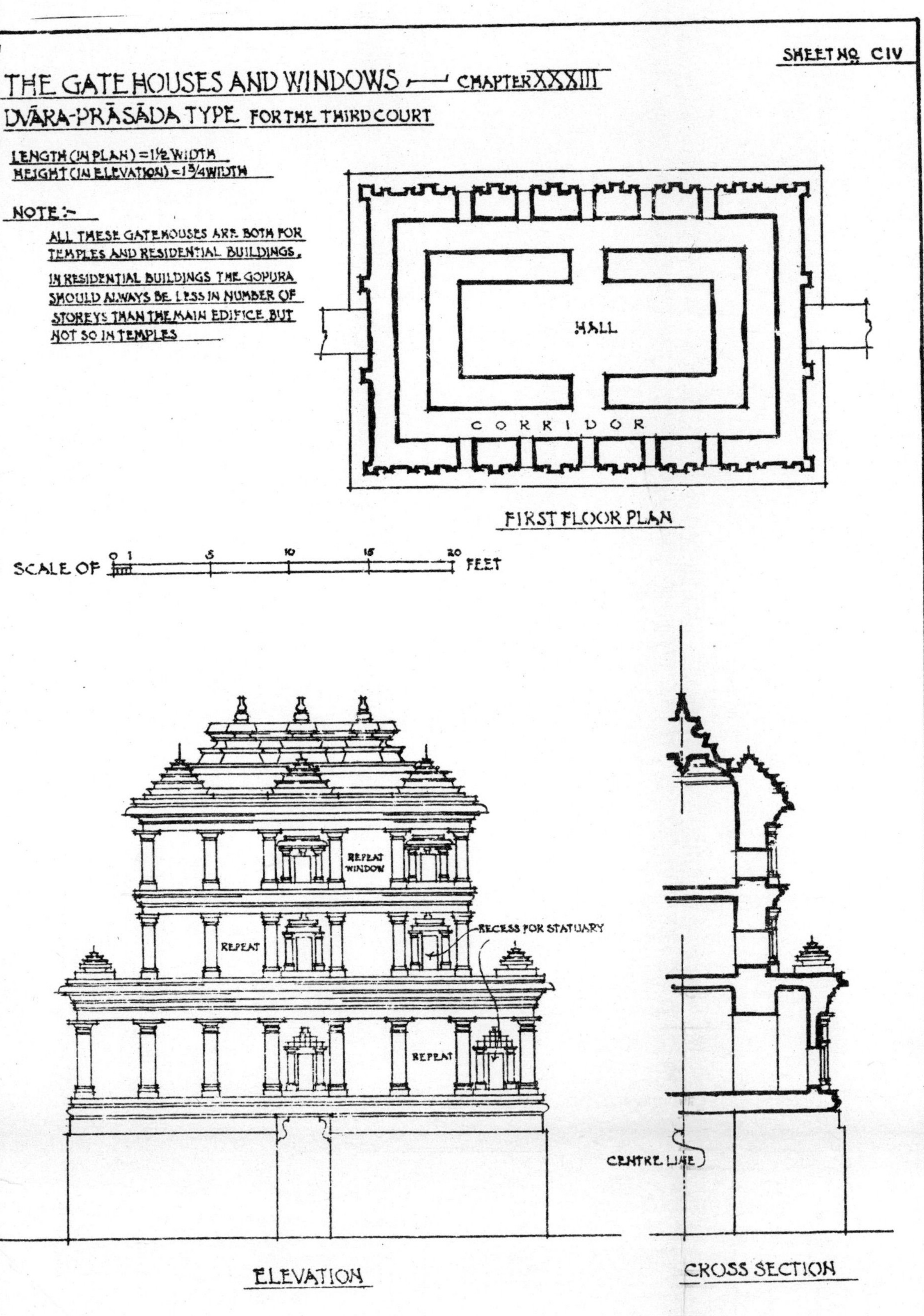
SHEET NO. CIV
THE GATE HOUSES AND WINDOWS — CHAPTER XXXIII
DVĀRA-PRĀSĀDA TYPE FOR THE THIRD COURT
LENGTH (IN PLAN) = 1½ WIDTH
HEIGHT (IN ELEVATION) = 1¾ WIDTH
NOTE :-
ALL THESE GATEHOUSES ARE BOTH FOR TEMPLES AND RESIDENTIAL BUILDINGS.
IN RESIDENTIAL BUILDINGS THE GOPURA SHOULD ALWAYS BE LESS IN NUMBER OF STOREYS THAN THE MAIN EDIFICE BUT NOT SO IN TEMPLES
HALL
CORRIDOR
FIRST FLOOR PLAN
SCALE OF 0 1 5 10 15 20 FEET
REPEAT WINDOW
REPEAT
RECESS FOR STATUARY
REPEAT
CENTRE LINE
ELEVATION
CROSS SECTION
S. C. MUKHERJI.

SHEET No. CV

[T]HE GATE-HOUSES AND WINDOWS — CHAPTER XXXIII

[DV]ĀRA-HARMYA TYPE FOR THE FOURTH COURT

[LE]NGTH (IN PLAN) = 2 WIDTH
[HEIGHT (IN ELEVATION)] = 2¼ WIDTH

[N]OTE:-

ALL THESE GATE-HOUSES ARE BOTH FOR TEMPLES AND RESIDENTIAL BUILDINGS

IN RESIDENTIAL BUILDINGS THE GOPURA SHOULD ALWAYS BE LESS IN NUMBER OF STOREYS THAN THE MAIN EDIFICE BUT NOT SO IN TEMPLES

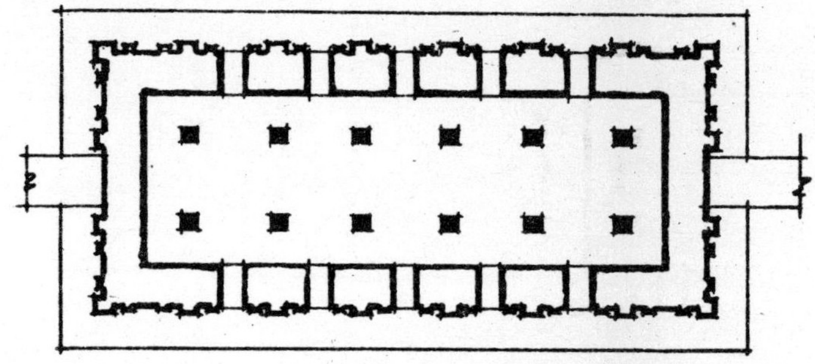

FIRST FLOOR PLAN

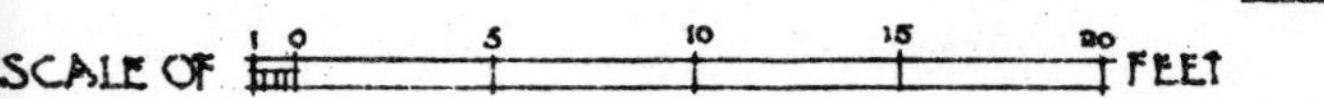

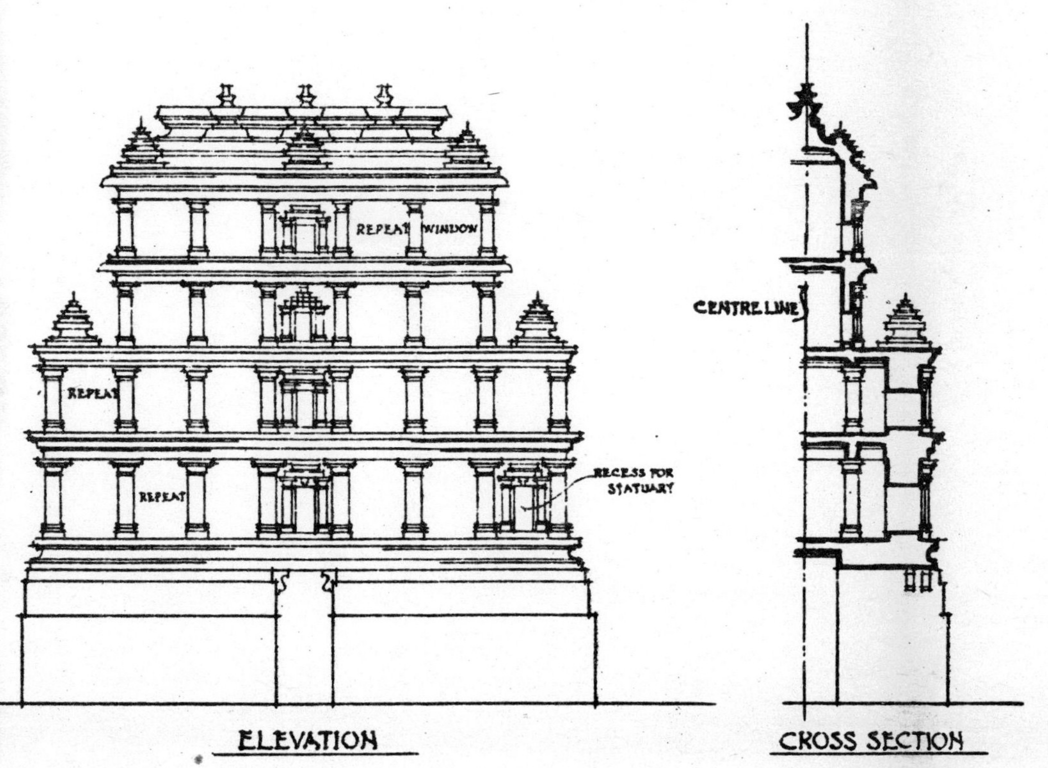

ELEVATION

CROSS SECTION

S. C. MUKHERJI.

SHEET NO. CVI

THE GATE-HOUSES AND WINDOWS — CHAPTER XXXIII

MAHĀ-GOPURA TYPE FOR THE FIFTH COURT

LENGTH (IN PLAN) = 2 WIDTH
HEIGHT (IN ELEVATION) = 2¼ WIDTH

NOTE:—

ALL THESE GATE-HOUSES ARE BOTH FOR TEMPLES AND RESIDENTIAL BUILDINGS

IN RESIDENTIAL BUILDINGS THE GOPURA SHOULD ALWAYS BE LESS IN NUMBER OF STOREYS THAN THE MAIN EDIFICE BUT NOT SO IN TEMPLES.

THE GATE-HOUSES MAY BE UPTO 17 OR 18 STOREYS IN HEIGHT

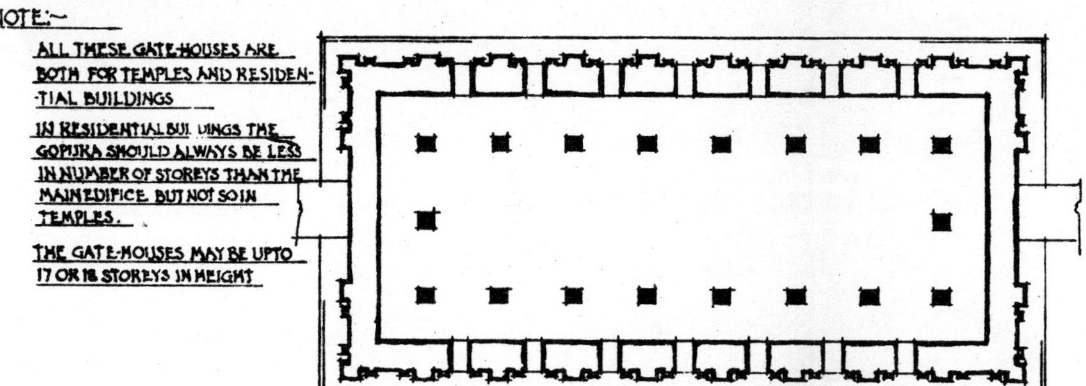

FIRST FLOOR PLAN

REPEAT
REPEAT
REPEAT
REPEAT
RECESS FOR STATUARY
CENTRE LINE

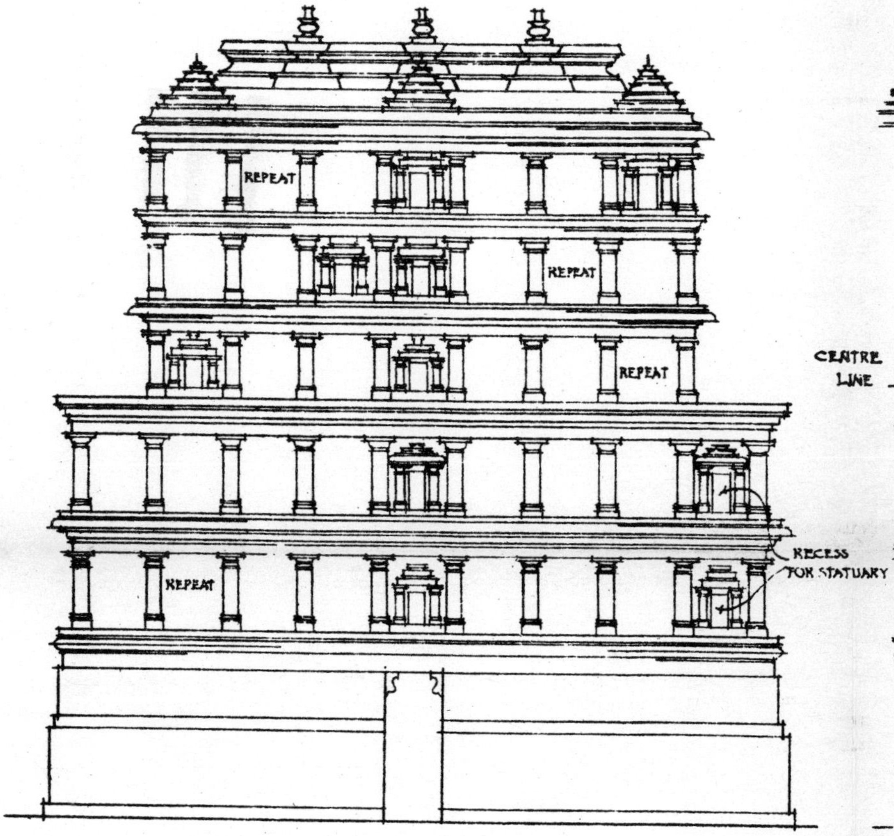

ELEVATION

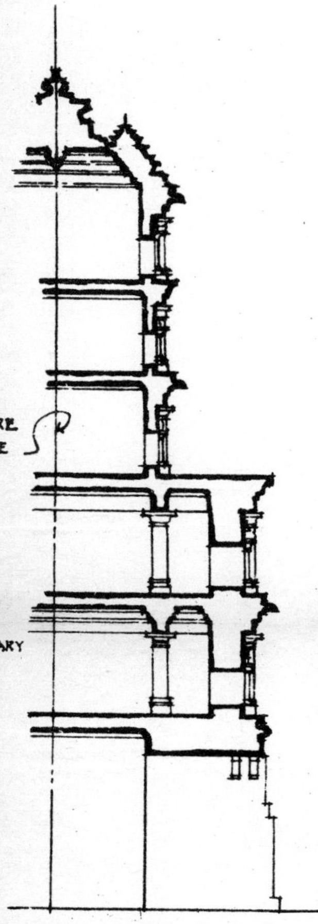

CROSS SECTION

S. C. MUKHERJI.

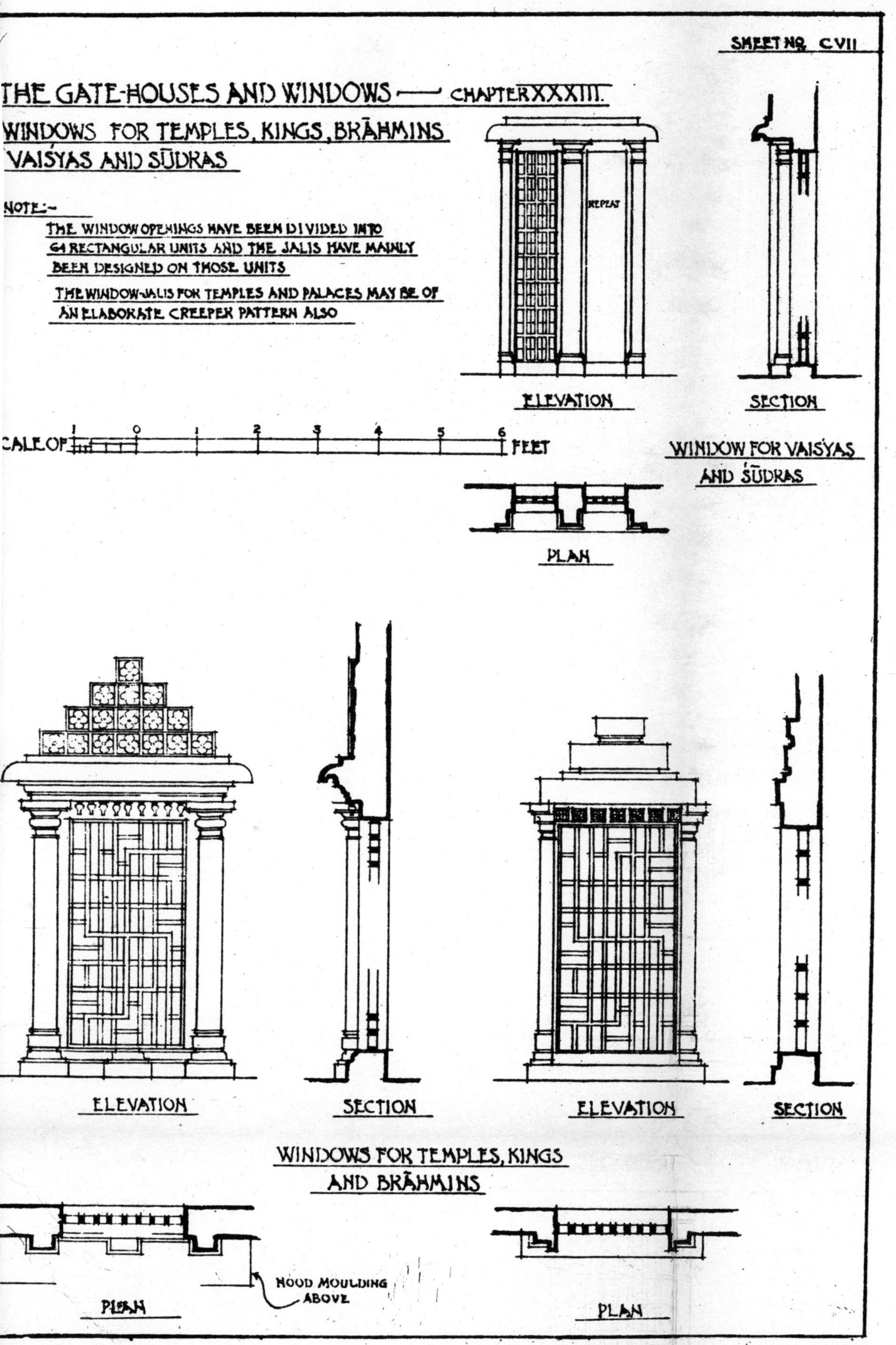
SHEET NO. CVII
THE GATE-HOUSES AND WINDOWS — CHAPTER XXXIII.
WINDOWS FOR TEMPLES, KINGS, BRĀHMINS
VAIŚYAS AND SŪDRAS
NOTE:-
THE WINDOW OPENINGS HAVE BEEN DIVIDED INTO
64 RECTANGULAR UNITS AND THE JALIS HAVE MAINLY
BEEN DESIGNED ON THOSE UNITS
THE WINDOW-JALIS FOR TEMPLES AND PALACES MAY BE OF
AN ELABORATE CREEPER PATTERN ALSO
REPEAT
ELEVATION
SECTION
SCALE OF 1 0 1 2 3 4 5 6 FEET
WINDOW FOR VAIŚYAS
AND SŪDRAS
PLAN
ELEVATION
SECTION
ELEVATION
SECTION
WINDOWS FOR TEMPLES, KINGS
AND BRĀHMINS
HOOD MOULDING
ABOVE
PLAN
PLAN

SHEET NO CVIII

THE PAVILIONS — CHAPTER XXXIV.

NOTE:-

THE PAVILIONS HIMAJA, NISHADAJA, VINDHYAJA SHOULD BE BUILT IN FRONT OF A MAIN EDIFICE.

IN HIMAJA TYPE, NOTHING ABOUT THE OMISSION OF MIDDLE COLUMNS IS MENTIONED.

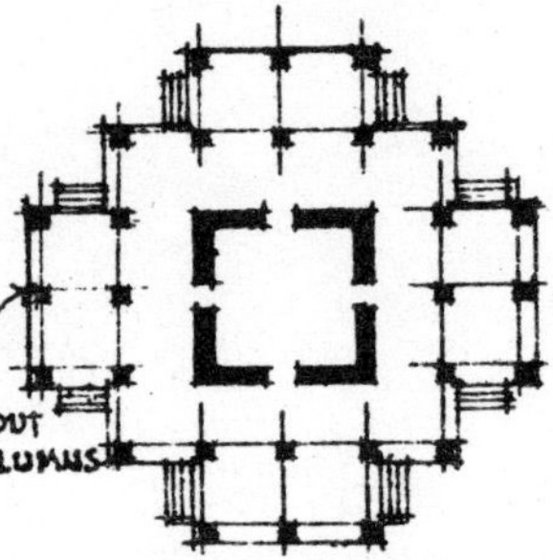

HIMAJA PAVILION
(WITH 4 PARTS SQUARE)

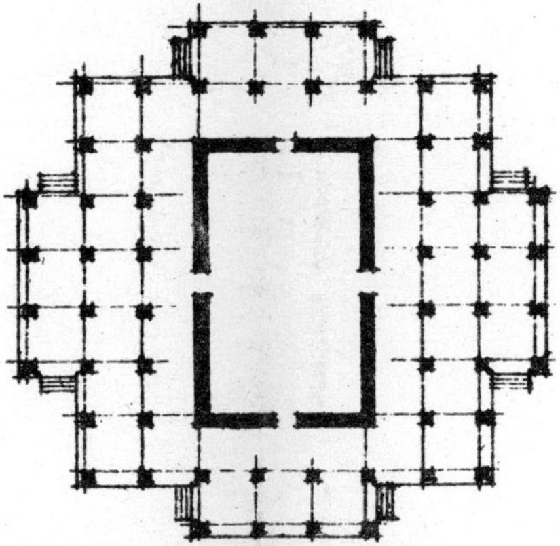

VINDHYAJA PAVILION
(WITH 7 PARTS SQUARE)

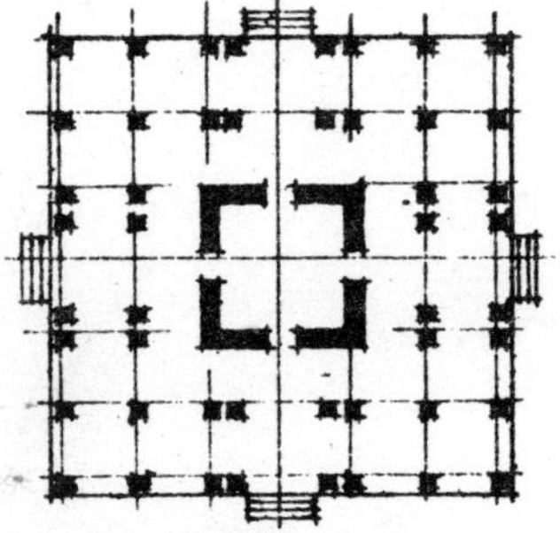

NISHADAJA PAVILION
(WITH 6 PARTS SQUARE)

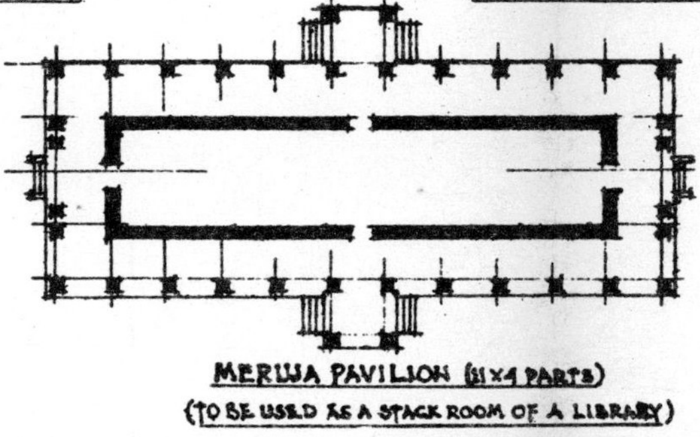

MERUJA PAVILION (11×4 PARTS)
(TO BE USED AS A STACK ROOM OF A LIBRARY)

S. C. MUKHERJI.

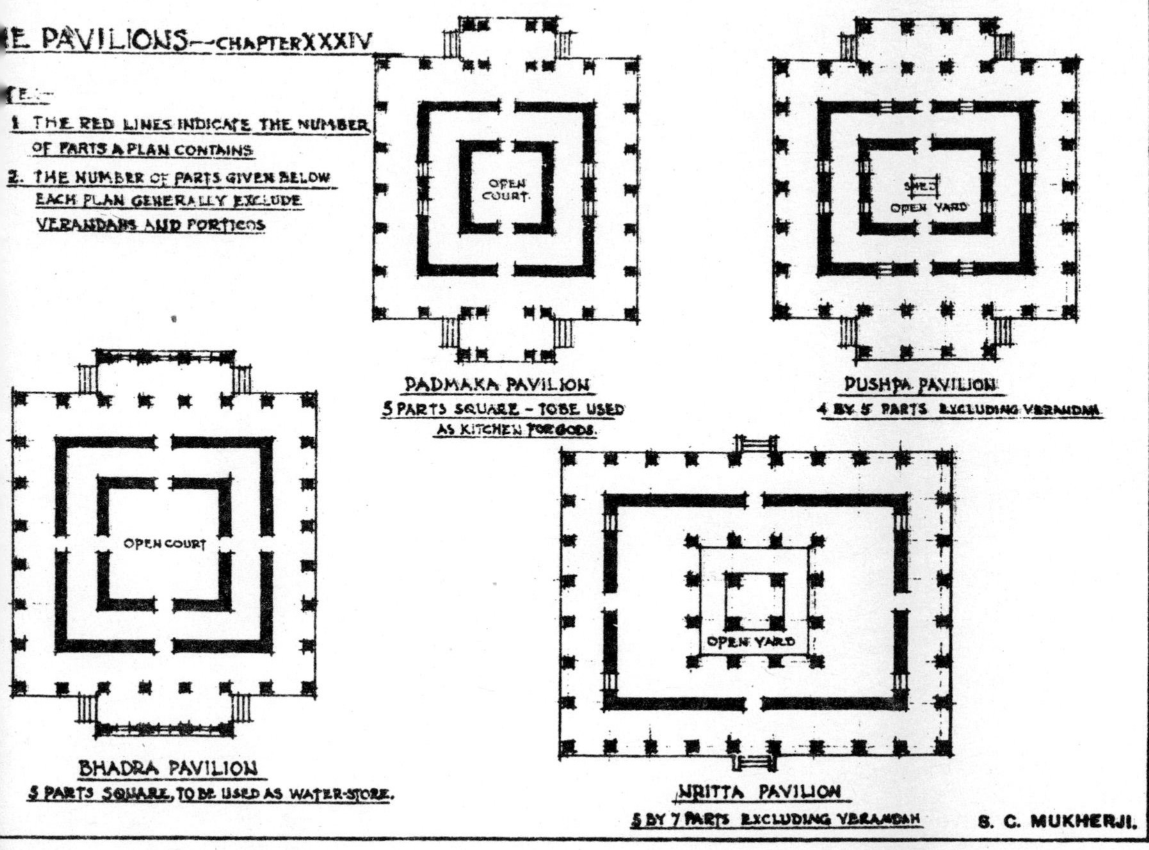
SHEET No. CIX
E PAVILIONS--CHAPTER XXXIV
TE:-
1 THE RED LINES INDICATE THE NUMBER OF PARTS A PLAN CONTAINS
2. THE NUMBER OF PARTS GIVEN BELOW EACH PLAN GENERALLY EXCLUDE VERANDAHS AND PORTICOS
OPEN COURT
PADMAKA PAVILION
5 PARTS SQUARE - TO BE USED AS KITCHEN FOR GODS.
SHED
OPEN YARD
PUSHPA PAVILION
4 BY 5 PARTS EXCLUDING VERANDAH
OPEN COURT
BHADRA PAVILION
5 PARTS SQUARE, TO BE USED AS WATER-STORE.
OPEN YARD
NRITTA PAVILION
5 BY 7 PARTS EXCLUDING VERANDAH
S. C. MUKHERJI.

SHEET No CX

THE PAVILIONS — CHAPTER XXXIV

NOTE :—

1. THE RED LINES INDICATE THE NUMBER OF PARTS A PLAN CONTAINS.
2. IN KŪLADHĀRANA PLAN EACH UNIT OF DEVISION REPRESENTS 2 PARTS.

PART SECTION

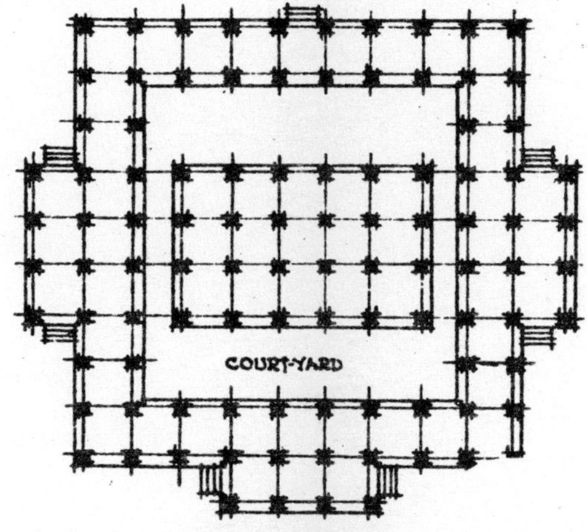

ASSEMBLY HALL

OF 100 COLUMNS, 9 PARTS SQUARE.

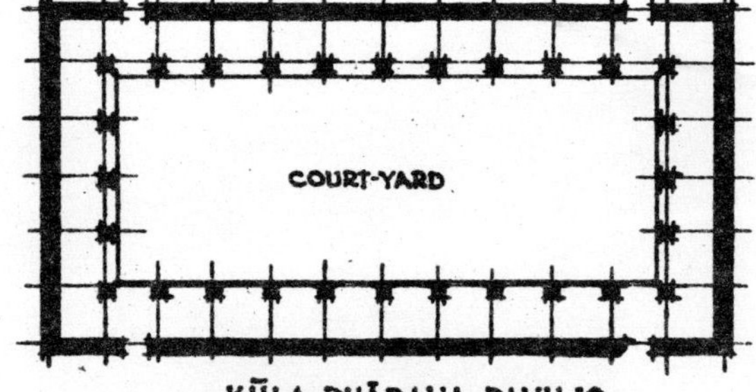

KŪLA-DHĀRANA PAVILIO[N]

24 BY 12 PARTS, TO BE USED AS A COW-[SHED]

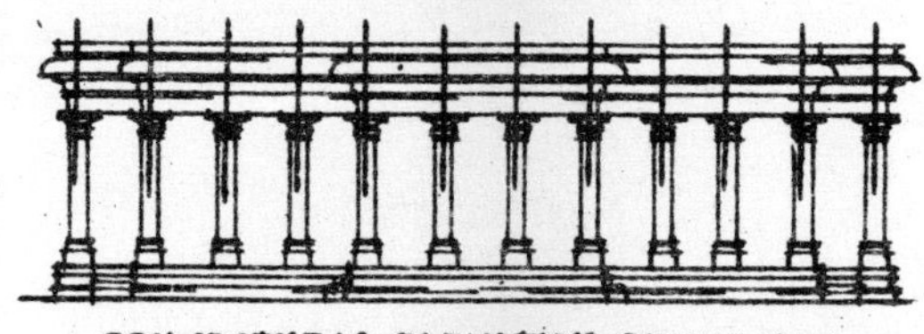

CONJECTURAL ELEVATION OF THE HALL

S. C. MUKHERJI.

SHEET NO CXI

THE PAVILIONS — CHAPTER XXXIV

NOTE :-

1. THE RED LINES INDICATE THE NUMBER OF PARTS A PLAN CONTAINS

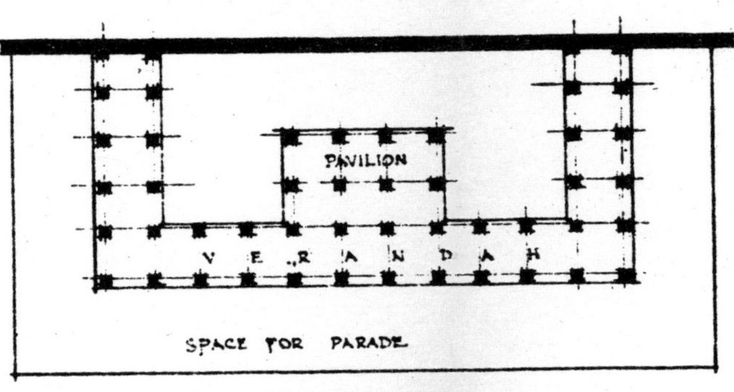

DRONA PAVILION

15 BY 7 PARTS, TO BE USED AS A PLACE FOR RAM-FIGHTING

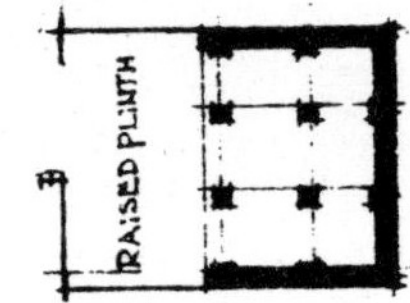

DHANĀDHIPA PAVILION

3 BY 4 PARTS INCLUDING PLINTH

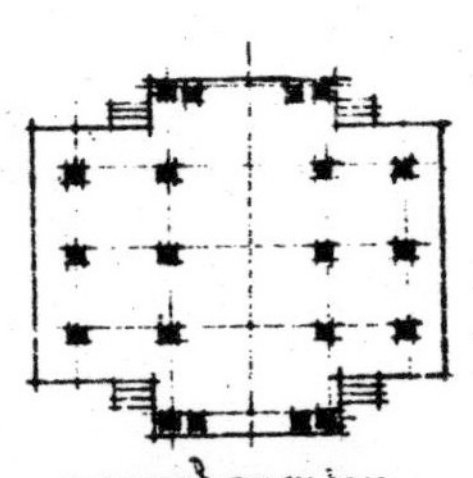

VIJAYĀ PAVILION.

4 BY 2 PARTS EXCLUDING PORCH ETC.

USED FOR WEDDING ETC.

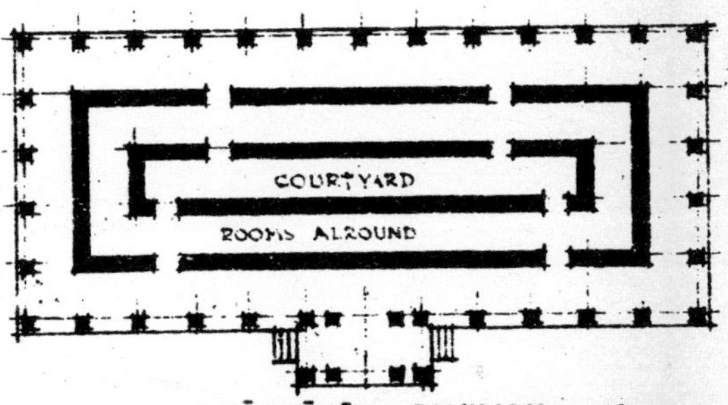

DHĀNYĀGĀRA PAVILION (FOR ŚŪDRAS)

10 BY 3 PARTS EXCLUDING VERANDAH AND PORCH

TREASURY

FOR KSHATRIYAS ETC.

5 BY 3 PARTS

S. C. MUKHERJI.

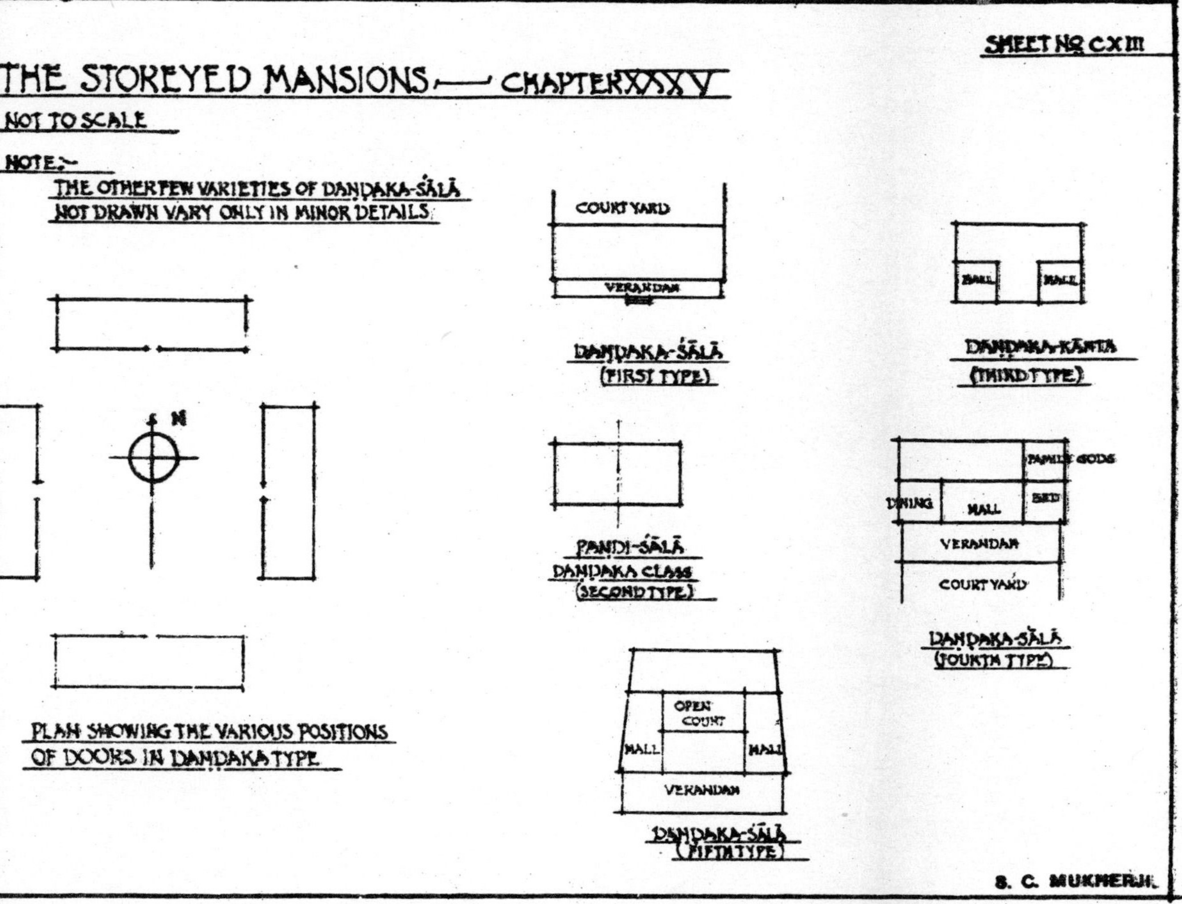
SHEET NO. CXIII
THE STOREYED MANSIONS — CHAPTER XXXV
NOT TO SCALE
NOTE:—
THE OTHER FEW VARIETIES OF DANDAKA-SĀLĀ NOT DRAWN VARY ONLY IN MINOR DETAILS.
N
PLAN SHOWING THE VARIOUS POSITIONS OF DOORS IN DANDAKA TYPE
COURT YARD
VERANDAH
DANDAKA-SĀLĀ (FIRST TYPE)
PANDI-SĀLĀ DANDAKA CLASS (SECOND TYPE)
HALL
HALL
DANDAKA-KĀNTA (THIRD TYPE)
FAMILY GODS
DINING
HALL
BED
VERANDAH
COURT YARD
DANDAKA-SĀLĀ (FOURTH TYPE)
OPEN COURT
HALL
HALL
VERANDAH
DANDAKA-SĀLĀ (FIFTH TYPE)
S. C. MUKHERJI.

SHEET No. CXIV

THE STOREYED MANSIONS — CHAPTER XXXV.

SVASTIKA AND MAULIKA TYPES

NOTE :—

THE TWO TYPES OF MAULIKA-ŚĀLĀ AND THE SECOND TYPE OF SVASTIKA-ŚĀLĀ (NOT DRAWN) VARY ONLY IN MINOR DETAILS AND IN SIZE

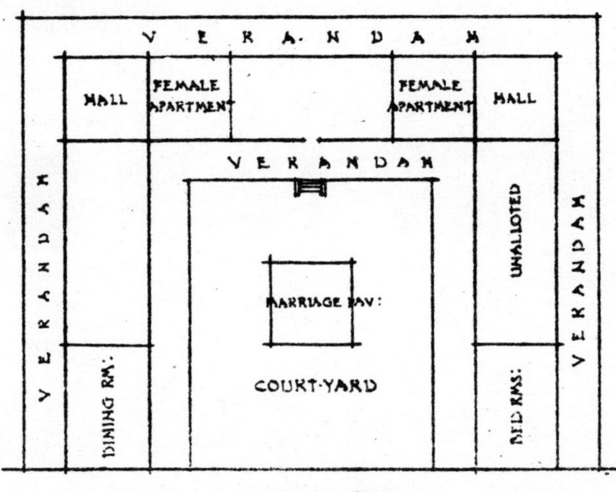

MAULIKA-ŚĀLĀ

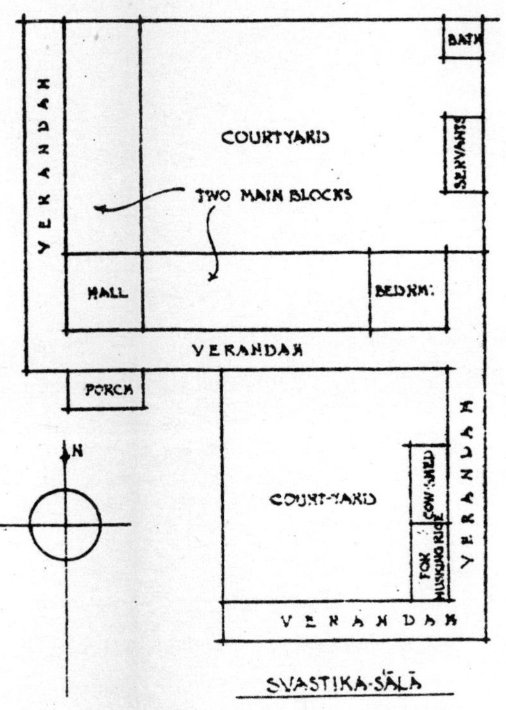

SVASTIKA-ŚĀLĀ

SCALE OF 0 5 10 15 PARTS

S. C. MUKHERJI.

SHEET No CXV

THE STOREYED MANSIONS — CHAPTER XXXV

CHATURĀLAYA AND SARVATOBHADRA TYPES

NOTE:-

THE OTHER VARIETIES OF THESE TWO TYPES VARY ONLY IN MINOR DETAILS

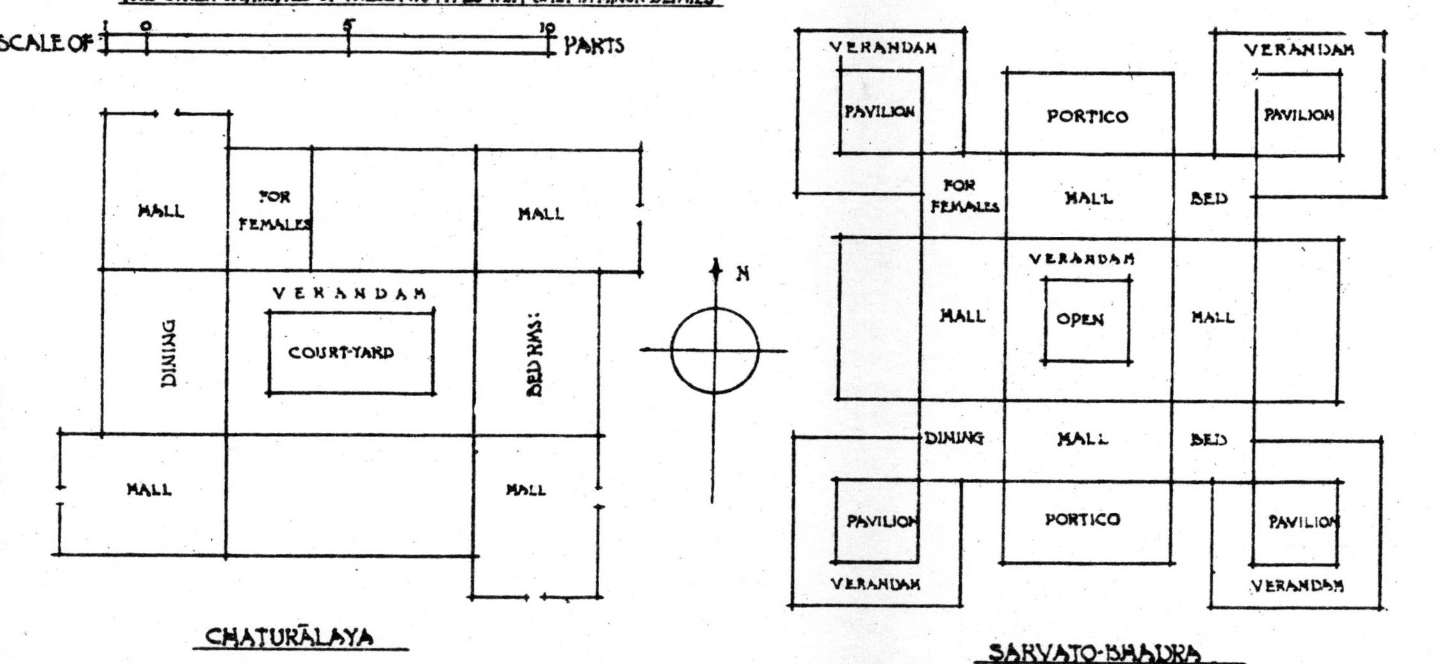

S. C. MUKHERJI.

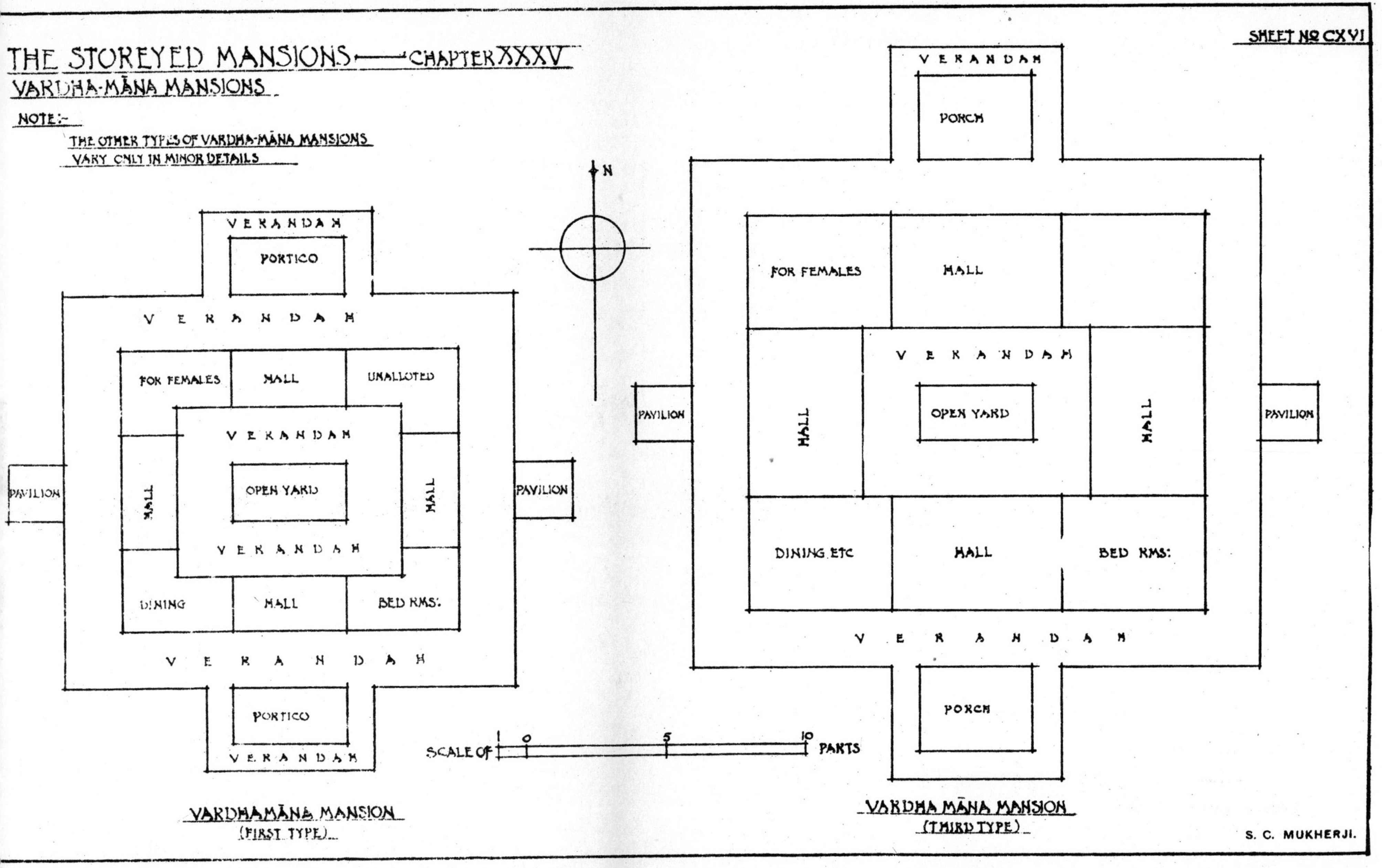
THE STOREYED MANSIONS — CHAPTER XXXV
VARDHA-MĀNA MANSIONS
SHEET NO CXVI
NOTE:-
THE OTHER TYPES OF VARDHA-MĀNA MANSIONS
VARY ONLY IN MINOR DETAILS
N
VERANDAH
PORTICO
VERANDAH
FOR FEMALES
HALL
UNALLOTED
VERANDAH
PAVILION
HALL
OPEN YARD
HALL
PAVILION
VERANDAH
DINING
HALL
BED RMS.
VERANDAH
PORTICO
VERANDAH
VERANDAH
PORCH
FOR FEMALES
HALL
VERANDAH
PAVILION
HALL
OPEN YARD
HALL
PAVILION
DINING ETC
HALL
BED RMS:
VERANDAH
PORCH
SCALE OF 0 5 10 PARTS
VARDHAMĀNA MANSION
(FIRST TYPE)
VARDHA MĀNA MANSION
(THIRD TYPE)
S. C. MUKHERJI.

THE DOORS — CHAPTER XXXIX

SMALL TYPE — SCALE 1 INCH = 1 FOOT

HEIGHT = 9 PARTS AND BREADTH = 5 PARTS

NOTE :-

CHAPTER XXXVIII GIVES ONLY THE POSITIONS OF DOORS IN TEMPLES AND RESIDENTIAL BUILDINGS

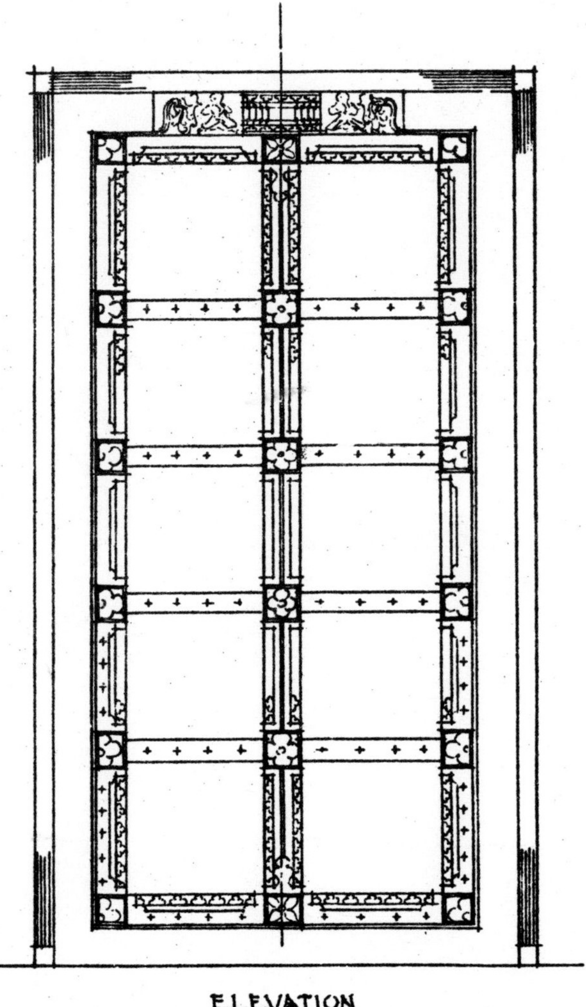

ELEVATION

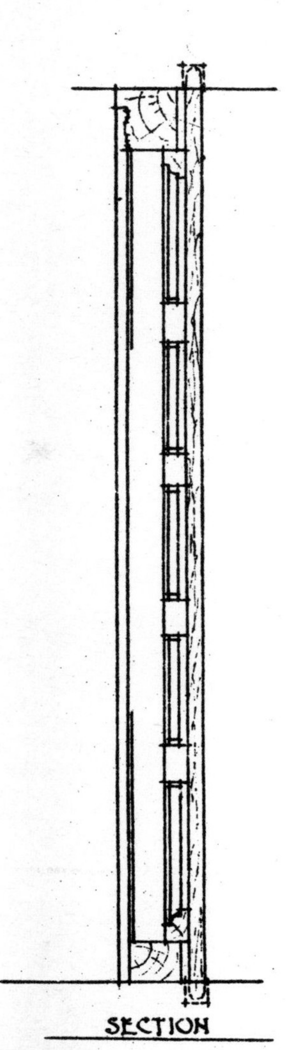

SECTION

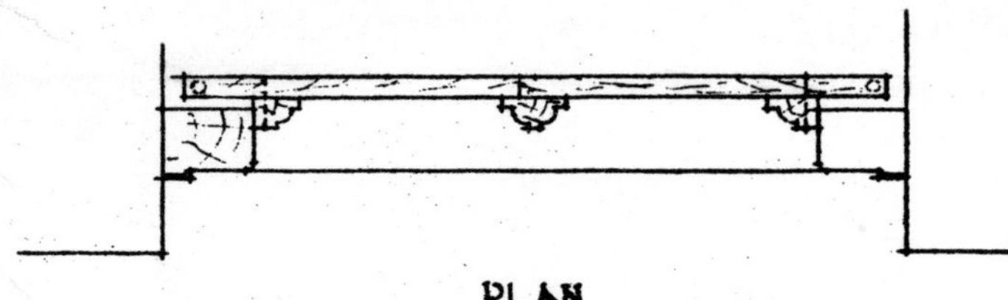

PLAN

S. C. MUKHERJI

THE DOORS — CHAPTER XXXIX

INTERMEDIATE TYPE— SCALE 1 INCH=1 FOOT

BREADTH=5 PARTS HEIGHT=9 PARTS

NOTE:-

CHAPTER XXXVIII GIVES ONLY POSITIONS OF DOORS IN TEMPLES AND RESIDENTIAL BUILDINGS

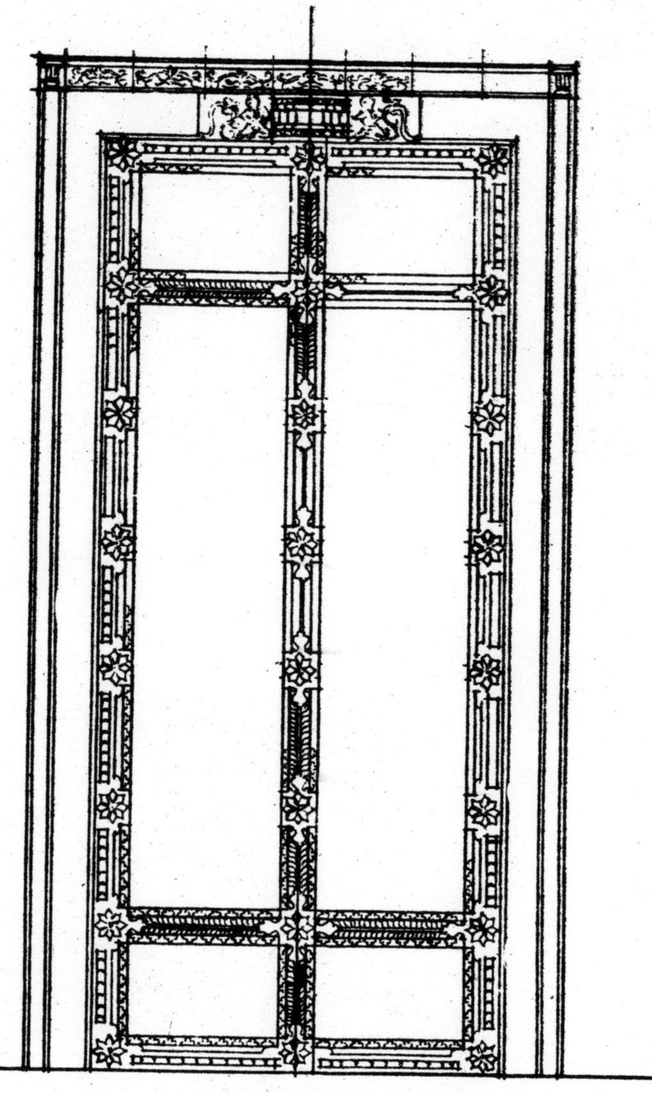

ELEVATION

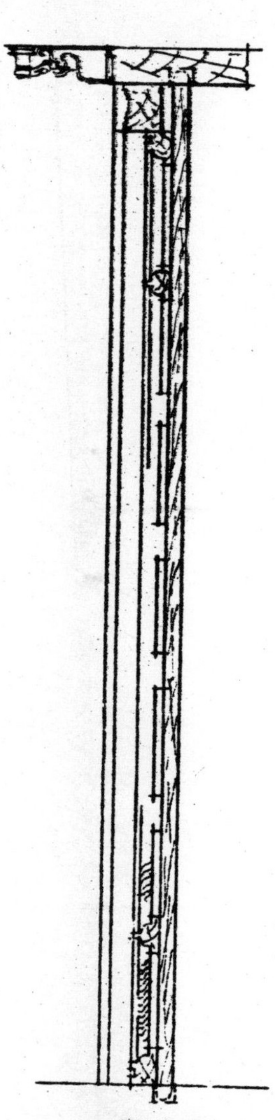

SECTION

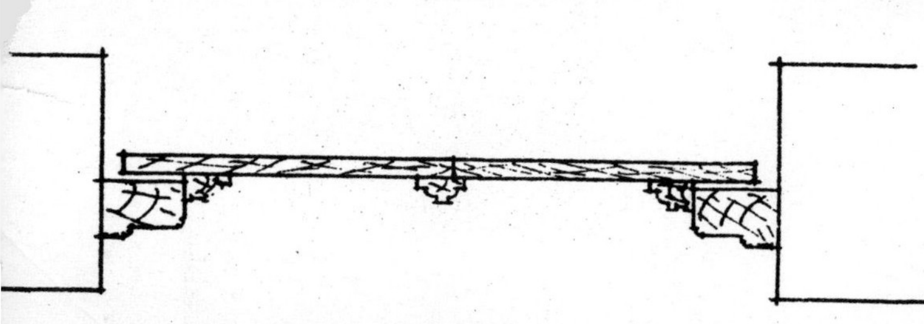

PLAN

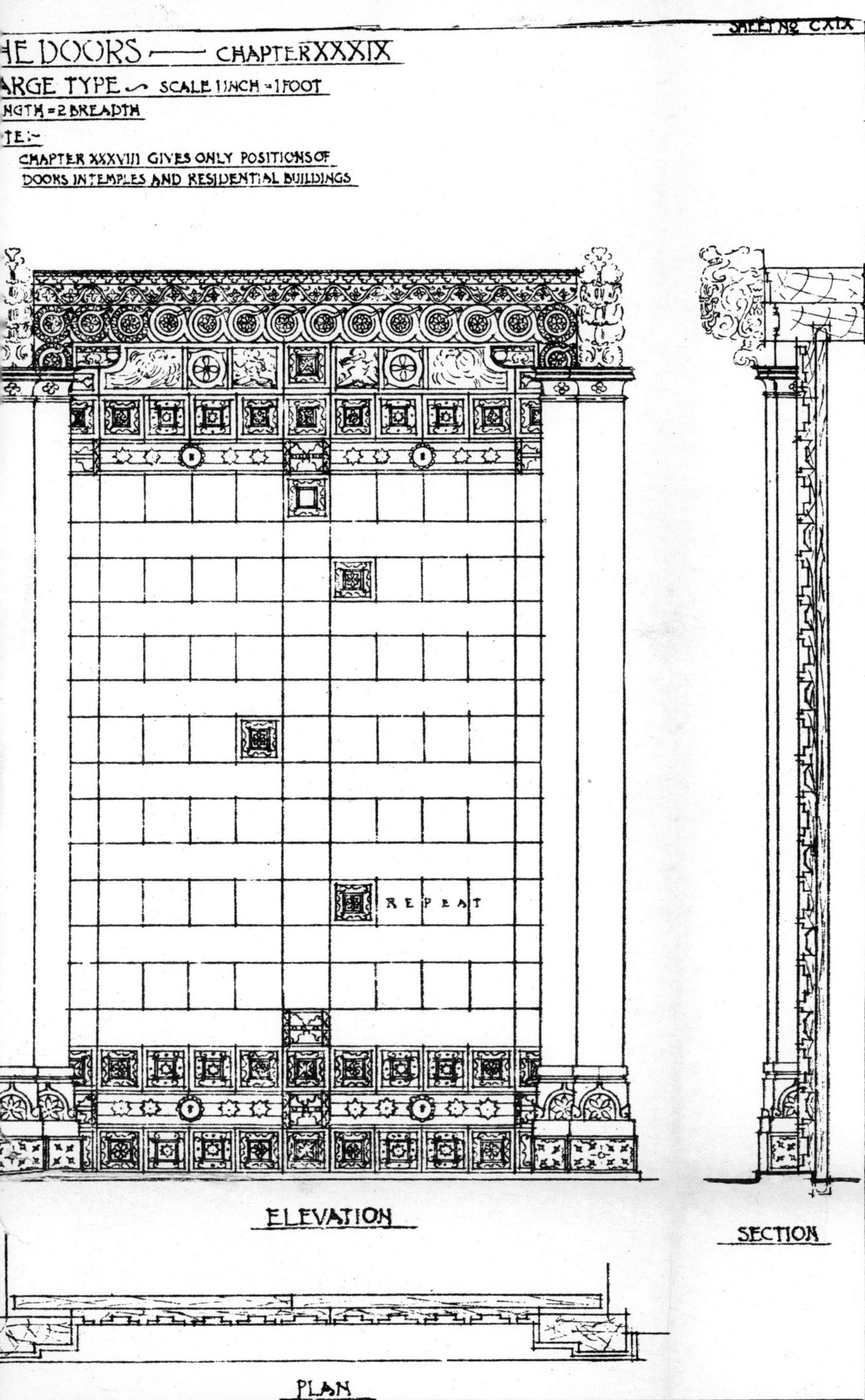
SHEET NO CXIX
HE DOORS —— CHAPTER XXXIX
ARGE TYPE ~ SCALE 1 INCH = 1 FOOT
NGTH = 2 BREADTH
TE:-
CHAPTER XXXVIII GIVES ONLY POSITIONS OF
DOORS IN TEMPLES AND RESIDENTIAL BUILDINGS
REPEAT
ELEVATION
SECTION
PLAN

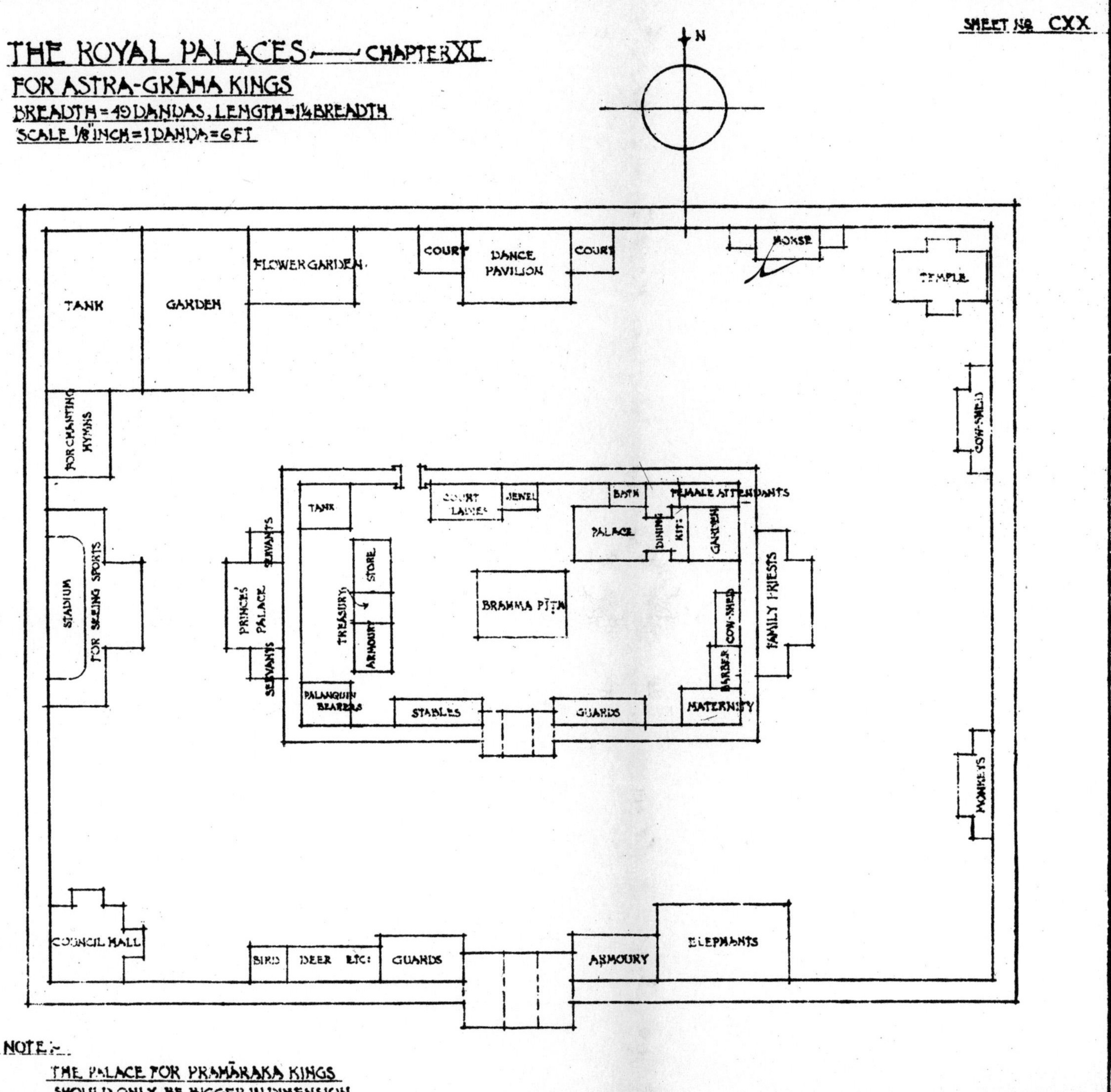
SHEET No CXX
THE ROYAL PALACES — CHAPTER XI
FOR ASTRA-GRĀHA KINGS
BREADTH = 49 DANDAS, LENGTH = 1¼ BREADTH
SCALE 1/8" INCH = 1 DANDA = 6 FT
N
TANK
GARDEN
FLOWER GARDEN
COURT
DANCE PAVILION
COURT
HORSE
TEMPLE
FOR CHANTING HYMNS
COW-SHED
STADIUM
FOR SEEING SPORTS
SERVANTS
PRINCES' PALACE
SERVANTS
TANK
STORE
TREASURY
ARMOURY
COURT LADIES
JEWEL
BATH
FEMALE ATTENDANTS
PALACE
DINING
KIT:
GARDEN
BRAMMA PĪTH
COW-SHED
BARBER
FAMILY PRIESTS
PALANQUIN BEARERS
STABLES
GUARDS
MATERNITY
MONKEYS
COUNCIL HALL
BIRD
DEER ETC:
GUARDS
ARMOURY
ELEPHANTS
NOTE :-
THE PALACE FOR PRAMĀRAKA KINGS SHOULD ONLY BE BIGGER IN DIMENSION
S. C. MUKHERJI.

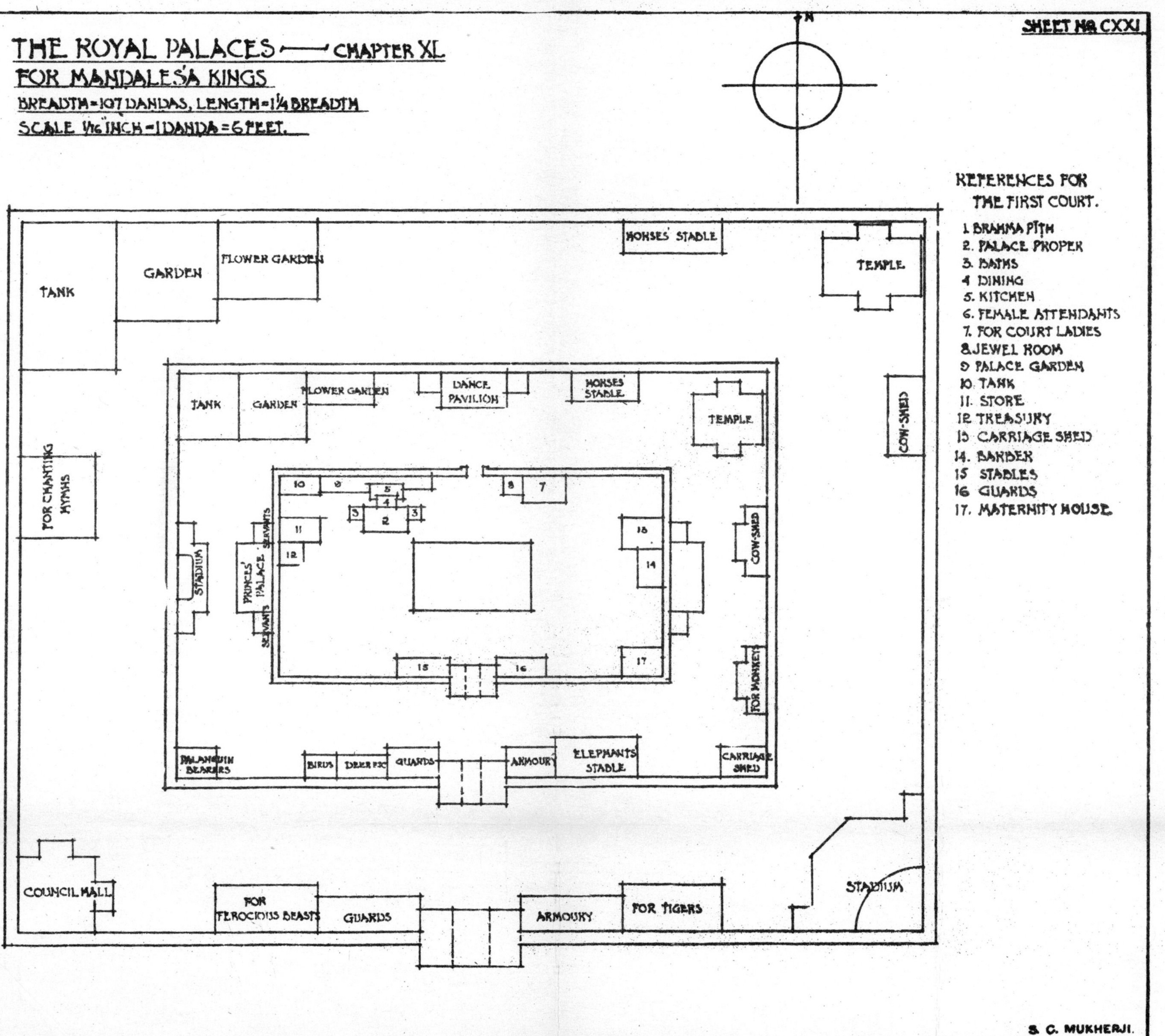
SHEET NO CXXI
THE ROYAL PALACES — CHAPTER XL
FOR MANDALESA KINGS
BREADTH = 107 DANDAS, LENGTH = 1¼ BREADTH
SCALE 1/16" INCH = 1 DANDA = 6 FEET.
N
REFERENCES FOR THE FIRST COURT.
1. BRAHMA PITH
2. PALACE PROPER
3. BATHS
4. DINING
5. KITCHEN
6. FEMALE ATTENDANTS
7. FOR COURT LADIES
8. JEWEL ROOM
9. PALACE GARDEN
10. TANK
11. STORE
12. TREASURY
13. CARRIAGE SHED
14. BARBER
15. STABLES
16. GUARDS
17. MATERNITY HOUSE.
TANK
GARDEN
FLOWER GARDEN
HORSES' STABLE
TEMPLE
FOR CHANTING HYMNS
COW-SHED
DANCE PAVILION
STADIUM
PRINCES' PALACE
SERVANTS
FOR MONKEYS
PALANQUIN BEARERS
BIRDS
DEER ETC
GUARDS
ARMOURY
ELEPHANTS STABLE
CARRIAGE SHED
COUNCIL HALL
FOR FEROCIOUS BEASTS
FOR TIGERS
S. C. MUKHERJI.

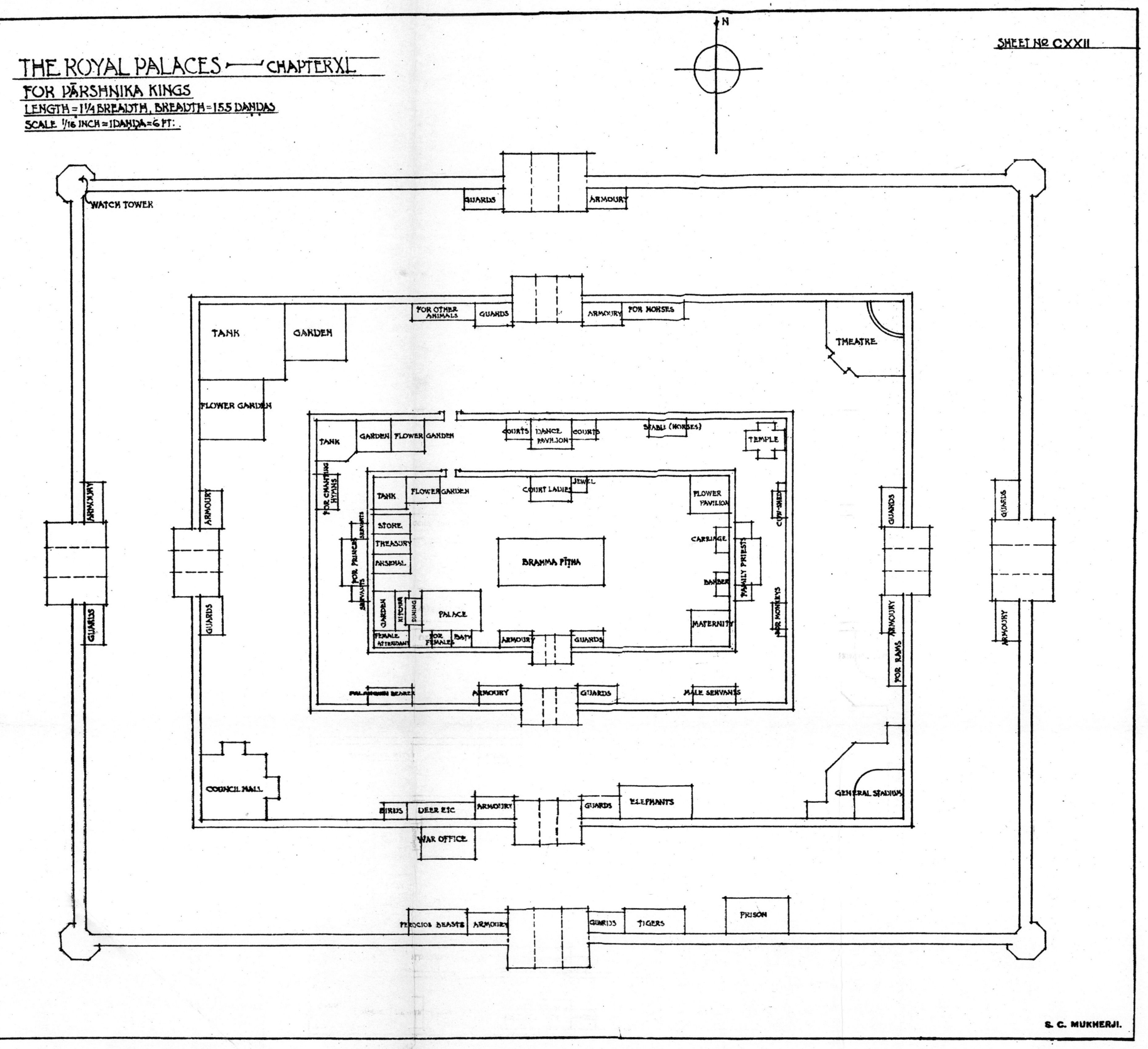
THE ROYAL PALACES — CHAPTER XL
FOR PĀRSHNIKA KINGS
LENGTH = 1¼ BREADTH, BREADTH = 155 DANDAS
SCALE 1/16 INCH = 1 DANDA = 6 FT.
SHEET No CXXII
N
WATCH TOWER
GUARDS
ARMOURY
FOR OTHER ANIMALS
FOR HORSES
TANK
GARDEN
THEATRE
FLOWER GARDEN
FLOWER
COURTS
DANCE PAVILION
STABLE (HORSES)
TEMPLE
FOR CHANTING HYMNS
COURT LADIES
JEWEL
FLOWER PAVILION
COW-SHED
SERVANTS
STORE
TREASURY
ARSENAL
FOR PRINCES
BRAHMA PĪTHA
CARRIAGE
FAMILY PRIESTS
BARBER
KITCHEN
DINING
PALACE
MATERNITY
FOR MONKEYS
FEMALE ATTENDANT
FOR FEMALES
BATH
FOR RAMS
PALANQUIN BEARER
MALE SERVANTS
COUNCIL HALL
GENERAL STADIUM
BIRDS
DEER ETC
ELEPHANTS
WAR OFFICE
PRISON
FEROCIOS BEASTS
TIGERS
S. C. MUKHERJI.

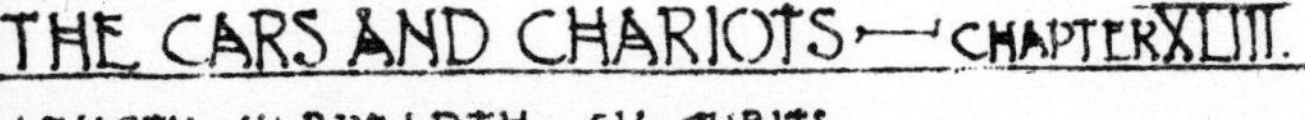

SCALE ¼ INCH = 1 FOOT

NOTE :-

THIS SHOULD BE BUILT IN WOOD

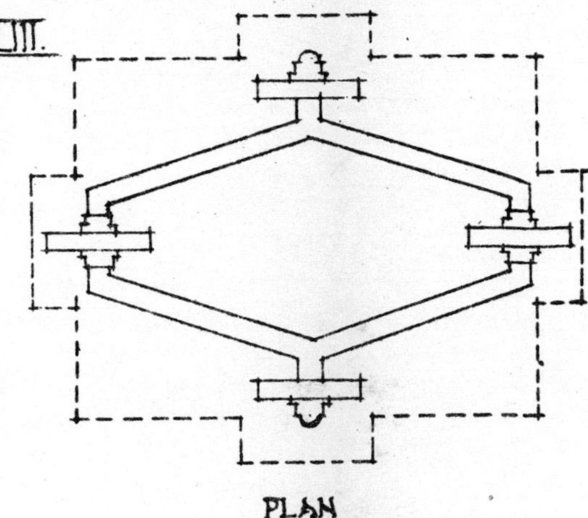

PLAN

OUTLINE SECTION

FRONT ELEVATION

SIDE ELEVATION

S. C. MUKHERJI.

THE CARS AND CHARIOTS — CHAPTER XLIII

TWO-STOREYED CHARIOTS

LENGTH = 1¼ BREADTH, BREADTH = 5½ CUBITS.

SCALE ¼ INCH = 1 FOOT

NOTE :-

THE CHARIOTS MAY BE UPTO 9 STOREYS IN HEIGHT.

OTHER STOREYS WOULD BE SIMILAR IN TREAT-MENT.

THESE ARE TO BE BUILT IN WOOD

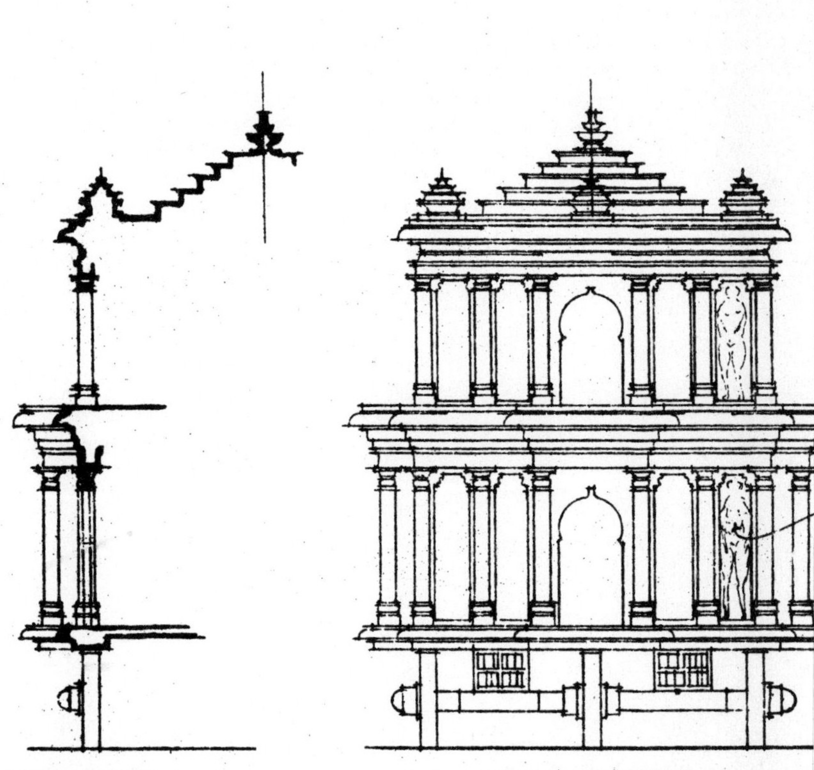

OUTLINE SECTION

FRONT ELEVATION

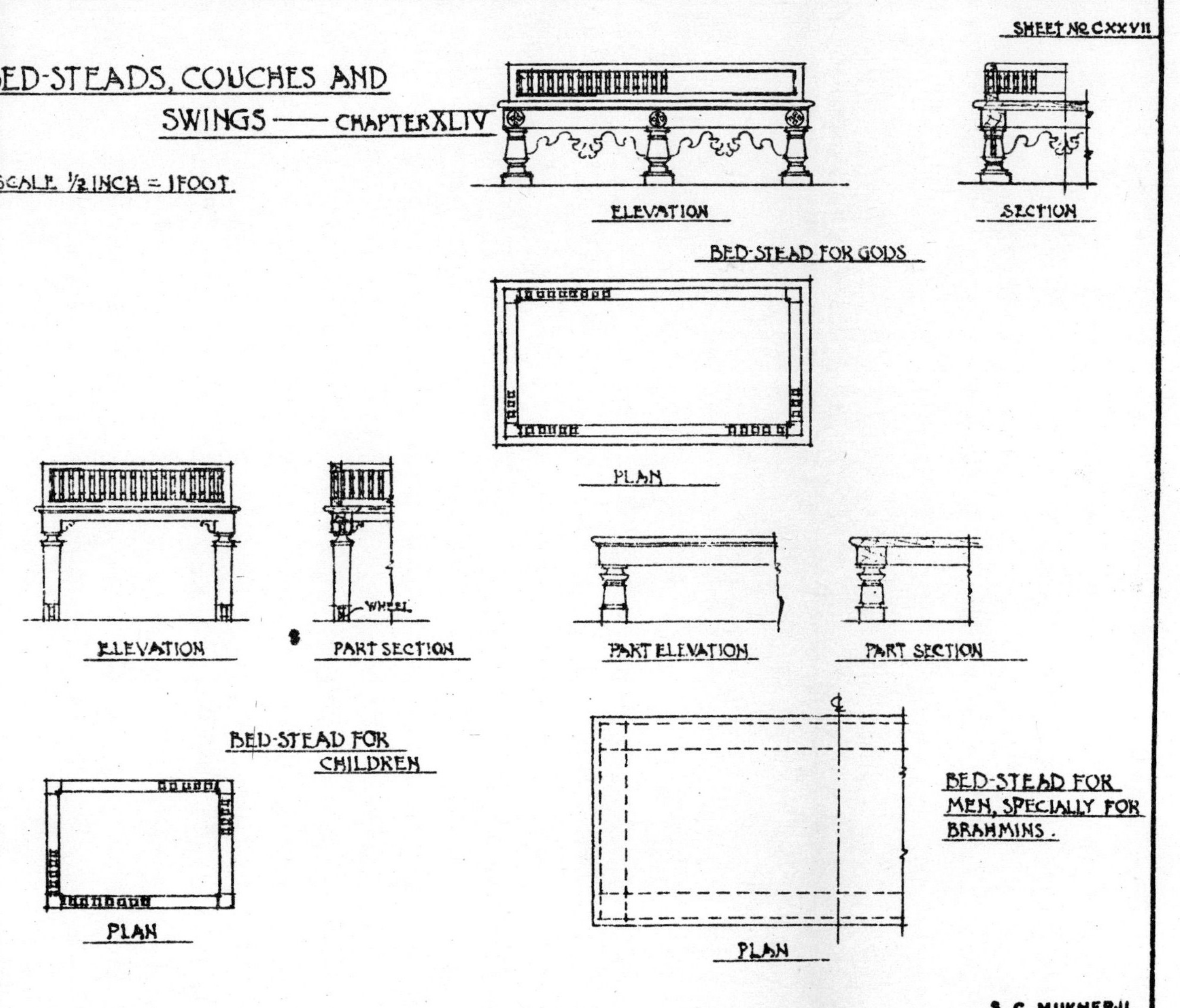
SHEET No CXXVII
BED-STEADS, COUCHES AND
SWINGS —— CHAPTER XLIV
SCALE 1/2 INCH = 1 FOOT.
ELEVATION
SECTION
BED-STEAD FOR GODS
PLAN
ELEVATION
WHEEL
PART SECTION
PART ELEVATION
PART SECTION
BED-STEAD FOR
CHILDREN
PLAN
BED-STEAD FOR
MEN, SPECIALLY FOR
BRAHMINS.
PLAN
S. C. MUKHERJI.

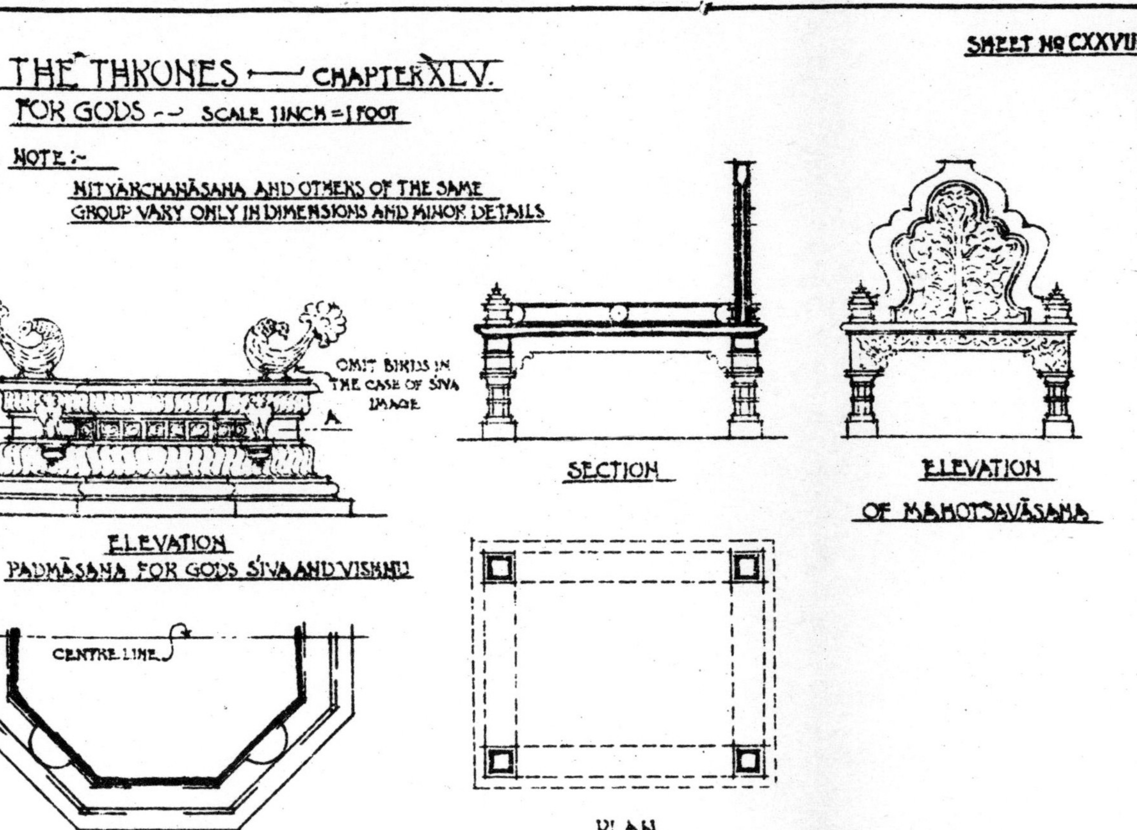
SHEET No CXXVIII
THE THRONES — CHAPTER XLV.
FOR GODS — SCALE 1 INCH = 1 FOOT
NOTE :-
NITYĀRCHANĀSANA AND OTHERS OF THE SAME
GROUP VARY ONLY IN DIMENSIONS AND MINOR DETAILS
OMIT BIRDS IN
THE CASE OF ŚIVA
IMAGE
A
A
SECTION
ELEVATION
OF MAHOTSAVĀSANA
ELEVATION
PADMĀSANA FOR GODS ŚIVA AND VISHNU
CENTRE LINE
PLAN
PLAN AT A.A.
S. C. MUKHERJI.

SHEET No. CXXIX

THE THRONES — CHAPTER XLV

FOR HIGHER ORDER OF KINGS SUCH AS CHAKRAVARTIN AND OTHERS

SCALE ½ INCH = 1 FOOT

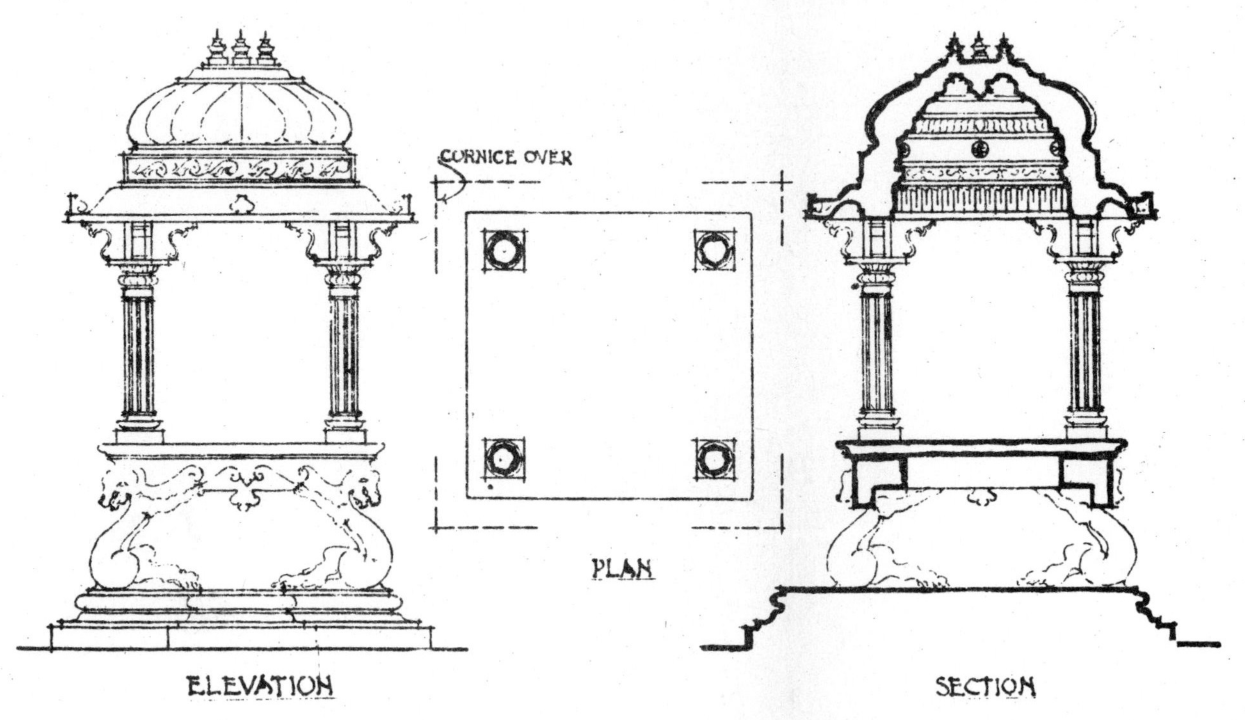

S. C. MUKHERJI

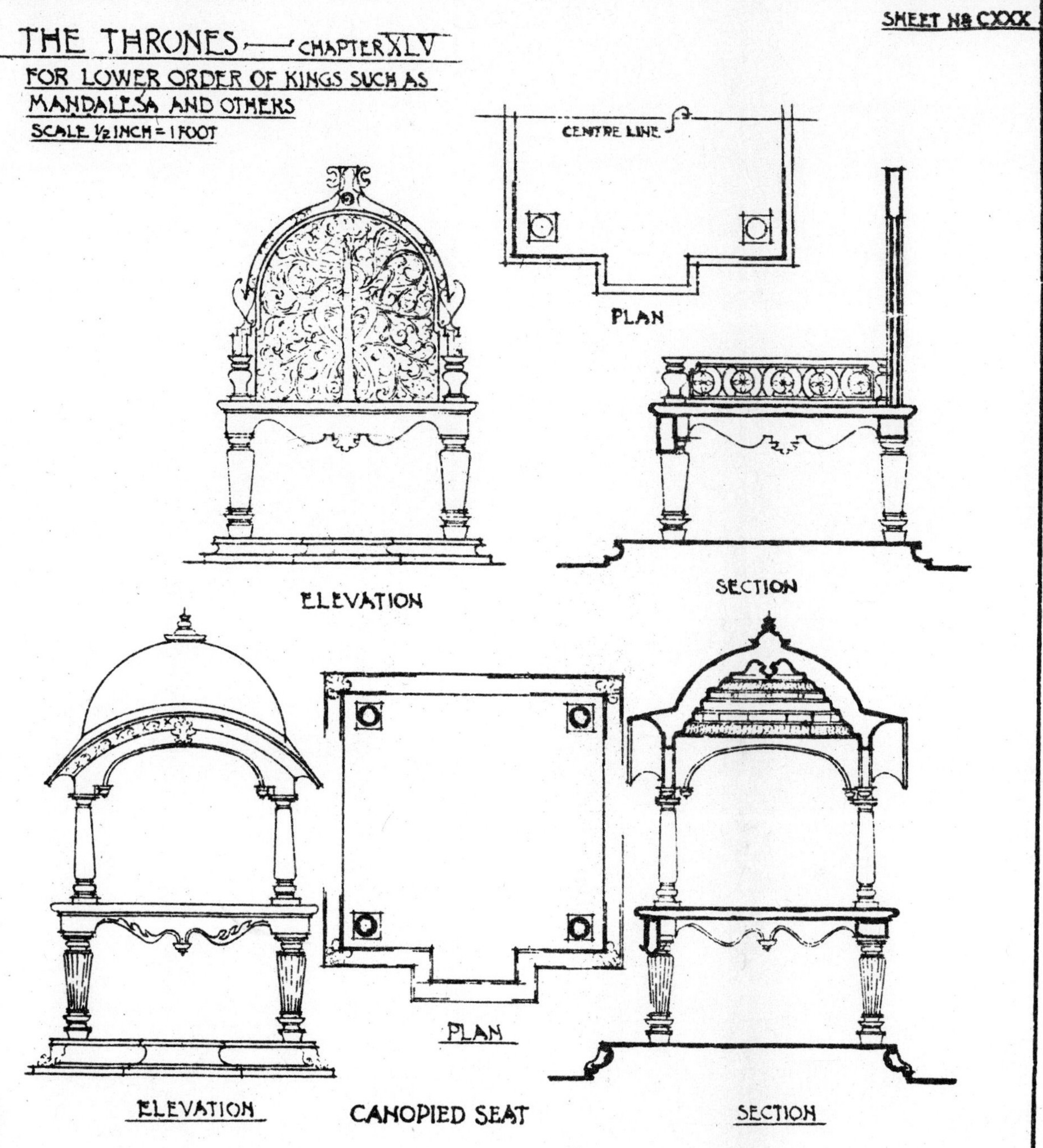
SHEET No CXXX
THE THRONES — CHAPTER XLV
FOR LOWER ORDER OF KINGS SUCH AS
MANDALESA AND OTHERS
SCALE 1/2 INCH = 1 FOOT
CENTRE LINE
PLAN
ELEVATION
SECTION
ELEVATION
PLAN
CANOPIED SEAT
SECTION
S. C. MUKHERJI.

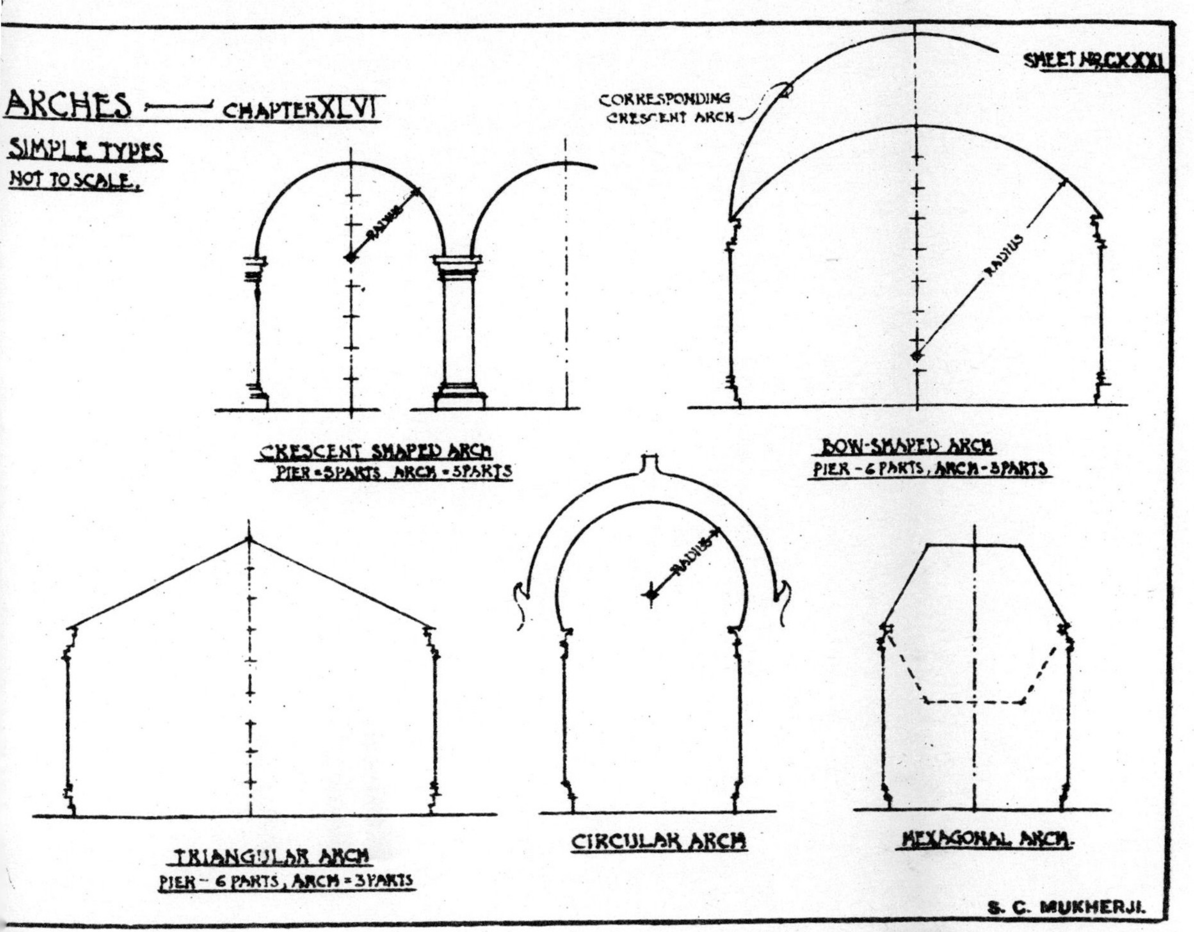
SHEET NO. CXXXI
ARCHES — CHAPTER XLVI
SIMPLE TYPES
NOT TO SCALE.
CORRESPONDING CRESCENT ARCH
RADIUS
RADIUS
CRESCENT SHAPED ARCH
PIER = 5 PARTS, ARCH = 3 PARTS
BOW-SHAPED ARCH
PIER - 6 PARTS, ARCH - 3 PARTS
RADIUS
TRIANGULAR ARCH
PIER - 6 PARTS, ARCH = 3 PARTS
CIRCULAR ARCH
HEXAGONAL ARCH.
S. C. MUKHERJI.

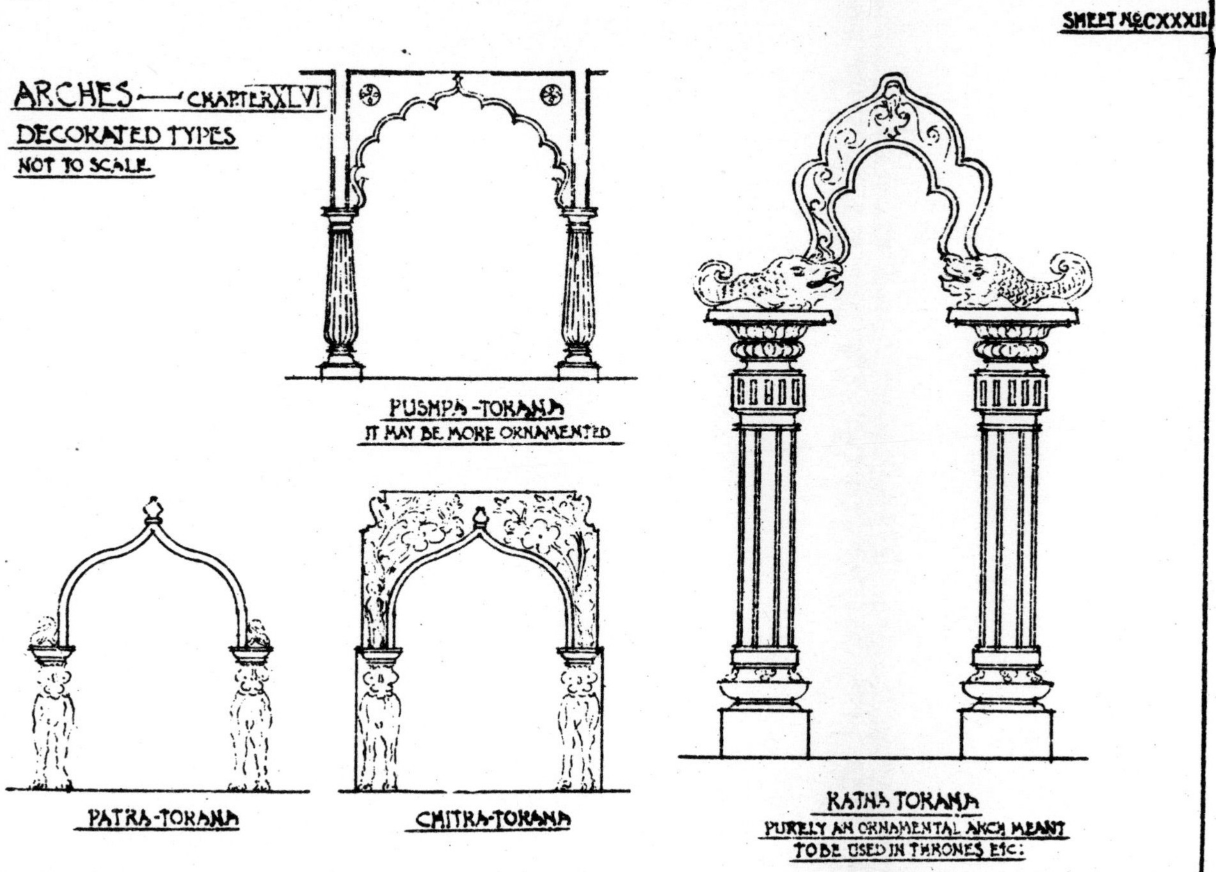
SHEET No CXXXII
ARCHES — CHAPTER XLVI
DECORATED TYPES
NOT TO SCALE
PUSHPA-TORANA
IT MAY BE MORE ORNAMENTED
PATRA-TORANA
CHITRA-TORANA
RATNA TORANA
PURELY AN ORNAMENTAL ARCH MEANT
TO BE USED IN THRONES ETC.

S. C. MUKHERJI

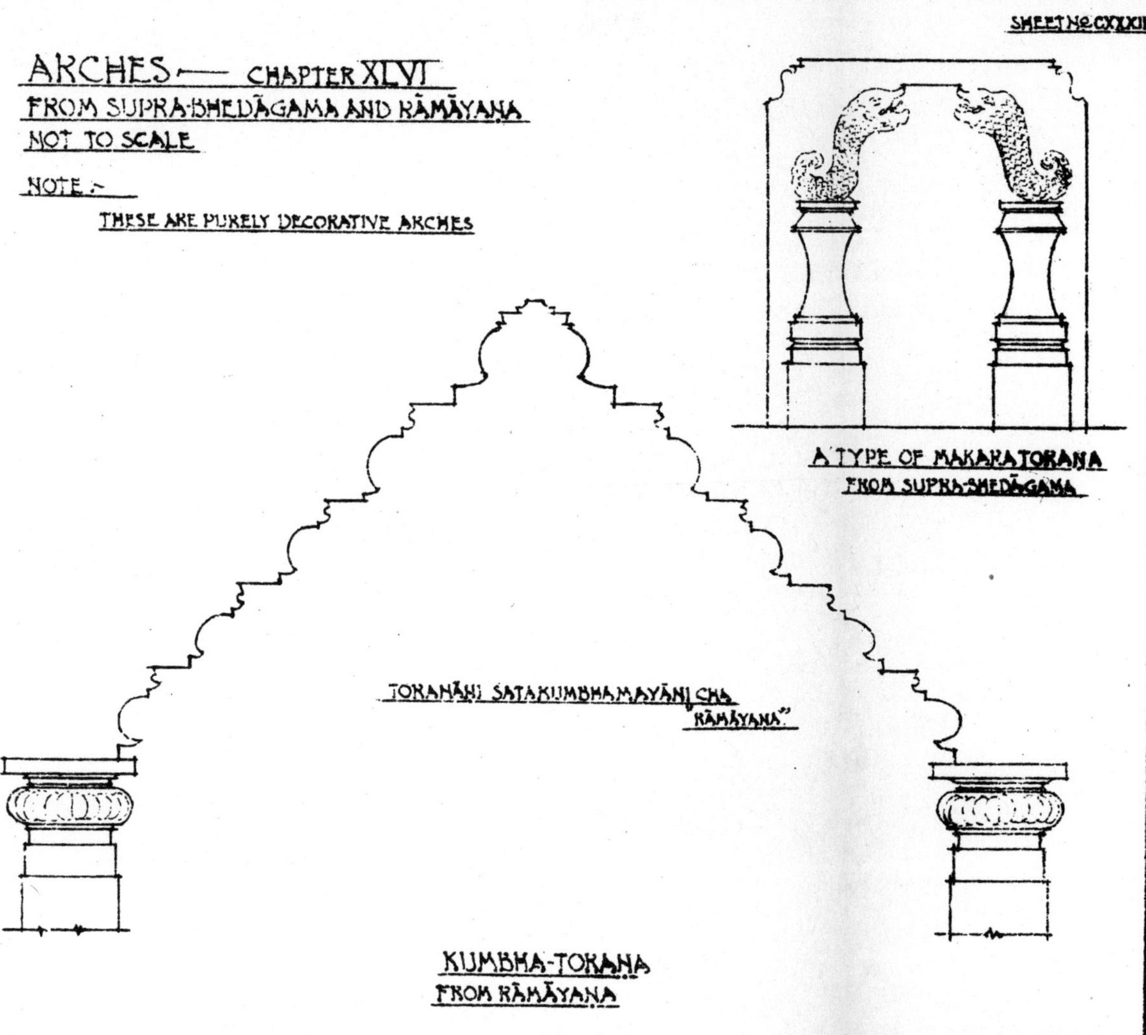
SHEET No CXXXIII
ARCHES — CHAPTER XLVI
FROM SUPRA-BHEDĀGAMA AND RĀMĀYANA
NOT TO SCALE
NOTE :-
THESE ARE PURELY DECORATIVE ARCHES
A TYPE OF MAKARATORANA
FROM SUPRA-BHEDĀGAMA
TORANĀNI SATAKUMBHAMAYĀNI CHA
"RĀMĀYANA"
KUMBHA-TORANA
FROM RĀMĀYANA
S. C. MUKHERJI.

THE CENTRAL THEATRE — CHAPTER XLVII

SHEET Nº CXXXIV

NOTE:-

1. THE MADHYA-RANGA IS MEANT TO BE USED IN EACH AND EVERY CLASS OF RESIDENTIAL BUILDINGS AND TEMPLES. THE ONE DRAWN HERE IS MEANT FOR A PALACE IN GENERAL.

3. THE HEIGHT IN ELEVATION IS 8 PARTS IN ALL BUT THE INTERNAL DIVISIONS HAVE NOT BEEN STRICTLY ADHERED TO.

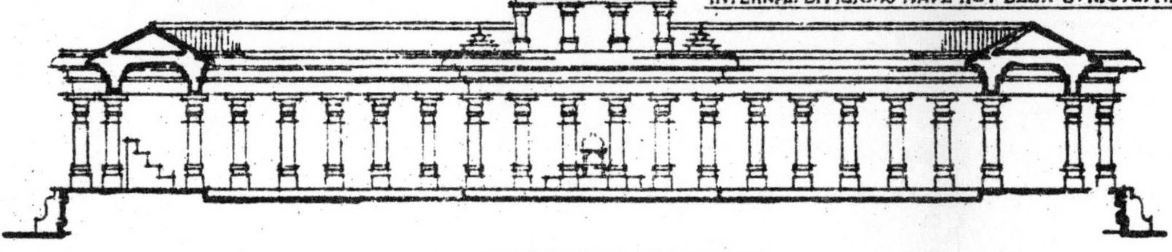

SECTIONAL ELEVATION

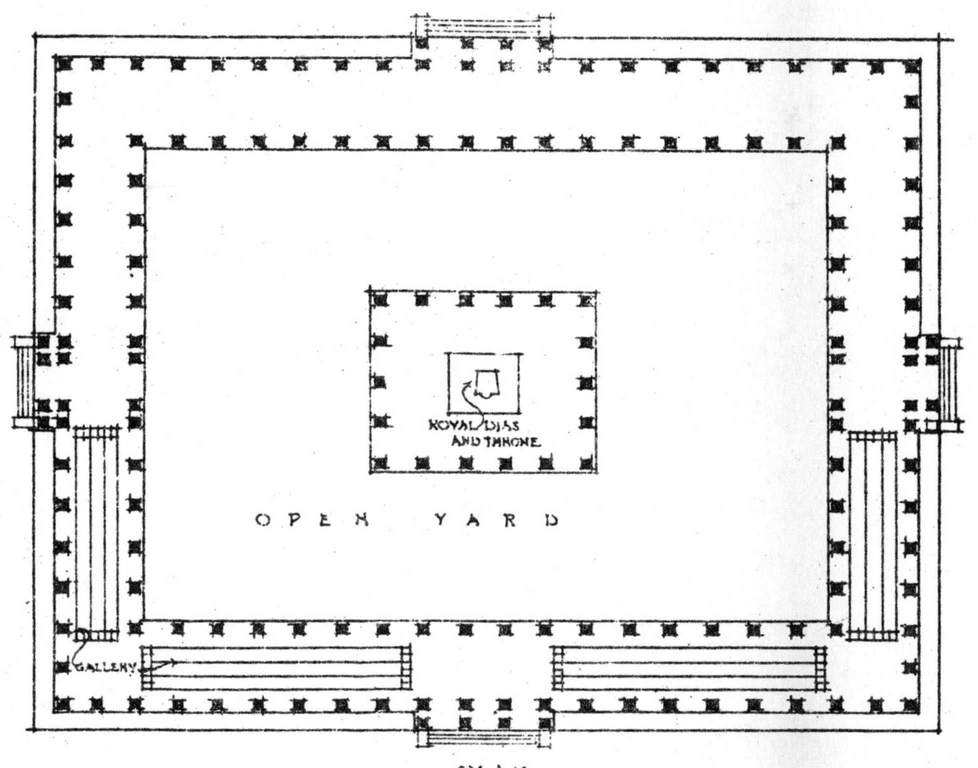

PLAN

SCALE OF 1 0 5 10 15 20 25 PARTS

S. C. MUKHERJI.

SHEET No CXXXV

THE ORNAMENTAL TREE — CHAPTER XLVIII

FOR THRONES OF GODS AND KINGS

NOT TO SCALE

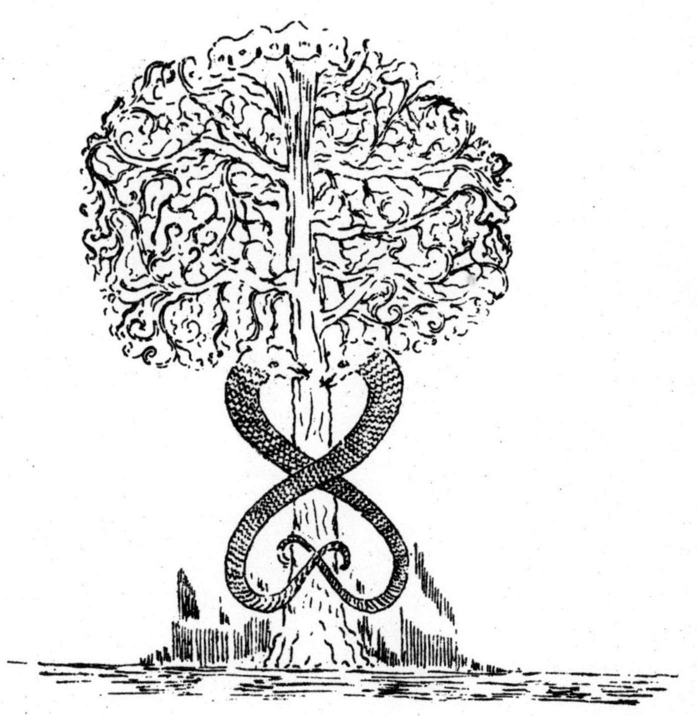

S. C. MUKHERJI.

SHEET No. CXXXVI

THRONES—CHAP. XLV

For Gods and Kings and their Consorts : Eighteen kinds varying in size plan and Ornaments

PADMASANA

K. S. Siddalinga Swamy.

THRONES—CHAP. XLV
For Gods and Kings and their Consorts : Eighteen kinds varying in size plan and Ornaments

PADMAKESARA

K. S. Siddalinga Swamy.

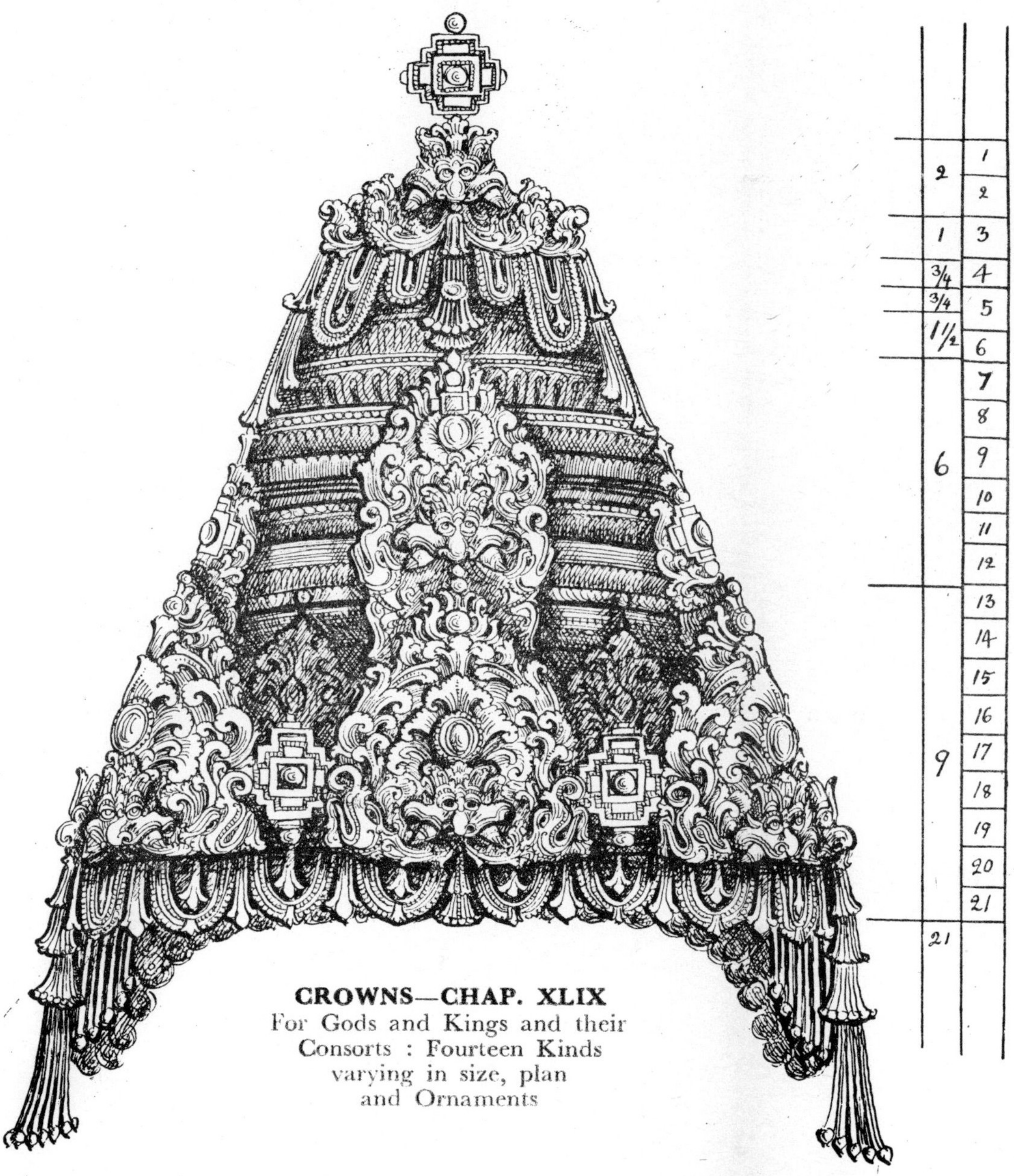

CROWNS—CHAP. XLIX
For Gods and Kings and their
Consorts : Fourteen Kinds
varying in size, plan
and Ornaments

JATA

K. S. Siddalinga Swamy.

CROWNS—CHAP. XLIX

For Gods and Kings and their Consorts : Fourteen Kinds varying in size, plan and Ornaments

MAULI

K. S. Siddalinga Swamy.

CROWNS—CHAP. XLIX
For Gods and Kings and their Consorts : Fourteen Kinds varying in size, plan and Ornaments

KUNTALA

K. S. Siddalinga Swamy.

ORNAMENTS—CHAP. L
Four Groups Comprising some Thirty Varieties

HARA
(CHAIN)

K. S. Siddalinga Swamy.

ORNAMENTS—CHAP. L

Four Groups Comprising some Thirty Varieties

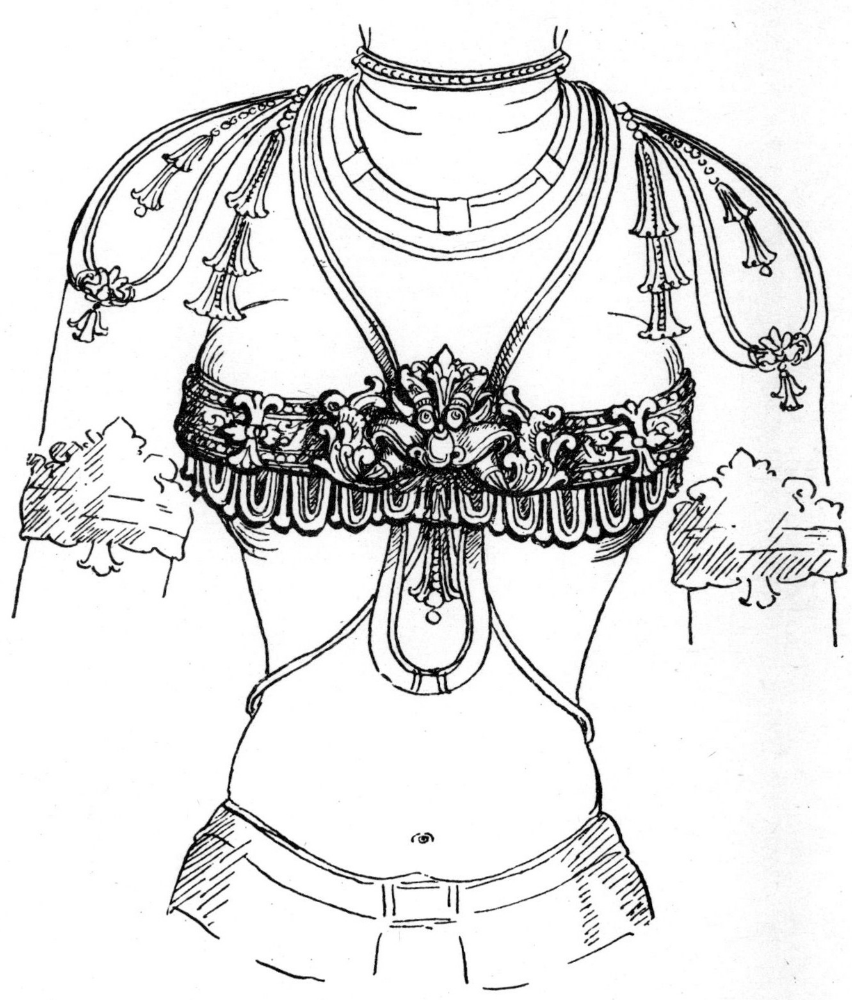

SUVARNA-KANCHUKA
(GOLDEN JACKET)

K. S. Siddalinga Swamy.

MANJUSHA
(BASKET)

K. S. Siddalinga Swamy.

ARTICLES OF FURNITURE—CHAP. L
Eight Groups comprising several varieties including Fifteen types of Cages

ARTICLES OF FURNITURE—CHAP. L
Eight Groups comprising several varieties including Fifteen types of Cages

DOLA
(SWING)

K. S. Siddalinga Swamy

A WITH SARASVATI AND SAVITRI
(OF LARGE TEN *TALA*)

THE TRIAD—CHAP.LI
Comprising Brahma, Vishnu and Siva

K. S. Siddalinga Swamy.

THE TRIAD—CHAP.LI

Comprising Brahma, Vishnu and Shiva

WITH LAKSHMI AND BHUDEVI
(OF LARGE TEN *TALA*)

K. S. Siddalinga Swamy.

THE TRIAD—CHAP.LI

Comprising Brahma, Vishnu and Siva

SARASVATI—GODDESS OF LEARNING
(OF TEN *TALA*)

K. S. Siddalinga Swamy.

FEMALE DEITIES—CHAP.LIV

There are sixteen Great Goddesses

MAHALAKSHMI—GODDESS OF FORTUNE
(OF TEN *TALA*)

K. S. Siddalinga Swamy.

FEMALE DEITIES—CHAP.LIV

There are sixteen Great Goddesses

JINA WITH ATTENDANT DEITIES
(OF LARGE TEN *TALA*)

K. S. Siddalinga Swamy.

JAIN IMAGES—CHAP.LV

ive groups: Siddhas, Sugandhas, Jinas, Arhats and Parsvakas and including Twenty Four Tirthankaras

BUDDHA
(OF LARGE TEN *TALA*)

K. S. Siddalinga Swamy.

BUDDHIST IMAGES—CHAP.LVI

There are several types
varying in details

KASYAPA
(OF EIGHT *TALA*)

K. S. Siddalinga Swamy.

SAGES—CHAP. LVII

Seven Great Sages Measured in three different Talas and varying in details

VIḌYADHARA
(OF NIṆE *TALA*)

K. S. Siddalinga Swamy.

THE MYTHICAL BEINGS—CHAP.LVII

Comprising Vidyadharas, Yaskshas
including Rakshasas and Nigrahas,
Gandharvas and Kinnaras

SAYUJYA
(OF TEN *TALA*)

K. S. Siddalinga Swamy.

DEVOTEES—CHAP.LIX

Comprising Four Classes Salokya, Samipya, Sarupya and Sayujya with Human Features but Super-Human Measures

GARUDA
(OF NINE *TALA*)

K. S. Siddalinga Swamy.

THE GARUDA IMAGE—CHAP.LXI

: in sitting, Erect or Walking Posture and in stationary or Movable Attitude

PLUMB-LINES

K. S. Siddalinga Swamy.

PLUMB-LINES—CHAP. LXVII

Numbering eleven, drawn through the Body of an image to find out the Perpendicular Horizontal Mesurement of and distance between Different parts of the Body in three postures and Four poses